RESTRAINING MYTHS

RESTRAINING MYTHS

Critical Studies of U. S. Social Structure and Politics

RICHARD HAMILTON
McGill University

SAGE Publications

Halsted Press Division
JOHN WILEY & SONS
New York–London–Sydney–Toronto

Distributed by Halsted Press, a Division of John Wiley & Sons, Inc., New York John Wiley & Sons, Inc., New York

Printed in the United States of America

Library of Congress Cataloging in Publication Data
Hamilton, Richard F
   Restraining myths.

   1. Social classes—United States. 2. United States—Politics and government—1945- 3. Political sociology. I. Title.
HN90.S6H36   1975   301. 5'92   75-1220
ISBN 0-470-34711-2

FIRST PRINTING

For Irene

CONTENTS

LIST OF TABLES

FOREWORD

One of the most crucial responsibilities of any field of study is the periodic reexamination of "conventional wisdom," or the body of information and theory which has been transmitted from prior research. Such a reappraisal often yields results so startling and unexpected that one is led to question if the principal goal of scholarly inquiry is actually the discovery of new knowledge. Instead, a major share of the time and energy of academic investigators is consumed by the effort to eradicate persistent myths and superstitions inherited from earlier studies. The duty of separating empirically verifiable facts from the unsupported generalizations and assumptions that permeate the literature is an onerous—but inescapable—obligation of the researcher.

Richard Hamilton's book, much like his earlier work on *Class and Politics in the United States,* demonstrates the value of this undertaking. In examining "centrist," "mass society," and "pluralistic" concepts of political behavior, he not only mounts a devastating attack on prevailing social science theories, but he also provides surprising and significant quantitative support for his criticisms. Thus, his work cannot be assessed solely as a valuable contribution to the study of political sociology, although it has amply achieved that standard. More important, the implications of his findings and his arguments seem to represent an opportunity for social scientists to reevaluate some of the biases contained in previous research and to develop a new approach to the study of social and political structures. The time has come to take a fresh look at the data and theories regarding the functions of the people in a democratic society.

The significance of this book, therefore, is derived in part from the importance of the subject. Theories of political behavior, are, fundamentally, statements about the capabilities of people to govern themselves. They represent an estimate by social scientists of the appropriate role of the public in the decision-making process and of the extent to which the society should approximate the standards of a true democracy. By emphasizing the limitations of the public (and especially persons at the lower end of the socioeconomic spectrum) and by stressing arguments that promote the perpetuation of the existing system, many sociologists and political scientists have contributed to a view of American politics that imposes severe restrictions upon public participation in the formulation of policy.

In part, this orientation probably can be attributed to the natural tendency of researchers to become overly enamored with the institutions and decision-makers they study. Political scientists who devote their lives and their careers to the analysis of legislatures, executives, or courts, for example, hardly may be expected to contend that those groups should be accorded less influence in the political process than the people. But the elitist implications of the perspective have undesirable consequences. Conventional theories have been "restraining myths" that deprive both social scientists and government leaders of a valuable source of insight concerning the goals and anxieties that permeate the everyday lives of ordinary citizens. As a result, the relationship between social scientists and rank-and-file members of the general public often has been characterized by mutual distrust and suspicion rather than by mutual respect and understanding.

Social scientists may be guilty of a serious disservice to the people. Instead of emphasizing the supposed talents of political elites and alleged limitations on the capabilities of the public, researchers might consider the possibility of theoretical developments which stress efforts to maximize rather than to restrict the abilities of all segments of the population. Political scientists and sociologists may be required to correct the severe injustices that have been committed by imposing unnecessary restraints upon human potential. Perhaps most important, attention might be devoted to plans for restructuring social and political institutions to permit the attainment of this potential. This is a task and a goal that extends beyond this book. By demonstrating the restraining character of existing theories of public behavior and the myths that have been perpetuated concerning the capabilities of the public, Richard Hamilton has taken an important step that may have revolutionary implications for the social sciences.

Harlan Hahn

PREFACE

This work was substantially completed when someone pointed out to me that it contained what has been called "grounded" theory. And then, shortly thereafter, I learned that it was also, quite unbeknownst to me, in the symbolic-interactionist and phenomenological traditions. There are even some ethnomethodological elements in it, at least so I have been told. It clearly involves an assumption of a systematic perspective. It may, or it may not, involve a structural-functional perspective. About that I am not entirely certain. The work is unquestionably dialectical in its character although it does not derive in any significant way from the dialectical materialist tradition. It is also historical, at least in some respects.

Lest there be any serious doubt about it, the observations contained in the previous paragraph are intended to be pejorative. Some social scientists find it impossible to proceed to the consideration of a given task without first spending twenty or thirty pages (at least) on something they call "theory." And many of them are in a state of nervous anxiety unless they can "locate" work in one of the "great" or "classic" traditions. In the process they might even spend some time considering the "metatheoretic" implications of their own observations.

Two decades ago C. Wright Mills undertook a very useful exercise. He took some of the more obscure formulations of a leading "theorist" and translated them into everyday language. In the process it was discovered that the original formulations did not go much beyond the commonplace. Mills's effort provided a rather important lesson. And yet, in the subsequent years, many of the people who sympathized with the Mills exposé have gone on to pick up and champion one or another of the florid vocabularies that have since become available in academia. By expressing themselves in recondite language—whether a distilled Parsonian or a Neo-Hegelian makes little difference—they think they have made a significant contribution to human wisdom. One might call it the "fetishism of academic commodities."

Juan Linz once suggested the comparison with a construction project. The massive structure is covered with scaffolding; people are at work everywhere. Building materials are delivered and stacked at the foot of the structure. Cranes then swing these materials aloft where they are "integrated" into the "ongoing" activity. Eventually the cranes are removed and the scaffolding comes down. And at that point one discovers that nothing is there—or maybe only a tiny bungalow. All the effort had gone into the elaborate scaffolding. Similarly much intellectual effort goes into fashioning and perfecting the "means," so much so that one loses sight of the end which, after all, is the development of knowledge, not the production of esoteric language.

In the chapters that follow, it has been assumed that the reader has at least a passing knowledge of the subject matter being considered and that it is possible to proceed more or less directly to the task. Almost everyone with any acquaintance with United States affairs, for example. knows what "backlash" is and knows the major explanatory claims providing the underpinning for this position. And so chapter 4, for example, opens up with some brief quotations, reminders only, and then turns immediately to consideration of the evidence. One critic, clearly a master guildsman, a true descendant of Sixtus Beckmesser, argued that the piece should not be published because it "lacked theory." Rather than obliging the guildsman and responding to his demand that all his squirrel's gatherings be recognized and duly noted, I have preferred another strategy, one which bypasses the obvious, the trivial, and the empty. Baroque architecture is one thing; that has considerable attraction. Baroque intellectualizing, however, is quite another matter.

I would like to thank the following persons for their advice and wisdom in commenting on the manuscript: Chandler Davidson, Lewis Dexter, William Domhoff, Paul Eberts, Maurice Pinard, Donald Von Eschen, Jonathan Wiener, and James Wright. None of these persons, to be sure, is responsible for the contents of this work.

For their labors in the field, I would also like to thank Brian Schechter and Suzanne Standard.

For their assistance, direct and indirect, I would also like to thank Irene Hamilton, Carl Hamilton, Tilman Hamilton, and Bruce Chase-Dunn.

The study would not have been possible without the resources provided by the Inter-University Consortium for Political Research of the University of Michigan and the Roper Center at Williamstown, Massachusetts. I wish to thank the members of those organizations, the researchers who undertook the original studies, and the respondents who cooperated on those studies. I would also like to thank the University of Wisconsin's Data and Program Library Service and its director, Alice Robbin, for her assistance. Again the responsibility for the interpretations is mine.

And finally I wish to express my appreciation to McGill University and to the Faculty of Graduate Studies and Research for their generous financial support of this project.

CHAPTER 1

RESTRAINING MYTHS

Social theories provide economical, simplified accounts of human affairs. Most theories also have some directive implications. Some are intended as an aid to and justification for interventions in human affairs. Some, on the other hand, provide arguments for not intervening in those matters or, alternatively, for limiting the character or extent of any intervention. Most theories contain some indication of the appropriate kinds of means one might use or, alternatively, that one might best avoid. Many theories, in other words, may be said to have a restraining or a directive character.

The restraints involved are not physical: it is not a matter of force. They are not even external restraints but rather are self-imposed. One might best describe them as prudential. At one time, for example, it was said that "the vapours" (evening airs) were bad for health. As a consequence, people who accepted the claim slept in their chambers with windows closed and drapes drawn. It seemed, after all, the wise thing to do. Where social theories suggest that certain procedures are bad for social health, one is likely to find a similar kind of prudential restraint. If it is felt that feeding the poor would encourage high reproductive levels (or that it would destroy incentives), one might, for fear of the coming famine or malaise, refrain from performing acts of simple human decency.

Where the claims of a theory prove to be unfounded but, nevertheless, are still widely accepted, one may speak of restraining myths. That term might be applied, for example, where it was discovered that the well-fed poor did not reproduce to excess or stop working but where, nevertheless, people still believed and acted as if they did.

The first aim of this work is to consider and bring evidence to bear on the major claims of some dominant social theories. Many of these claims, to anticipate the findings, are found to be unsupported. The point then, already indicated in the title, is that we are dealing with restraining myths.

A second aim of this work is to consider the reasons for the persistence of these myths. These claims, as will be seen, have been peculiarly immune to empirical assessment. They have only infrequently been subjected to study and, even where some research has been done, the theorists and commentators have avoided recognition of the lessons.

This work will be focused on three major traditions that dominate in much of contemporary discussion. These are: the "centrist" social science position, the major concern of this work, the "mass society" theory, and the pluralist theory. It is useful to give a brief outline of each of these theories so as to provide an initial summary mapping of the territory to be explored.

The first tradition, which for lack of a better term may be referred to as the "centrist" position of the contemporary social sciences, derives from the revisionist Marxist view of the world, specifically from the work of Eduard Bernstein.[1] This recharting of the Marxist landscape puts a major stress on the emergence of a separate "new middle class" consisting of salaried white-collar workers. This group is said to be different from wage-earning blue-collar workers. The earliest formulation of this position argued that there were substantial differences in the income, education, life chances, life-styles, and, most important, in the "consciousness" of white-collar and blue-collar employees. The initial formulations saw the white-collar group as intervening between the bourgeoisie and proletariat to form the "center" which moderated the political struggle, preventing the clash of opposites anticipated in the unrevised Marxist formulations.

In Weimar Germany (and in later discussions of the Weimar experience) the initial portrait of social health was changed for one indicating serious pathologies. The "old middle class," consisting of independent businessmen, small proprietors, and artisans, are bypassed by modern institutional developments. They find themselves crushed by big business and big labor and burdened by the requirements of big government. Suffering considerable stress in "modern society," it is not too surprising that they wish to return to a more amicable nineteenth-century arrangement, one in which they were more or less at the center of things and in which "bigness" was no threat. Their politics, then, at least so it is claimed, are reactionary. They are the irreconcilables as far as modern institutional arrangements are concerned; and they provide a ready supply of alienated and disaffected persons who are available for mobilization by rightist political movements.

The Weimar variant also finds some pathological elements in the situation of the white-collar workers, particularly those who are poorly paid, those who are "lower middle class." They find themselves "losing position" with respect to the blue-collar workers. Filled with a sense that they ought to have some degree of distinction setting them apart from manual workers, they too, like the independent middle class, react by supporting reactionary, restorationist movements. These two segments together, that is, the small businessmen and the poorly paid white-collar workers, constitute the "lower middle class," a category which is seen as playing a key role in the development of fascism in Europe and elsewhere.

In a still later development, in the United States of the 1950s, blue-collar workers, like the lower middle classes, also come to be portrayed as a "dangerous class," as a group that is intolerant of political, ethnic, and racial minorities and as indifferent or hostile to the democratic "rules of the game." This refers to the widely accepted claim of a "working-class authoritarianism."[2]

A peculiar inversion of the previous world view occurs in this new development. In the Marxian and in the revisionist views, the bourgeoisie and their immediate employees (who would now be called the upper middle class) were portrayed as conservative if not reactionary, as hostile to the rights of minorities and as not especially concerned with the niceties of democratic procedure. In the social sciences of the 1950s, the upper and upper middle classes came to be portrayed as champions of democracy, as the

principal source of liberal virtue. They were credited with protecting individual rights and democratic procedures against the
mass intolerance found in the working and lower middle classes.
While the upper and upper middle classes never came to be
described as economic liberals, they were defined as "responsible";
insofar as means allow, they would do the right thing for the
society and for the major groups in it.

The restraining lessons contained in this viewpoint are very
clear. Democracy is a flimsy and unstable thing depending on
passive, acquiescent masses. Were these masses to be aroused, it
would be impossible for the small numbers of the upper and upper
middle classes to withstand the force of their outrage. Key to the
maintenance of the democratic arrangement and to the securing of
the rights of minorities is this passivity and acquiescence. It would,
to all appearances, be somewhat foolhardy to intervene in any way
that would arouse the slumbering masses. The viewpoint, in short,
encourages restraint in making contact with, in activating, in
organizing, or in supporting "interest group" representation from
among the manual workers and the lower middle classes. The
lesson, very simply, is that it would be dangerous to do otherwise.

There is, to be sure, a corrective process operating which, over
the long term, should yield a more wholesome condition. The
changes in the labor force (more and more people being employed
in "middle class" jobs), improvements in living standards, higher
educational levels, and greater involvement in voluntary associational activity should all aid in the creation of more tolerant and
responsible outlooks. The size of the "threatening masses" will be
steadily reduced as they come to be "integrated" into the society.
This also involves a lesson in restraint. It says that things will be all
right in the future and that the best strategy is to let these
ineluctable processes continue their albeit somewhat slow course.
There is little provision for, or discussion of, interventions. Other
than encouragement of "more and more" education, there is
nothing said about active interventions into, or planning of, occupational development in society. The favored stance with respect
to voluntary associational activity is one of *laissez-aller*. [3]

This centrist position, basically, is a theory of stratification. It
delineates the classes present in the society, indicates something
about the attitudes and orientations of these classes, and says

something too about the trends thought to be in process. In this work we will examine the claims made about the attitudes of those found in each of these key segments of the society. Specifically, we will assess the claim about the conservative or reactionary propensities of the old middle class, that is, of the independent businessmen, most of whom are said to be economically marginal and consequently rather desperate (in chapter 2). A parallel examination will be made of the new middle class, in particular, of the "lower middle" salaried white-collar workers (in chapter 3). Following through on another strand of the above discussion, we will examine the claim of a "working-class authoritarianism." Specifically this will consist of an examination of the attitudes of white workers and white middle classes toward the question of the rights of blacks (chapter 4). Another context in which upper middle class responsibility and working-class irresponsibility is sometimes claimed involves foreign affairs. The policy choices presented with respect to the Korean and the Viet Nam wars provide an opportunity for assessing these claims (in chapter 5).

The second of the theories is the "mass society" theory. This view has a very ancient heritage, stemming originally from the experience of ancient Rome. In more recent times there has been an English version which was derived from the French Revolutionary experience as analyzed by Carlyle and popularized by Dickens. There is also a French stream of development which begins with the same revolutionary events; in this case the analysis was supplied by Taine, Le Bon, and others. In Germany the experience of Nazism was analyzed within the same broad perspective by Emil Lederer, Sigmund Neumann, Hannah Arendt, and many others.

The major claim in this viewpoint is that the masses have been "uprooted." They have no base, no anchoring traditions; modern society with its corrosive competition, industrialization, and urbanization has left individuals "free" but at the same time isolated, alone, and anxious. The consequences for the masses are very much the same as those indicated for the lower middle class in the centrist theory. The masses experience strains and stresses and, lacking any kind of serious defense, are easily led by the clever and/or irresponsible.

There are two major variants in this tradition, one conservative and one radical (or perhaps better, "critical"). In the conservative variant the threat comes "from below." It is the "irresponsible demagogue," one who "proffers" what are called "easy solutions," who is seen as the threat. This line of theorizing too has a restraining lesson. Because the masses are characteristically portrayed as irrational and volatile, as not too intelligent, and also as appetitive (having insatiable demands), their participation, once again, is said to be "destabilizing." The lesson is again one of the dangers of arousal.

There is little offered in the way of practical suggestion in most such accounts. Because "in a free society" there is not much that can be done to hinder the free expression of any interested "demagogue," the characteristic stance is largely hortatory, admonishing the reader to avoid the suasions of any such persons.

There is a parallel here to the centrist theory in that the upper and upper middle classes are again portrayed as "responsible," as doing what they can to contain the influence of those engaging in socially deleterious behaviors. The example of the elites in closing ranks against the demagogue Senator McCarthy is frequently cited as the exemplary instance of this kind of responsibility. Another kind of restraining effort comes in the definition of persons or movements as "demagogic" and hence "irresponsible." Where people accept the basic world view and where they also accept such "definitions" (one might also consider the use of the term "denunciations"), the effort again serves to restrain behavior. Those who might otherwise follow an innovator or an insurgent movement would be discouraged from doing so.

The radical or critical variant of the mass society theme sees the threats coming from above. Shrewd and calculating elites control the mass media and manipulate the media content so as to generate support from the helpless (because isolated and powerless) masses. In some left theories, this effort provides the key to the stability of the system; the consciousness of the masses has been formed by these distant elites who have made use of all the sophisticated technology of the age. They are in a position to control the very consciousness of the masses and can engineer consent (not just acquiescence). The manipulative efforts of these all-powerful elites also extends to voluntary organizational activity which, in this view, provides merely another area for the exercise of influence.

The restraints in this case are somewhat different from those previously discussed. This reading, while not inviting alliance with upper classes, seriously restricts the kinds of approaches to "the masses." If one does not have control, or at minimum significant access to "the media," it would be impossible to have any serious impact on the general population. Moreover, given the disparity in the means involved (the ruling elites having the "sophisticated" techniques, the best that money can buy, while the entire opposition is left with more humble workaday tools), the outcome can never be seriously in doubt. Roughly the same may be said with respect to the use of the voluntary associations: "they" have the money and the technique; the opposition has only very feeble resources.

The disparities are such, in some readings at least, as to immobilize. With the ruling elites having "the power" and their opponents having nothing, any struggle is hopeless. This reading, in short, would make use of the theory as an explanation or justification for the claim that nothing can be done. It is the argument of the "sophisticated," "knowledgeable," or "realistic" commentator who truly appreciates where "things are at."

Another alternative reading based on the same line of theorizing also closes out direct discussion with "the masses." Because they, the masses, are "doped up" or, to use a much-favored expression, "narcotized," there is no possibility of reaching them through a direct approach. The alternative is to intervene in such a way as to break the "mechanism" and, thereby, to shock the masses out of their torpor. Demonstrations in which the police are provoked or enticed into an attack on the general populace, for example, are held to serve this purpose. Violence and terrorism, to the extent that such acts serve to disrupt routines and force people out of their accustomed channels, also prove useful in "creating consciousness."

The character of the restraint in this case involves a restriction of the range of means that might be considered. Here again, if the theoretical judgments are unsound or inadequate, what one has is a restraining myth. Some of the demythologizing appears in chapter 5, which, although focused on the centrist claims, also proves to have some relevance to the mass society claims in particular by allowing some specification of the question as to just which groups constitute the "manipulated masses." Chapter 6 takes up the question of the sophisticated manipulators and their "chilling" techniques and raises the question about just how "expert" they really are. This is, in effect, an evaluation study, one that asks about the actual impact of their "technique."

The third of the major restraining lines of theorizing is the pluralist view. The key claim of this position holds that "power" has been dispersed; each segment of the population now has resources allowing some influence in collective decisions. The key agency for the exertion of this influence is the volunatry association. These associations are seen as weapons in the hands of the general population, weapons that allow achievement of their aims and defense of their interests. A key implicit assumption is that the associations are agencies of and representative of the grass roots. Chapter 7, the final substantive chapter, contains an exploration of the supposedly democratic character of some voluntary associations, the focus being on small business organizations. The assumption that one is dealing with an agency representing grass roots sentiment proves to be unwarranted.

If one accepts the pluralist claims, that is, if one believes that "power" has been divided and effective influence is now available to all major segments of the population, that belief would inhibit any attempt to initiate further redistribution of resources. Such a belief would serve, once again, as a restraint on behavior. If it was believed that the organizations present in the society were genuine emanations from and expressions of grass roots sentiment, then, where the expression was conservative or reactionary in tone, it would inhibit any appeals in the name of liberal or left alternatives. Where the judgments of the organizations as democratic and as true reflections of sentiment prove to be mistaken, one would again be dealing with restraining myths. The misperceptions of underlying grass roots opinion would have the effect of immobilizing those who might otherwise take action if they were not intimidated by the sense that the other major forces in the society were against them.

A variant on the pluralist theme argues that the division of power occurs among the elites. They are not (or are no longer) of one mind about the issues of the day. The various segments of the elites put forward their package programs, run different political parties, and present their offerings to the mass electorate for what, in essence, is a ratification. Borrowing the "working-class authoritarianism" notion, the argument is developed that this limited ratifying choice is the best possible democratic arragement. This variant then also provides justification for restraining the options that might otherwise be undertaken.

The major task of this work is to bring evidence to bear on key claims of these influential social theories. Put somewhat differently, the task is to show that the theories which supposedly provide straightforward factual analyses of social affairs contain important unfounded empirical judgments. All social theories have implications for political choices, favoring some and discouraging others. The point to be argued here is that some key elements of the theories under consideration are not empirically supported and that therefore the consequent restriction in the range of choice is unjustified.

The final task here is to give some indication as to why these unsupported claims have been so easily accepted, in some instances, for decades. This final concern involves an excursus into what has sometimes been called the "sociology of knowledge," which is to say, it will be concerned with indicating the social sources or roots of a persistent misinterpretation. This task will be undertaken in the final pages of the chapters and in some greater detail in the concluding chapter of this work.

Most restraining myths, for obvious reasons, would be conservative in nature. Most demythologizing of such ideologies would be radical or "critical." It will be noted that in the above review there is one formulation that does not fit this pattern, the "left" or "critical" mass society view. The descriptions of the "mass society," when taken together with a portrayal of an omnicompetent power elite or ruling class, are intended to provide "realistic" alternatives to mythological pluralistic accounts. The point being made here is that both accounts contain important mythological elements.

In rejecting the mythology of the moderates, one is not obligated to accept an alternative mythology of the "critical" left. The latter mythology also provides its restraints, rejects some practical options, and argues for others. Many of the favored options, because of the essentially mythic character of the fundamental assumptions, prove to be self-defeating. The definitions of "the masses" are insulting. There is an assumption of ignorance and gullibility which certainly would have little appeal. Many of the actions undertaken in the name of "the people" are so transparently manipulative as to discourage any "mass" support. Many of the initiatives that stem from acceptance of the mass society perspective are manifestly detrimental to the interests of the masses, a fact that also discourages support. The precondition for a ready belief in the adequacy of the mass society theory is distance from and ignorance of the masses. It is, to use a standard cliché, "no accident that" the mass society theorists, with rare exceptions, come from very distant aristocratic or upper middle class ranks.

Restraining myths, in short, are not the exclusive property of the political right or of the "moderate" center. The task, with respect to all theoretical orientations, as C. Wright Mills once put it, is to "get it straight." All kinds of things from Mills's work are cited for hortatory effect but this lesson, curiously, is rather remarkable for its absence. The primary task in this work is to do what he advised, to get it straight.

Thus far the discussion would suggest that the effort is largely negative. People have believed theory A or B, and these beliefs have limited or directed the initiatives they were willing to undertake; evidence to be presented shows these beliefs to be ill-founded and the self-imposed restraint to be unjustified. That effort, in essence, takes one back to the zero-point; one might well then ask what is to be put in place of the rejected theories.

There is an alternative envisaged. Much of what is contained in the following chapters, in fact, is based on this alternative orientation. For lack of a better name, this will be referred to as the group-bases approach. It assumes, as the cornerstone assumption, that values, attitudes, and outlooks are learned, supported, and reinforced in primary group settings, that is to say, within intimate, face-to-face, personal relationships. A person has a given constellation of religious, moral, and political outlooks because he or she has been raised among people who have instilled those beliefs and who, later in life, have reinforced them. All important elements of one's outlook would ordinarily be learned within the family, in school, in the immediate community, and from various groups of friends and possibly from co-workers within that community.

All of this, to be sure, is rather commonplace. It is close to the heart of the sociological perspective which, traditionally, has seen attitudes and behaviors as the result of social influences. It is the central focus of a subarea within sociology, social psychology, which is concerned with the social determinants of individual attitudes and behavior. And, even without the aid of an eminent scholarly tradition. The proverbial "man on the street" has recognized this range of experience as having a very considerable impact in determination of outlooks.

The group-bases viewpoint becomes important, that is, it becomes noncommonplace in a number of ways. When attention is focused on alternative theories, on those placing the emphasis elsewhere, to call attention to the rather fundamental realism of the group-based position is not as commonplace or trivial as it first seems to be. When attention is focused, as in the centrist position, on a range of "class" determinants and these are emphasized to the near exclusion of all others, then a "reminder" does become important.

Centrist theorizing places a heavy stress on economic rewards and deprivations as *the* source of attitudes and behavior. It is useful to consider, by way of illustration, the case of two upper middle class men, both of whom are employed as accountants in the same firm. Both, in other words, have approximately the same "life chances" or level of well-being. But, rather than having similar outlooks, the one, a Catholic, is a Democrat in politics, is liberal on economic issues, and is opposed to abortion. The other is white and Protestant, a Republican, conservative on economic issues, and in favor of abortion. The differences in outlook are to be accounted for in terms of the differences in early training and in contemporary social pressures and influences. They are, on the whole, rather friendly at work but, except for rare occasions, they rarely discuss political parties, political issues, religion or religious issues. They live in different communities, the one being composed largely of upper middle class Catholics and the other of upper middle class Protestants. In this case it is pointless to talk, as in centrist theorizing, of *the* upper middle class, as if it were all of a piece, as if that life contained a set of inexorable determinants that forced a given response of all its members. One must ask the question: which upper middle class? And the analysis of each segment must contain an account of the social roots of the outlooks. The purely "economic" analysis will not suffice.

A similar argument, with appropriate differences to be sure, may be made with respect to the attitudes generated by anomic conditions as in the mass society theory. And still another challenge may be made with respect to the presumed sweeping impact of the mass media in another variant of the mass society theory.

These statements are not meant to deny these theories in their entirety. One might very well have a substantial clustering of group-based attitudes in a society; but, among the relatively few isolates who are linked to the society only by a television set, one might find support for the mass society theory. Both explanations, in other words, may be operating; however, the significant question then is the relative importance of each.

The group-bases approach may become noncommonplace in another way. To the extent that the approach has been used "social psychologically," it has tended to treat attitudes of one person (nowhere located in the social structure) as linked to the attitude of another (similarly unlocated). If one were to undertake a more systematic charting of the groups in the society and of their locations in the social structure, the approach might well prove more useful. The lower class, in such a case, would be seen as a collection of subgroups X, Y, and Z, each with a distinctive cultural heritage which was passed on over the generations. Although they face similar economic problems, the same stresses and strains, these problems are handled within the frameworks of the separate and diverse subgroup traditions. Those traditions, moreover, appear to persist independently of the economic "determinants" impinging on the class.

There is still another way in which the approach may be used or elaborated in a noncommonplace way. In great measure the group-bases approach has been used to explain or account for continuities in attitude. Children hold the same political beliefs as their parents, the same religious beliefs, the same moral standards: that is the dominant tendency. But there is always a segment who break with the tradition and adopt alternative outlooks. Rather than simply treating them as "exceptions" or as "deviant cases," their experience may be analyzed to discover the sources of change. These changes may also be accounted for in terms of the social bases framework. The most familiar example would be that of the person who comes to be subject to a different range of social determinants. Ordinarily a family will train a child in a set of attitudes and also will play some role in "placing" that child in the society. In most instances that would involve a setting in which the attitudes would be supported and reinforced. There is, however, some "displacement" that occurs. The son of the working-class Democrat, for example, "arrives" in a strongly Republican upper middle class milieu, and in that context, being subjected to new and different pressures, he changes his political allegiance.

One may trace the various changes in circumstance experienced within the population, and, given the initial assumption, one should be able to show associated changes in attitude. This would be true, presumably, with farm-to-city movement, with inter-regional movement, and so forth.[4]

The changes discussed in the above paragraphs might be referred to as routine: they appear in the course of normal, everyday life with the attitudinal and value changes being essentially unintended by-products of the changed location in the society.

In addition to these unintended by-product changes, we have the direct, systematic attempt to change attitudes or behavior. Because of the dominance of mass society theorizing, there is a tendency to think of media campaigns in this connection. One can always produce the telling case from recent experience—or what at least appears to be the telling case. Many changes in the political landscape, however, have been the result of concerted campaigns involving personal activity and influence. These changes were the product of extensive organization and campaigning on a person-to-person basis.

Possibly the most important case of this kind of effort was the electoral success of the National Socialists in Germany between 1928 and 1932 when they went from 3 to 37 percent of the total vote in five years. On the North American continent the initial success of the Cooperative Commonwealth Federation in Saskatchewan was due to the same kinds of influence. And, in more recent times, the success of Senator Eugene McCarthy and later of Senator McGovern in primary elections appears to have been largely linked to this "personal influence" factor.[5]

In such cases, clearly, one's analysis must focus on the activists who are carrying the new political lesson. One must ask such questions as who they are, what motivates them, what lessons they offer, and how their "audience" reacts to them. In essense one must treat the development as a social movement and provide an explanation of its dynamics.

A movement does not operate in a vacuum. The success or failure of the movement will, to some degree, be determined by the existential problems facing people and by the extent to which the new lessons appear to provide viable solutions. The character of the new militants, whether they are seen as serious or frivolous, as plausible or implausible, as helpful or threatening, will also play a role in determining their success or failure.

In the ordinary run of things, insurgent activists are not present. The usual election is dominated by media efforts orginating "at the top" of the established parties. Some limited personal efforts by a tiny minority of the population are undertaken, this referring to the local or grass roots activities of the party faithful. In such routine electoral efforts, one would expect the hold of the traditional social pressures to dominate—because there are no other significant influences present to challenge that "hold." In such instances it is to be expected that the electoral outcome would rather closely match the results of earlier elections. In essence, the tendency to vote for the party of one's father (and friends and associates) would be greatest in such circumstances.

Major cataclysms, wars and depressions mainly, provide incentives to break with traditional choices. Actually making a break, however, is another matter. It assumes there is an alternative present, one that is seen as plausible. In the ordinary run of things, that is not likely: established political parties are subject to a range of determinants that tend to keep them moving in their distinctive channels. If a new movement were to make an entry onto the political stage, it would ordinarily be aided by the presence of a cataclysm: the latter encourages the search for an alternative. At the same time the new movement would have to be able to present itself as providing the alternative, one that was both serious and plausible.[6]

A brief summary may be useful at this point. In the lives of most people one will find a set of existential concerns (with bread and butter, jobs, inflation, war) and a set of interpersonal relations. Within the latter context, one will find, typically, support for preferred or approved solutions to these existential problems: one takes such and such an attitude toward them; one is right in doing some actions and wrong in doing others; some political agencies are approved, others disapproved. And it is this set of social supports which provides the continuity observed in mass political behavior—despite the continuous flow of new events, despite the apparent (to the outsider) irrationality of many of the results. When seen "from the inside" however, from the perspectives of the persons involved, the chosen solutions might make a great deal of sense.

A third factor increasingly intervenes in this setting, that is, the stimuli experienced through the distant, impersonal mass media. It would be a mistake to discount the role of the media entirely. The question being posed here concerns the kinds of and amount of influence. The available studies on the subject during election campaigns suggest a very limited role, largely because positions are so thoroughly rooted in personal involvements. The role of the media has been largely one of providing information, of reawakening slumbering political identities, and reinforcing preexisting political loyalties.[7]

One can also consider a fourth factor, the possibility of new activists appearing on the scene. This involves a different kind of analysis; but, at the same time, it is still an analysis of small group dynamics. In this case, however, it would be the activities of those wishing to set a new direction as opposed to those of groups bearing the old directions. There is little point in dwelling on the role of new activists since, in most of what follows, we will be concerned with those groups sustaining more or less traditional political directions.

The discussion to this point has been very formal. It is useful to add some elements of substance to this portrayal. The question of class and class cleavages has been considered at some length elsewhere and will be taken up in still more detail in later chapters. Some handed-down claims about the location of cleavages (the key division being between blue- and white-collar workers, or that separating the affluent skilled workers from others in the blue-collar ranks) have been rejected in previous work. The most important cleavage to be observed within the generality of the American population (that is, laying aside the tiny and exclusive upper class for the moment) is that separating the upper middle class from the rest of the population. The latter category, essentially, refers to the combination of blue-collar and lower middle class families. By rough, rule-of-thumb measurement, this category constitutes about three quarters of the nonfarm population.[8]

In some ways this point is obvious from even the most casual observation of the American scene. The upper middle classes live in separate communities on the edge of the larger cities. They therefore have a separate territorial base; their children are born and raised in those communities, they go to school there, and have all their friends living there. They leave to spend time in universities that are, once again, rather separate and exclusive upper middle class enclaves. And then, in the normal upper middle class life, one returns to the upper middle class communities in which the entire remainder of one's life will be spent.[9]

Upper middle class careers may begin with relatively low-level jobs, but these are followed by a series of planned moves to positions of even higher responsibility and remuneration. The upper middle class, after all, staffs the leading full-time technical and administrative positions in public and private bureaucracies. Accordingly their incomes will, again in the typical case, show continuous improvement throughout the economically active career. This stands in sharp contrast to the income pattern associated with lower middle class or working-class careers. Those families have a pattern of increased earnings to middle age followed by some decline in later years. This means that the upper middle class is able to have a "style of life" that is beyond the reach of the other elements in the population. Analyses that focus on mean income figures for occupational groupings but which fail to recognize the differences in career patterns needlessly confuse matters.

The upper middle class, in short, has a separate territorial base.[10] They are the recipients of the "best" education in the society, that is, education in the "quality" schools. And they have an income pattern that sets them apart from the majority of the society.

Although rarely specified, there is at least implicit in academic discussion a strong suggestion that the lower middle class also possesses a separate territorial base. This appears to be a doubtful conclusion. A limited investigation of the American experience showed that the so-called lower middle class occupations were not clustered territorially in separate communities but rather were scattered throughout what is, in its majority, blue-collar territory. The lower middle class, in other words, forms a small minority population located in all working-class areas of the cities.

Given the lack of territorial base one may also suspect, at least as an hypothesis, the lack of a separate consciousness. Rather than placing the emphasis on "differences," on a lower middle class desire to maintain distance from blue-collar workers and blue-collar traits, this observation invites one to think in terms of an opposite hypothesis. The lower middle class white-collar workers may well come from the same families as the blue-collar workers. Rather than thinking of each other as different classes, the actual experience may well involve thoughts of uncles, aunts, cousins, brothers, and sisters. And "maintaining distance" in such a case would have quite different meaning from establishing status claims vis-a-vis a distant and personally unknown class. The common territory would also mean (again in all likelihood) that the blue-collar and white-collar workers had gone to the same school and possibly also to the same church. There is also a likelihood that they were and still are together in the same "peer groups."

If this is in fact true, one would anticipate shared attitudes and outlooks, not dissimilarity of views. The evidence assembled on this question does support this position. It is to be noted by way of precaution, however, that this is speaking of broad aggregates: the entirety of the lower middle class compared with all blue-collar workers or with blue-collar workers at the same level of earnings. The detailed study, the examination of the white-collar workers living next to the blue-collar worker in the urban neighborhood, that kind of study has yet to be undertaken. All that can be said at this moment is that the logic of the situation would suggest similarity and that the aggregated evidence from surveys supports the position argued here.

There is another kind of cleavage present in the society which has been established in virtually every available study, cleavage along religious and/or ethnic lines. Within the upper middle class there is some segregation of these suburban communities, some having Catholic predominance, some Protestant, and some Jewish. And the same holds within the working-class/lower middle class category; segregation into black and white subcommunities is one very significant dimension with religious and ethnic divisions among whites also playing some role. Given all the talk in the thirties, forties, and fifties about acculturation and assimilation, the remarkable fact in the late sixties and early seventies is the rediscovery of the persistence of these "traditional" divisions. It would take very exceptional circumstances to yield any other result; to the extent that people like to live near relatives and friends and stores and community facilities servicing one's own personal and/or groups' interests, that will yield a clustering. Where assimilationist and mass society viewpoints anticipate a random distribution of populations (or at least a strong tendency in that direction), the actual experience is a persistent nonrandom tendency.

Related to this consideration one finds differences associated with region and size of community. Whites in the South, overwhelmingly, are Protestant and Anglo-Saxon. Outside the South, white Protestant Anglo-Saxons tend to be located in rural areas and in smaller towns. They too, therefore, are provided with a separate territorial base, the precondition, ordinarily, for a separate consciousness.

Previous work in the area has shown different political tendencies to be dominant within these separate ethnic/religious communities. In all comparisons the white Protestants are more likely to be Republicans and more likely to be conservative on economic issues than are the other groups.[10] This holds even when examining the differences within a class. There too the traditional influences appear to dominate and to outweigh any specific "class" determinants. The white Protestants in the middle-sized and smaller communities, moreover, are somewhat more likely to be Republican and conservative than their counterparts in the cities.

A similar picture appears when one considers questions relating to tolerance and civil rights. The white Protestants, in all comparisons, appear to be less tolerant than are Jews and Catholics although the differences are not large. This pattern holds, once again, even within classes suggesting the persistence of subcultural determinants.

The explanation for the difference is not as easy to establish as the fact itself. The white Protestants are more likely to be living in homogeneous circumstances in the smaller communities. That is to say, they are less likely to have contact with blacks or with other white ethnic groups. Part of the explanation may lie in these isolated circumstances which, everywhere, are associated with ethnocentrism and chauvinist outlooks. Dominant majorities in all countries are less concerned with civil rights than are minorities, hence a self-interest factor may also be involved. There are many other factors one might speculate about: fundamentalist ministers preaching the inferiority of the children of Ham may have left a heritage lasting to the present day. Or racist lessons contained in the press and magazines of former decades read by white Protestants may have left a similar heritage.

The main point of this review is that the actual attitudes have a pattern to them which is consonant with the group-bases position; the outlooks, in other words, tend to be systematically related to these subcultural bases. This approach appears to provide a more adequate understanding of the facts and the dynamics of mass opinion than the centrist position with its near-exclusive focus on "class" and class-related determinants. In many instances, faced with the actual evidence, one must ask the question—Which lower middle class?—since white Protestants, Catholics, and Jews differ so considerably. Were one to make a "pure" class analysis, it would obscure the actual results by averaging a number of diverse patterns.

Probably the least adequate of the theories considered here is the mass society viewpoint. The group-bases approach was originally intended as an empirically grounded response to that position. In this respect it has had considerable success. The mass society portrait offers a huge, ill-defined, and undifferentiated "mass." The sources of strain suffered by the masses are delineated only in the most sweeping, "large brush" outlines. Attempts at detailed testing of the claims are almost entirely absent. The group-bases claim, by comparison, finds a highly differentiated "mass." The individuals within that "mass," in their various subgroups, have all kinds of supports and protections from the vagaries of the outside world.

The group-bases account touches only obliquely on the claims in the standard pluralist repertory. The "groups" in the group-bases theory are not active, innovative pressure groups envisioned in the pluralist theory. They are, rather, smaller and more intimate units in which one rests and relaxes. Rather than being instruments for the fighting of political battles in the larger society, these smaller, "primary" groups are passive and defensive. They (or· rather, the political "experts" within the groups) define the world within the framework of the received intellectual traditions, interpret new data as it comes in from "outside," help to screen out the attempt to manipulate, and so on. But all of these activities, unlike the voluntary association in pluralism, are defensive. These primary groups protect their members against efforts in the outside world; they do little to change it.

This is not to say that the routine efforts of the primary groups are adequate for the task at hand. Because they are small, they are relatively powerless. Against a powerful and well-organized city hall, they might be next to useless when the bulldozers appear at the door to begin the urban renewal project. The "received traditions" of some primary groups may even weaken them in any struggle. If, for example, a part of the tradition is the notion that one "can't fight city hall," that debilitating definition—another restraining myth—would prove very helpful for the administrators and developers who send out the bulldozers. In the ordinary run of things, the defenses of the primary group are going to be rather limited.

Their importance, however, does not lie in this particular sphere, that is, in the actual struggle for power, in the ongoing "political process." The importance of such groups lies elsewhere: they train their members in the traditional outlooks of the group, and they reinforce belief patterns and punish deviations from approved judgments and behavior. The importance therefore is in their role in determining or setting mass outlooks.

Nothing has been said about the validity of the claims passed on as part of the subgroup traditions. Clearly much of the tradition in such cases is going to be handed-down gossip, distilled folk wisdom, the wit and wisdom of small-town, village, and country ancestors, plus considerable amounts of sheer misinformation. Seen from one perspective, these traditions may provide the core of what has been called "false consciousness." On the other hand, the knowledge passed on within those channels might be very adequate to the circumstances. There is always the problem that knowledge and practice which are rational and appropriate from the perspective of the group in question might seem "irrational" and "false" from the perspective of distant intellectuals. In any event the truth or falsity of any given claim is an empirical matter and not one to be determined by declaration.

This approach too, like the others criticized here, has some restraining or directive implications. There is, first of all, a difference in the research directives. To gain knowledge about the social bases present within a society is a much more difficult and complex task than the offering of a few sweeping claims about the "mass society" or about the stresses and strains attributed to a few major classes. This is one of the major reasons for the relative unpopularity of this position: it demands a much more detailed kind of work than is required of other positions.

Second, the problems involved in the generation of social

change are much more complex than in the views that have been criticized. To change attitudes, outlooks, and behavior, one would have to be able to intervene with "social influences" on a personal or grass roots level. One would need a large group of activists bearing the new lessons, or alternatively, one would need to inspire a large number of current group leaders to become active in promulgating the new lesson and supporting the new direction.

These practical options clearly require a considerable amount of work if one is to be effective. Only in the fairy tale does the elimination of the restraining myth give place to a nonrestraining reality. The more likely alternative is a restraining reality. Although much work is demanded in order to change things, this alternative theoretical position does not needlessly immobilize (through fear of the threatening masses) or rely on spectacular, self-defeating, magical solutions (such as the use of terror, or the expectation that the "coming collapse of capitalism" will perform the educational task). "Getting it straight," Mills noted, does not always yield a happy or cheery result. The position outlined here, nevertheless, offers more grounds for hope, than the needlessly, unrealistically restraining alternatives.

NOTES

1. For a more detailed discussion of this and the other two positions (together with appropriate references), see Richard Hamilton, *Class and Politics in the United States* (New York: John Wiley, 1972), chap. 2.

2. Seymour Martin Lipset, *Political Man* (Garden City, N.Y.: Doubleday, 1960), chap. 4.

3. There are, to be sure, some detailed specifications that could be added. A poverty program, for example, called for "maximum feasible participation" of the poor and many "community organizers" were enlisted to train the poor in the skills of voluntary associational activity. This was one of the few instances in which the practice was not *laissez-aller*. One was dealing with a deprived minority here, one which was not especially threatening (or as it is sometimes put "destablizing"). The relations with this "underclass" constituted another demonstration of upper or upper middle class responsibility. The latter groups were going far out of their way to aid a group that could not make it on their own. The same kind of maximum

feasible participation was not envisaged for the "middle American" blue-collar workers. A few years after this episode the presidential advisor in this area advocated a policy of "benign neglect" as a substitute for the maximum feasible participation.

4. See Hamilton, *Class and Politics*... op. cit. The theory of group-based politics is discussed on pp. 49-63. The political correlates of the movements mentioned in the text are also discussed, with supporting evidence, in that work.

5. On the Nazis see Richard Hamilton and James Wright, *New Directions in Political Sociology* (Indianapolis: Bobbs-Merrill, 1975). For the CCF in Saskatchewan, see S. M. Lipset, *Agrarian Socialism* (Berkeley: University of California Press, 1950). Eugene McCarthy's primary campaigns are described in Lewis Chester, Godfrey Hodgson, and Bruce Page, *An American Melodrama: The Presidential Campaign of 1968* (New York: Viking Press, 1969), pp. 78 ff.

6. See Maurice Pinard, *The Rise of a Third Party: A Study in Crisis Politics* (Englewood Cliffs, N.J.: Prentice-Hall, 1971).

7. The standard work in this connection is that of Joseph T. Klapper, *The Effects of Mass Communication* (Glencoe: The Free Press, 1960). An important specification, however, is to be found in John P. Robinson, "Perceived Media Bias and the 1968 Vote: Can the Media Affect Behavior After All?" *Journalism Quarterly* 49 (1972) 239-246. See also the references in *Class and Politics*..., *op. cit.*, pp. 79-80.

8. Ibid., pp. 214 ff.

9. On the territorial bases question, see ibid., pp. 159 ff.

10. On the political and attitudinal correlates of religion and ethnicity, see ibid., chaps. 5 and 11.

CHAPTER 2

THE POLITICS OF INDEPENDENT BUSINESS

BUSINESS AND POLITICS—THE RECEIVED CLAIMS

The conventional picture of independent businessmen portrays them as political and economic conservatives. In the United States they are said to be Republican in persuasion, overwhelmingly so, and to lean heavily toward the conservative wing of that party. They are said to be opposed to most kinds of government aid and support programs, especially to those associated with the so-called Welfare State. They are also, again so it is said, hostile to labor unions since these organizations drive up costs and make it more difficult for the independents to compete against the giant firms. The independents, in short, are thought to be hostile to or, at minimum, to have ambiguous feelings about three of the major institutional clusterings of contemporary capitalist societies, that is, "big government," "big business," and "big labor." Their hostility toward these three "modern" developments makes them a special reservoir of reaction on the contemporary scene. They have an "interest" in returning to premodern conditions, that is, to a setting in which "they" were the predominant force in society, in which there was no threatening competition from the giants, no

AUTHOR'S NOTE: This chapter is a sequel to a paper written ten years ago with Paul Eberts. Entitled "The Myth of Business Conservatism," it was presented at the American Sociological Association meetings in Montreal in September, 1964. I wish to express my appreciation for his advice and assistance on this chapter. He also did the work for note 24.

strain produced by the costs and demands of government, and no pressure from labor.[1]

In many of these formulations one finds independents treated as if they were all *small* businessmen. "With very few exceptions," one author states, "proprietorship today is limited to small businesses." And these independents in turn are portrayed as economically marginal, as just barely getting along, as existing on the edge of disaster. Implicit in such readings is the assumption that an independent who "makes it," who achieves a financial success, will change his status: he will become a big businessman, a member of the bourgeoisie, or a salaried manager (to be sure, one with a large initial share in the ownership). The sense of these formulations is that independents form a residual class, the class of persons who have not "made it." This formulation, as we shall soon see, is seriously misleading.

A recent variation on the basic theme does make a distinction between small and not-so-small independents. It is useful to quote at some length:

> . . . the spread of new wealth led to a rise of status insecurity on various levels. The most obvious example was the *nouveau très riche* whose numbers had indeed multiplied from 1940 to 1950. The man who amasses wealth himself feels more insecure about keeping it than do people who possess inherited wealth. He also feels more aggrieved about social reform measures which involve redistribution of the wealth, as compared with individuals, still wealthy, who have grown up in an old traditionalist background, with the values of tolerance associated with upper class aristocratic conservatism. . . .
>
> While the most important significance of the newly wealthy lies in the power which their money can bring, rather than in their numbers, there is a mass counterpart for them in the general population, the small independent businessmen. Statistical data on social mobility in the United States indicate a great turnover in the ranks of these groups. . . .
>
> These small businessmen, perhaps more than any other group, feel constrained by progressive social legislation and the rise of labor unions. They are squeezed harder than large business, since their competitive position does not allow them to pay increases in wages as readily as can big firms. Governmental measures such as social security, business taxes, or various regulations which require filling out forms all tend to

complicate the operation of small business. In general these people are oriented upward, wishing to become larger businessmen and take on the values or imagined values of those who are more successful.[2]

In this formulation, one which is clearly in the "centrist" social science tradition, independents are set in opposition to responsible old wealth and, implicitly, to the more secure and responsible salaried employees. The independents, big and small, are reactionary in orientation; they do not accept the basic contemporary institutional developments and wish to return to the *status quo ante*. Responsible managers and the traditional wealthy, by comparison, accept and approve these innovations.

Where a distinction is made between big and small independents, as in the quotation being discussed, it is in terms of the motivations of the two subgroups. Small independents react because of objective strains in their lives. The reactions of large independents are based more on social psychological considerations; they feel "more insecure" and they feel "more aggrieved" about reform measures.

There is a historical dimension to the argument. Presumably children of successful first generation entrepreneurs, that is, children of those who first "made it," would have more moderate influences in their lives. The fathers were "educated" in their own firms, in the struggles to work their way up, to ward off the competition, and so on; the children, on the other hand, are educated in the "better" schools. They would learn something of that "aristocratic conservatism" and also some sense of security about their wealth and position, a sense denied to their fathers.

The major task of this chapter is to assess the adequacy of this portrayal. In the order in which they are discussed, the concerns are: first, the claims about the economic condition of independents; second, their presumed allegiance to conservatism, specifically, in the United States, to Republicanism; and third, their attitudes toward social welfare legislation.

The initial discussion contrasts independents with other major occupational groups of the society, salaried professionals, managers and officials, clerical and sales personnel, and manual workers. This allows us to test all variations of the business conservatism thesis. The first step in the analysis shows the claim that all or nearly all independents are small to be unsupported. It still makes sense, nevertheless, to compare independents, large and small together, with other middle class groups since the Lipset-Raab variant has claimed that both segments share rightist propensities. The second and third steps of the analysis cast doubt on that claim. In the fourth step, later in the chapter, the question of internal differentiation within the independent category will be considered. This allows a further, more precise test of both the original and the variant claims. The comparison of independents and salaried middle class categories also proves helpful in assessing some claims made about the latter. We will be referring back to these tables in the course of our discussion in chapter 3.

It may be noted initially that the available evidence does not sustain most of the conventional expectations. It may also be noted that most of the conventional accounts fail to consider other possible explanations for the behavior of this group. Social factors, such as the rural-urban location of independents, their regional location, religious persuasions, educational level, and family political traditions, are all remarkable merely for their absence. It is ironic that an eminently un- or anti-Marxian tradition of sociology should have so easily and so thoroughly accepted a crude Marxian viewpoint. Some speculations about the reasons for the misperception and for the narrow focus are presented in the final discussion of this chapter.

Counted as independent businessmen are all self-employed males other than those classed as independent professionals. The 1964 and 1968 surveys (discussed below) indicate that independents thus defined constitute approximately 15 percent of the active nonfarm population. A small number of self-employed skilled workers and other manuals have also been included in this category. One might question this reworking of the U.S. census procedures. The question is whether an artisan, a manual worker who sells his product in a commodity market as opposed to selling his services in a labor market, is best counted as a manual worker or as an independent businessman when in fact he is both. The procedure adopted here makes the provisional assumption that dependence on the demands and uncertainties of a commodity market would be a more salient determinant of his political behavior than would his activity doing manual labor.

In this respect the procedure used here follows the assumptions of the tradition outlined above. The use of this procedure also makes possible a more precise comparison with West European studies which, if based on official occupational categories, separate artisans (or *Handwerker*) from other manual workers. This procedure does not in any way foreclose consideration of the immediate question at issue. A consideration of the orientations of manual and nonmanual independents will be made at a later point.

The presentations are limited to male heads of households and to housewives classified according to their husbands' occupations. The main reason for doing this is the assumption that other males would be either retired, unemployed, or students, and that inclusion of these categories would add a number of obscuring considerations unrelated to the principal concern. The focus on male heads of households stems from the same concern, to allow direct attention to the presumed effects of independent versus dependent occupational status. Were we to take the occupations of persons (rather than of male househeads) a number of complications would be introduced, such as a very different sex composition of the occupations (e.g., there being very few independent businesswomen), a disproportionate number of widows and divorcees, and a different age distribution of employed men and women. To focus on occupations of individuals in short would mean introducing a large number of nonoccupational considerations which would obscure the intial relationship and force the use of detailed control tables. The procedure adopted here builds in these controls from the start.[3]

There is, on the whole, relatively little empirical work on the subject of independent businessmen.[4] For the most part the received lines of analysis have been passed on from commentator to commentator without any serious attempt being made to assess the basic claims. A major reason for the absence of studies evaluating these claims is that most research follows the U.S. census in the delineations of occupational categories, and the census makes use of a composite category, "Managers, Officials, and Proprietors." In addition, as has been noted, some independents are classed elsewhere in the census categories, according to their activity instead of their relationship to employer or to the market. Most published census material therefore does not allow examination of proprietors; and most surveys, unless they happened to include a question on self-employment versus employment by others, are also not in a position to address the questions raised in the theoretical tradition outlined here.

The various national election studies of the University of Michigan's Survey Research Center do permit this separation. These studies provide the basis for the assessment made in the following pages.[5] In addition, results of some smaller studies will be presented and evidence from some of the few previous researches will be cited. Because of the distinctive features of the 1964 and 1968 campaigns, both of which contained elements that should have appealed to independent businessmen, the major focus will be on those two studies. The 1952 and 1956 studies will be covered but in much less detail.

The major comparison will be with three categories of salaried employees, with those groups which have been called the new middle class. The three categories are: the combined managers and officials, the salaried professionals, and the combined clerical and sales employees. There is a convention in the contemporary social sciences which treats managers and professionals as "upper" middle class and clerical and sales employees as "lower," it being thought that there are clear and significant differences between them in terms of education, income, prestige, and other indicators of good or not-so-good living. As will be seen shortly, that characterization is not very adequate. Any suggestion, therefore, that one group is a "lower" and the other an "upper" middle class is to be avoided. Although it is frequently claimed that independents, too, are "lower" middle class, this is also open to question. The present task, in any event, is one of discovery or assessment rather than a priori determination.[6] For the sake of completeness, results for the small number of independent professionals and relatively small number of foremen are included in the presentation. And last but not least, also for completeness, the results for manual workers are presented.

THE ECONOMIC CONDITION

Possibly the most important single comment one could make about the economic condition of the independents would be to note the relatively wide dispersion of their incomes. The incomes of managers and officials and of salaried professionals tend to cluster in the middle and higher ranges. Clerical and sales incomes tend to cluster in the middle ranges, but the independent business category is distinctive in having a fairly high percentage in both higher and lower income categories. They are, in short, less homogeneous with respect to income than other middle class groups (Table 2.1).

One may summarize the findings as follows. Independent businessmen and the clerical and sales category contain the largest proportions of economically marginal families of the six middle class categories delineated here. To that extent the received formulations have some validity. It would, however, be a mistake to describe all families in those categories as marginal since the majority of both are in either the middle or higher income ranges.[7]

The objective facts of income are one thing, the subjective appreciations another. It is possible that because of differing backgrounds and expectations two groups might have identical incomes and widely differing levels of satisfaction, one group, perhaps, feeling it had finally arrived and another feeling it had lost its standing and had been declassed. The objective income level, in short, might have little relationship to the level of satisfaction. For this reason it is necessary to make an independent inquiry, rather than assuming the connection.

Looking at the levels of satisfaction or dissatisfaction expressed in 1964, one finds half of the independents saying they are pretty well satisfied and another two-fifths saying they are more-or-less satisifed. Although some 38 percent fell into the low income categories, only 9 percent of independents said they were not satisfied with their current financial standing. Hence, neither in terms of objective income levels nor in terms of subjective appreciations of that income is the picture one of widespread, majority stress. *Some* stress is indicated, but in both cases that is a minority phenomenon.[8]

The 1964 study allows exploration of two other related dimensions, the respondents' assessments of the trend in their personal finances over the past few years and their expectations with respect to the coming years.

TABLE 2.1
OCCUPATION, INCOME, AND ASSESSMENT OF ECONOMIC CONDITION:
Married, Economically Active Respondents (Survey Research Center, 1964 and 1968)

	Old Middle Class		New Middle Class				
	Independent Business	Independent Professional	Managers, Officials	Salaried Professionals	Clerical Sales	Foremen	Manuals
Family Income, 1964							
To $4,999	22%	—	7%	4%	15%	9%	25%
$5-$5,999	16	—	4	8	20	9	14
$6-$7,499	4	—	14	19	18	22	26
$7,500-$9,999	20	27%	24	23	23	22	21
$10-$14,999	25	7	32	29	17	38	11
$15,000 or more	13	67	20	17	5	—	2
N=	(116)	(15)	(102)	(104)	(98)	(32)	(425)
Family Income, 1968							
To $5,999	20	—	8	4	9	5	23
$6-$7,999	15	9	5	14	21	16	32
$8-$9,999	19	14	17	14	26	14	18
$10-$14,999	16	23	37	40	34	51	26
$15-$24,999	17	27	21	22	5	14	2
$25,000+	12	27	11	5	4	—	—
N=	(118)	(22)	(75)	(132)	(76)	(37)	(350)

1964:Q.42. We are also interested in how people are getting along financially these days. So far as you and your family are concerned, would you say that you are pretty well satisfied with your present financial situation, more-or-less satisfied, or not satisfied at all?

	Independent Business	Independent Professional	Managers, Officials	Salaried Professionals	Clerical Sales	Foremen	Manuals
Pretty well satisfied	50	69	60	48	37	35	42
More-or-less satisfied	40	19	35	42	47	56	42
Not satisfied at all	9	13	6	10	15	9	15
N=	(127)	(16)	(104)	(105)	(99)	(34)	(427)

TABLE 2.1 (Continued)

	Independent Business	Independent Professional	Managers, Officials	Salaried Professionals	Clerical Sales	Foremen	Manuals
1964:Q.43. *During the last few years, has your financial situation been getting better, getting worse, or has it stayed about the same?*							
Getting better	47	41	65	67	63	59	54
Stayed the same	38	53	34	27	28	24	37
Getting worse	16	6	1	7	9	18	9
N=	(128)	(17)	(103)	(105)	(99)	(34)	(431)
1964:Q.44. *Now looking ahead and thinking about the next few years, do you expect your financial situation will stay about the way it is now, get better, or get worse?*							
Get better	51	41	61	65	66	42	56
Stay way it is	40	59	32	33	30	48	39
Get worse	9	—	7	2	5	9	5
N=	(117)	(17)	(101)	(104)	(96)	(33)	(412)
1968:Q.1. *We are interested in how people are getting along financially these days—would you say that you and your family are better off or worse off financially than you were a year ago?*							
Better off	40	50	56	54	49	48	39
Same	48	50	23	24	35	39	45
Worse off	13	—	20	22	16	12	16
N=	(96)	(20)	(64)	(113)	(63)	(33)	(307)
1968:Q.3. *Now looking ahead—Do you think a year from now you people will be better off financially, or worse off, or just about the same as now?*							
Better off	29	55	54	50	55	42	35
Same	65	45	43	42	36	55	54
Worse off	6	—	3	8	9	3	11
N=	(84)	(20)	(61)	(109)	(58)	(33)	(267)

Without going into the details, one may note in summary that there are no sharp differences between independents and the salaried middle class. There are, nevertheless, some tendencies which would support the claims discussed previously.[9] Independents are somewhat more pessimistic in their assessment of past economic trends and are also more pessimistic about the future. The largest of these differences was with respect to the 1968 assessment of the future, this amounting to approximately 20 percentage points.

There is still another line of exploration one may undertake at this point. It would be easy to assume that the differences reported here, small though they may be, still result from the ineluctable processes of modern capitalist development. The dominance of the received line of theorizing could easily lead one to rest with that assumption. But it is clearly possible that the ever-familiar "other factors" might be present.

It is possible, for example, that independents are disproportionately located in the South, that entire region being characterized by relatively low incomes. Were that true, the meaning of the low income would probably be different because the assessment of the same "objective" amount might be more favorable in an area of relatively lower prices. According to the 1964 study, 27 percent of the independent businessmen were to be found in the South (which includes the border states). Forty-eight percent of the low income independents, however, taking the cutting line at $6,000, were Southern. Although the poorer independents are disproportionately Southern, the majority of the independents expressing dissatisfaction with their earnings were not Southern. A similar disjunction appears also in another comparison. Poorer independents tend to be located in the smaller communities. (This assertion holds for both Southern and non-Southern regions.) Dissatisfaction, however, tends to be greatest in the larger cities.

One other point is worth attention. Perception of an unfavorable past trend and anticipation of an unfavorable future are both strongly related to age. The group who are 55 years or older are extremely pessimistic.

The "strains" to be found in the ranks of the independents, in other words, appear to be linked to the frailties or disabilities of age rather than to the dynamics of advanced capitalism. With stress concentrated in the older age groups, the likelihood of a significant reaction developing within this category, in particular the development of an active, permanent rightist movement, would seem to be limited. It would be unlikely both because of the economic limitations of elderly and marginal independents and because most people begin retiring from active political effort at this age. The other part of the picture involves young independents. They reported relatively high levels of satisfaction and very favorable recent trends. They also have high expectations for the future.[10]

It is possible to make an assessment of still another feature of the independent businessman's condition. Because of difficulties in his economic situation, because of his helplessness and inability to control or, in many instances, even to influence his situation, his response supposedly is one of frustration and anger. It is this special psychological syndrome that provides the explosive force to his reaction—when it comes.

The 1964 Survey Research Center study contained a Political Efficacy Index which combined four questions tapping the sense of being able to understand and to have an influence on political events. If the assumptions of the received line of theorizing are correct, one should discover a widespread sense of helplessness indicated among independents and, by contrast, there should be a sensed ability to control indicated in the new middle classes, particularly among managers and salaried professionals. The sense of political efficacy among the independents is lower than that of the other two groups, but, as in the previous results, the differences were small ones.[11]

An examination of responses to the detailed questions, in this case using the improved formulations of the 1968 study, showed rather erratic results. Some questions did show support for the claim of "powerlessness" felt by independents. They were the most likely of the middle class groups to feel that public officials did not "care much at all" about people like themselves. They were also the most likely to report that voting was their "only way" to "have any say" about how the government runs things. And they also had the highest percentage saying that they could not really understand the affairs of government. Still, some new middle class groups closely approximated their sense of powerlessness in their responses to these questions. The most significant disaffection was indicated in response to a question about not having "much say" in political affairs. Seven out of ten of the independents agreed with that statement. This did not, however, make them a specially disaffected group, since the sentiment was shared pretty much across the board; there was less sensed powerlessness among the salaried professionals (only six out of ten) and somewhat more among the manuals (eight of ten).[12]

In summary we may note that independents do have a larger economically marginal subgroup than other middle class categories. It should, nevertheless, be noted that this by no means indicates that all independents are marginal. Independents were also more likely to report unfavorable recent economic trends and to anticipate a bleak future than were the new middle class segments although once again only a minority of them do so. And finally there is some, albeit very fragmentary, evidence showing a tendency for independents to feel powerless, more so than for some of the new middle class categories. It cannot be stressed too much that all of these differences involve *tendencies*. The occupational category in question is "somewhat" less well off or somewhat more disaffected than the others. In no case do we have sizable, categoric differences. In short, there is very little basis provided in this evidence for a theory of world historic significance.

These differences do, however, all run in the "right" direction, that is, they do provide some, albeit limited, support for the received claim. That degree of economic stress and that degree of sensed powerlessness could provide, if the theory were adequate, at least some basis for the well-known business conservatism and/or reaction.

POLITICAL PARTY PREFERENCES

The second major claim made about independent businessmen involves their conservatism. Their political outlooks, presumably, are forced on them by the stresses of their economic condition.

The received formulations rarely say anything about frequency distributions, independent businessmen being treated characteristically as a monolith, all subject to the same strains, all reacting in the same way. This has typically been taken to mean monolithic support for Republican candidates, and the more conservative the Republican the better. In the South, at one time at least, there was an obvious variant on this theme; there, independents would support conservative Democrats. In recent years, however, with the "emergence of a two-party South" and the development of a "viable" Republican alternative, the region's independents could and presumably would come out for a conservative Republican as opportunities presented themselves. One such opportunity appeared with the candidacy of Barry Goldwater in 1964.

The available evidence does not support the expectation of monolithic Republicanism. A majority of independent businessmen in the 1964 study identified themselves as Democrats (Table 2.2).[13] In fact, all middle class groups (with the single exception of the small number of independent professionals) had majorities saying they were Democratic. Even when one compares relative sizes of the Republican minorities, independents still do not stand out as especially conservative. The Republican percentage for independents is the same as that for the salaried professionals, below that of the managers and officials and somewhat above that of clerical and sales employees.

The 1964 election provided an occasion for assessing the claim that independents prefer conservative Republicans, those aligned with or supporting nineteenth-century, laissez-faire positions. That election did present a candidate who offered something of an old-style conservative line. In sharp contrast to the "me tooism" of the so-called liberal Republicanism which had dominated the party from the candidacy of Wendell Willkie through that of Thomas E. Dewey and up to Dwight D. Eisenhower, Barry Goldwater offered "a choice, not an echo." If independent businessmen were attracted by such old-style themes, they had the opportunity to demonstrate by their voting in that particular season.[14]

The basic result (taking the votes and the expressed preferences of the nonvoters) is very simple: the claim is not supported.[15] A

TABLE 2.2
OCCUPATION AND PARTY PREFERENCE: SAME BY REGION:
Married, Economically Active Respondents (Survey Research Center, 1964 and 1968)

	Old Middle Class		New Middle Class				Manuals
	Independent Business	Independent Professional	Managers, Officials	Salaried Professionals	Clerical Sales	Foremen	
Party Identification, 1964*							
Democrat	61%	40%	55%	61%	68%	58%	76%
Republican	39	60	45	39	32	42	24
N=	(113)	(15)	(94)	(99)	(90)	(31)	(385)
1964 Vote**							
Democrat	62	59	52	64	68	63	80
Republican	38	41	48	36	32	38	20
N=	(112)	(17)	(96)	(98)	(91)	(32)	(388)
Non-Southern Respondents							
Party Identification							
Democrat	53	38	50	58	68	54	72
Republican	47	62	50	42	32	46	28
N=	(86)	(13)	(64)	(74)	(53)	(24)	(285)
1964 Vote*							
Democrat	61	57	55	64	76	69	81
Republican	39	43	45	36	24	31	19
N=	(84)	(14)	(64)	(70)	(55)	(26)	(288)
Southern Respondents							
Party Identification, 1964							
Democrat	85	***	67	68	68	***	87
Republican	15		33	32	32		13
N=	(27)		(30)	(25)	(37)		(100)

TABLE 2.2 (Continued)

	Independent Business	Independent Professional	Managers, Officials	Salaried Professionals	Clerical Sales	Foremen	Manuals
Southern Respondents							
1964 Vote*							
Democrat	64	***	47	64	56	***	79
Republican	36		53	36	44		21
N=	(28)		(32)	(28)	(36)		(100)
Party Identification, 1968							
Democrat	63	35	58	47	64	62	72
Republican	37	65	42	53	36	38	28
N=	(99)	(20)	(62)	(126)	(75)	(34)	(306)
1968 Vote**							
Democrat	44	35	27	35	47	29	47
Republican	45	60	56	58	39	50	36
Wallace	12	5	17	7	14	21	16
N=	(101)	(20)	(64)	(117)	(64)	(34)	(295)
Non-Southern Respondents							
Party Identification, 1968							
Democrat	57	25	51	43	67	58	70
Republican	43	75	49	57	33	42	30
N=	(70)	(16)	(45)	(86)	(60)	(26)	(208)
1968 Vote***							
Democrat	43	33	33	38	53	36	49
Republican	50	67	54	56	37	43	42
Wallace	7	—	13	6	10	21	9
N=	(74)	(15)	(46)	(81)	(49)	(28)	(203)

TABLE 2.2 (Continued)

| | Old Middle Class | | New Middle Class | | | | |
	Independent Business	Independent Professional	Managers, Officials	Salaried Professionals	Clerical Sales	Foremen	Manuals
Southern Respondents							
Party Identification, 1968							
Democrat	76%	***	76%	55%	53%	***	78%
Republican	24		24	45	47		22
N=	(29)		(17)	(40)	(15)		(98)
1968 Vote							
Democrat	44	***	11	28	27	***	43
Republican	30		61	64	47		24
Wallace	26		28	8	27		33
N=	(27)		(18)	(36)	(15)		(92)

* See note 13 for explanation.

** Combines both votes and the preference of non-voters. See note 15 for explanation.

*** Too few cases.

fair-sized majority of independent businessmen favored the Democratic candidate, Lyndon Johnson, in that election. Independent businessmen, moreover, were not distinctive as far as the size of their Republican minority is concerned. The Republican percentage was little different from that for salaried professionals and was only slightly larger than the figure for clerical and sales employees. The distinctive center of conservatism was found among managers and officials, 48 percent of them having voted for or favored the Goldwater candidacy.

It is possible, of course, that this result is confounded by the regional factor. A separate examination of the non-Southern respondents, however, did not alter the picture in any significant way. The highest levels of conservatism were still found among managers and officials and among the small group of independent professionals. There is also no support for the conventional hypothesis within the South. The parallel claim about the special "moderation" of managers is not supported.[16] In the South the latter group actually shows a small majority in favor of the Goldwater candidacy.[17]

The overall pattern of party identifications in 1968 is very similar to that observed in 1964. The only important difference appears among salaried professionals, a small majority in 1968 indicating a Republican identification. Independent businessmen again show a Democratic majority.

The 1968 election campaign provided an opportunity to vote for a different kind of insurgent candidate but one who "should have" attracted the independents. The Wallace candidacy came with all the standard fundamentalist themes, a dominant one being the reestablishment of something called "order" and another being a reduction in the power of the federal government. The evidence, however, does not show any special attraction felt within the ranks of independents. The overall percentage for Wallace is below that among managers and officials and roughly equal to that of the clerical and sales group. Independents, together with the clerical and sales group, also had relatively high levels of support for the Democrat, Hubert Humphrey, eschewing the "moderate" Republican Richard Nixon.

There was a considerable defection from normal Democratic

levels, this being indicated by the differences between the party identification and voting percentages. But even here, shifting occurred across the board and was not especially pronounced among independents.

Even when the 1968 result was broken down by region, there still was no support shown for the standard expectation. Non-Southern independents had a higher level of Democratic identification than either managers and officials or salaried professionals. The highest level of Democratic sentiment appeared among clerical and sales employees, this being 10 percentage points greater than among independent businessmen.[18]

This lack of distinctiveness in party orientations of independent businessmen was also indicated in a number of other studies. A detailed presentation and discussion of these other results would not be justified. A brief summary, however, does indicate that the 1964 and 1968 results do not stand alone, that is, they are not "exceptional" or "erratic" studies.

The 1956 Survey Research Center study showed very similar results in regard to both party identifications and voting. In this study, independents did prove to be slightly more Republican than both managers and officials and salaried professionals, the differences amounting to 2 and 5 percentage points, respectively. But again all major groups were Democratic in their majority. In the voting that year salaried professionals stood out as the most Republican, but otherwise there were no major differences between the various segments of the middle class.

In the 1952 Survey Research Center Study independents proved to be the most Democratic in identification of the major middle class groups, although again this was a matter of only a few percentage points. In regard to 1952 voting, the first of the Eisenhower elections, they were undistinguished among middle class segments, neither the highest nor the lowest in Republican voting, all these segments varying between 61 and 71 percent Republican.

An examination of a large National Opinion Research Center (NORC) study, a nationwide survey done in 1955, showed independent businessmen to have the lowest level of Republican identification, that being 36 percent (N=156). The next lowest figure was 46 percent (N=134) among the clerical and sales employees.

All five studies reviewed thus far were based on national samples. Four of the five show independent businessmen as essentially no different from other segments of the middle class. And in one, the NORC study, the evidence goes slightly against the assumption of independent business conservatism.

A study of the Detroit area population from 1958 also showed independent businessmen to have the lowest level of Republican identification. This was only 3 percentage points below the clerical and sales category, but the figure was well below managers and salaried professionals. A reanalysis of another community study, done in Elmira, New York, in 1948, also showed the independents to be slightly below the clerical and sales employees in the level of both Republican identification in the 1948 voting. The highest Republicanism was among managers and officials and salaried professionals.

The basic conclusion to be drawn from this review of seven studies, five national and two local, is that *none* of them supports the assumption of independent business conservatism.[19]

This lack of distinctiveness is all the more surprising given some of the background characteristics of independent businessmen. They are somewhat more likely to have come from farm families than is true of those in the three major new middle class categories and, an obvious correlate, they are more likely to have been raised in rural areas and in small towns. They also tend to be still living in those locations. And, a third characteristic of the category, they are older on average than the other groups. In this respect the differences are very pronounced, independent business, after all, being one line of enterprise without mandatory retirement. All three of these characteristics are ordinarily associated with higher levels of Republican sentiment. It seems likely that a comparison with these factors controlled would show independents to be even less Republican, relative to their new middle class peers, than this presentation has indicated.[20]

ATTITUDES TOWARD ECONOMIC ISSUES

It is possible that party identifications and candidate choices do not provide an adequate indication of actual issue orientations.

Those preferences may be part of a tradition or heritage passed on within a family, within an ethnic group, or within a region. Although a majority of independent businessmen favor the more "liberal" of the two parties, their issue orientations might be conservative in character.

Inquiry into this matter does not support this alternative "saving" assumption. Once again the basic picture is one of no support for the conventional hypothesis.

We may consider first a question on the power of the government in Washington, whether or not it is excessive. In 1964 a majority of independents, 56 percent, indicated they thought the federal government was too powerful.[21] This result would appear to support the original line of speculation about the special hostility independents feel for the "threatening" costs and powers of government. In this respect, however, the independents proved to be very similar to other middle class segments (Table 2.3).

When it comes to specific federal government contributions, we find a somewhat more complicated picture. Majorities of all major middle class groups oppose federal government aid to education. The differences between those groups, once again however, are not very large. It will be noted, in passing, that a somewhat larger percentage of blue-collar workers favor such aid, a distribution of attitudes which goes against another of the standbys of the conventional imagery, specifically the notion of middle class responsibility and working class indifference or irresponsibility.

Asked whether the federal government should guarantee a job and a good living standard, middle class ranks exhibit a fairly uniform majority opposition, but again there is little difference between independents and the various categories of the salaried employees. Once again, blue-collar workers show a different pattern, half of them favoring a government role in this area.

When respondents were asked about a federal government role in guaranteeing medical care for the general population, a slight majority of independents proved to be in favor of such government action. Once more the independent-salaried distinction proved to be of little importance: all major middle class groups have approximately the same percentage in favor of that effort.

The 1968 study indicated that the level of concern over "government power" had increased somewhat as compared to 1964. As of 1968 independent businessmen had the highest level of concern over this question of any of the major middle class categories. The level of objection was 10 percentage points above that of the clerical and sales employees, this being the largest difference indicated.

There had also been some shifting on the school aid question over the four years with greater opposition to federal aid indicated in the later study. Here too independent businessmen were the most conservative of the major middle class groups although again the differences were small, the largest being only 7 percentage points.

Approximately three out of four independent businessmen in the 1968 study opposed a federal government role to guarantee jobs and living standards. This level was slightly below that of managers and officials but above that of salaried professionals and clerical and sales employees (by 11 and 13 percentage points, respectively).

The overall trend during the four years with respect to medical care was toward increased support for federal aid, this despite the opposite trend in concern with "government power." A majority of independents at this point in time thought the government should help, a level which was about average for middle class segments of the population.

The 1956 Survey Research Center study contained some questions similar to those used in the later studies. Again only a brief summary is practical. A question on a federal role to help pay school building costs found 80 percent (N=103) of independents approving. A similar level was found among clerical and sales employees (81 percent, N=103), and both figures were slightly higher than the level for the managers and officials (74 percent, N=92) and the salaried professionals (71 percent, N=95). A question on government help so as to provide doctor and hospital care at low cost found 61 percent (N=103) of independents agreeing, followed by 58 percent (N=100) of clerical and sales employees, 52 percent (N=89) of managers, and 49 percent (N=93) of salaried professionals. And a question on a federal government job guarantee (no mention this time of living standards) found 65 percent

TABLE 2.3
OCCUPATION AND ECONOMIC ISSUES:
Married, Economically Active Respondents (Survey Research Center, 1964 and 1968)

	Old Middle Class		New Middle Class				
	Independent Business	Independent Professional	Managers, Officials	Salaried Professionals	Clerical Sales	Foremen	Manuals

1964: Q.15,15A Some people are afraid the government in Washington is getting too powerful for the good of the country and the individual person. Others feel that the government in Washington has not gotten too strong for the good of the country. Have you been interested enough in this to favor one side over the other (if yes) what is your feeling, do you think the government is

	Independent Business	Independent Professional	Managers, Officials	Salaried Professionals	Clerical Sales	Foremen	Manuals
Too powerful	56%	56%	55%	49%	52%	50%	36%
Not too powerful	44	44	45	51	48	50	64
N=	(84)	(16)	(77)	(85)	(73)	(20)	(260)

1964: Q.16,16A Some people think the government in Washington should help towns and cities provide education for grade and high school children, others think this should be handled by the states and local communities. Have you been interested enough in this to favor one side over the other (if yes) which are you in favor of?

	Independent Business	Independent Professional	Managers, Officials	Salaried Professionals	Clerical Sales	Foremen	Manuals
Federal help	32	31	34	35	37	45	46
State and local	62	69	66	65	63	55	54
N=	(101)	(13)	(85)	(81)	(78)	(29)	(331)

1964: Q.17,17A In general, some people feel that the government in Washington should see to it that every person has a job and good standard of living. Others think the government should just let each person get ahead on his own. Have you been interested enough in this to favor one side over the other. (If yes) do you think that the government

	Independent Business	Independent Professional	Managers, Officials	Salaried Professionals	Clerical Sales	Foremen	Manuals
Should help	30	29	25	37	29	35	52
Should not	70	71	75	63	71	65	48
N=	(89)	(14)	(83)	(75)	(76)	(26)	(311)

1964: Q.18,18A Some say the government in Washington ought to help people get doctors and hospital care at low cost, others say the government should not get into this. Have you been interested enough in this to favor one side over the other (if yes) what is your position? The government in Washington

	Independent Business	Independent Professional	Managers, Officials	Salaried Professionals	Clerical Sales	Foremen	Manuals
Should help	54	23	52	53	51	56	71
Should not	46	77	48	47	49	44	29
N=	(103)	(13)	(75)	(83)	(79)	(27)	(330)

TABLE 2.3 (Continued)

	Independent Business	Independent Professional	Managers, Officials	Salaried Professionals	Clerical Sales	Foremen	Manuals
1968:Q.19,19A Government power*							
Too powerful	68	55	60	62	58	69	49
Not too powerful	32	45	40	38	42	31	51
N=	(94)	(20)	(64)	(106)	(59)	(29)	(238)
1968:Q.20,20A School aid**							
Government aid to education							
Federal help	29	47	36	34	31	24	38
State and local help	71	53	64	66	69	76	62
N=	(95)	(17)	(59)	(116)	(59)	(25)	(283)
1968:Q.21,21A Medical care**							
Should help	58	60	66	52	58	58	73
Should not	42	40	34	48	42	42	27
N=	(98)	(15)	(58)	(102)	(59)	(26)	(266)
1968:22,22A Job and living standard**							
Should help	26	43	22	37	39	23	45
Should not	74	57	78	63	61	77	55
N=	(96)	(14)	(59)	(94)	(62)	(30)	(293)

* With one small change, question the same as in 1964.

** Same as 1964.

(N=65) of independents agreeing, 67 percent (N=97) of clericals, 51 percent (N=85) of managers, and only 33 percent (N=101) of salaried professionals.[22]

The evidence from these national studies, to summarize, does not support the assumption of independent business conservatism. The best overall summary would note merely the absence of significant differences between the major middle class segments. There was fragmentary support for the claim indicated in the responses to some of the questions in the 1968 study, but the small percentage differences indicated are scarcely of the order that would warrant the creation of, or in this case the maintenance of, a significant body of theorizing. The evidence from the 1956 study, it will be noted, went in the opposite direction; in that study independent businessmen, together with the clerical and sales employees, proved the most liberal of the major middle class categories.

One of the community studies discussed previously contained a range of economic liberalism questions somewhat more extensive than those discussed above. This study, the Elmira inquiry of 1948, also contained questions with explicit evaluations of both union and big business performance.

The first of these questions proved to be one of the few discovered in this entire review which showed a near monolithic conservatism among businessmen, only one person in eight among them *opposed* to the Taft-Hartley Law (Table 2.4). This low percentage in opposition to the law, however, was a matter of 5 and 9 percentage points in the respective comparisons with managers and salaried professionals.

None of the other evidence from this study supports traditional expectations. The study was a panel study. Interviews were conducted in June, in August, and once again in October; and the final result was picked up with a mailed questionnaire. A June question asking about reinstituting price controls showed 43 percent of the independents favoring that possibility, a level higher than that of the three other middle class groups. The same question in October showed an across-the-board increase in the percentages favoring a restoration of price controls. By then approximately half the independents, who, it will be remembered,

TABLE 2.4
OCCUPATION AND ECONOMIC LIBERALISM: Married, Economically Active Respondents (Elmira, 1948)

	Occupation of Head of Household				
	Independent Business	Managerial* Executive	Salaried Professional	White* Collar	Manuals
August Q.26c	And you personally—are you for the Taft-Hartley law or against it?				
% against	12%	17%	21%	41%	51%
N=	(51)	(29)	(28)	(36)	(257)
June Q.27.	Do you think it would be better to put price controls back on some things, or let things work out as they are now without price controls?				
% for controls	43	27	38	37	47
N=	(106)	(52)	(39)	(89)	(439)
August Q.25c	How do you personally feel about this—are you in favor of putting back price controls on some things or of leaving prices without controls as they are now?				
% for controls	52	49	49	63	66
N=	(86)	(41)	(35)	(70)	(367)
October Q.39	How do you personally feel about this—are you for or against having the government sponsor more public housing projects?				
% favoring public housing	80	63	75	84	92
N=	(81)	(40)	(36)	(70)	(359)
June Q.26	With which of these four statements do you come closest to agreeing? 1. Labor unions in this country are doing a fine job. 2. While they do make some mistakes, on the whole labor unions are doing more good than harm. 3. Although we need labor unionism in this country, they do more harm than good the way they are run now. 4. This country would be better off without any labor unions at all.				
% choosing 1 or 2	42	48	44	49	68
N=	(106)	(52)	(39)	(89)	(446)
October Q.22	Same as above.				
% choosing 1 or 2	64	64	54	53	77
N=	(86)	(39)	(37)	(73)	(359)

TABLE 2.4 (Continued)

	Independent Business	Managerial* Executive	Salaried Professional	White* Collar	Manuals
June Q.28	During the past ten years there have been a number of corporations that sold one billion dollars or more of goods each year. Which of these four statements come closest to describing your feelings about a corporation that does this much business? 1. It is dangerous for the welfare of the country for any companies to be this big and they should be broken up into small companies. 2. While it may be necessary to have some very large companies, we should watch their activities very closely and discourage their activities as much as possible. 3. There may be some drawbacks to having such large companies, but on the whole they do more good than harm to the country. 4. It is foolish to worry about a company just because it is big; large companies have made America the kind of country it is today.				
% choosing 3 or 4	72	77	72	82	73
N=	(105)	(53)	(39)	(88)	(418)

* Category labels are changed somewhat following those used in this study.

are thought to be hostile to all kinds of government bureaucracy and red tape, were in favor of that kind of government action.

A question on government sponsorship of public housing projects, an effort which in some circles at that time was thought to mean the coming of socialism, found 80 percent of the independents approving those government measures.

In June of 1948 respondents were asked to choose from among four assessments of the activities of labor unions. Approximately two-fifths of the businessmen gave either unqualified approval or, the more frequent response, felt that they were doing "more good than harm." Their level of approval was not significantly different from that of other middle class groups. When the question was repeated in October, there was again an increase in approval to be noted, this occurring in all six categories. At that point the level of approval among independent businessmen had risen to 64 percent, a level which, together with that of managers and officials, was the highest of the middle class segments.

In June of 1948 there was a similar question asked about large corporations. At that time 72 percent of independent businessmen indicated either full or qualified approval of those corporations and their actions. In this respect they were not at all distinguished; all occupational segments in Elmira indicated equivalent levels of support for the "billion dollar" corporation.

The Elmira evidence, to summarize, shows one fragment of support for the received hypothesis, this being the extremely high level of conservatism indicated in the response to the Taft-Hartley question. For the rest, however, the results contained no support for the business conservatism hypothesis. In October of 1948 half of these independent businessmen were in favor of price controls, something which would certainly bring "government bureaucracy" into very close and direct contact with their own affairs. There was a very sizable majority in favor of government sponsorship of public housing projects. And, contrary to the assumption of hostility toward labor and big business, as of October, a majority indicated support for *both* of these institutional developments. Except for the Taft-Hartley question, where smallish percentage differences in favor of the received hypothesis appeared, there was no distinctive pattern of opinion to be found among independents.[23]

The review of the evidence as conducted to this point indicates that those lines of theorizing which have asserted that independents constitute a special source of reaction, of opposition to the major contemporary institutional developments, and, in particular, of opposition to government-supported welfare innovations, appear to be mistaken. Almost all differences discovered here are small ones, at best a matter of a few percentage points. In some instances, it will be noted, the small difference is even in the opposite direction from that predicted by the theory, that is, independents prove to be *more* liberal than the other middle class groups.

In summary, the evidence considered thus far provides very little support for the hypothesis of independent business conservatism. Comparisons with salaried middle class segments in the areas of party identifications, party choices, and economic issue orientations provide no *systematic* evidence to support the basic claim. Most comparisons show no difference, and some even indicate reversal, that is, that independent businessmen are more "liberal" than the middle class categories.[24]

When social commentators assert, as they have for some decades, that strains suffered by independent businessmen lead to conservative politics and rightest propensities, it is clear they have not been thinking in terms of miniscule percentage differences between that group and their supposedly more moderate and responsible middle class peers. Although rarely indicating anything about magnitudes or frequencies, these formulations clearly involve the assumption of sizable differences. That assumption is not justified by the present review of evidence.

There are some objections one might raise about the adequacy of this test of the claim. It might be objected that these studies did not occur during "crisis" conditions: only then would the "real test" come.

There is very little that can be offered by way of assessing this alternative. Economic crises come in two basic varieties, inflationary and deflationary. The studies reviewed here, extending from 1948 (the Elmira study) through to the 1968 inquiry of the Survey Research Center, cover two decades in which conditions have alternated between recessions and relatively mild inflation. The studies at hand are best for providing some limited indication of the impact of the inflationary phase of these cycles.

There was a general rise in prices between 1964 and 1968 (and continuing into the immediately following years) such that the 1968 study allows some assessment of the reaction to an inflationary trend. As judged by their voting in 1968 (shown in Table 2.2), there was no special tendency for independent businessmen to turn in a rightist direction at that time.

The only other bit of evidence on the impact of inflationary pressures appears in the 1948 Elmira study. Wartime price controls had only recently been lifted and had allowed one of the largest general price increases of the entire century. A number of giant strikes occurred, stimulated by the inflation, which crippled the economy and dominated the headlines for weeks. There were also, in the investigations of domestic communism, many occasions for generation of alarm and for convenient scapegoating.

Despite the turbulence of the period, the evidence showed that the independent businessmen of Elmira reacted with *increased* sentiment in favor of labor unions and *increased* sentiment in favor of a reimposition of price controls (Table 2.4). Given the clear choice that year between Republican Thomas E. Dewey and the Democratic president, Harry S. Truman, the "fighting liberal," independent businessmen tended, moreso than the various salaried middle classes, to favor the latter. The preference of Elmira's independent businessmen for the "liberal" Truman is also indicated in a national study. The 1952 Survey Research Center study asked a retrospective question about the 1948 vote, and that too showed a disproportionate Democratic preference.[25]

There is much less evidence available on the impact of a serious depression such as that of the thirties. The limited studies that are available, however, do not support the expectation of conservatism or of a rightist reaction.

A study done in Chicago in 1937 came up with quite the opposite result. Over half the small business owners favored New Deal policies. The sentiments expressed on a wide range of issue questions do not suggest monolithic, or even predominant, rightist sentiment. Two-fifths of the small businessmen said it was "the fault of the capitalist system" that there were so many poor and unemployed. Four-fifths said wealthy businessmen had too much influence in running national affairs. In contrast to the Lipset claim that "these people are oriented upward wishing to become larger businessmen . . . ," this Chicago study found 77 percent thinking that business leaders and executives "get too much" pay. By comparison, 68 percent of them thought unskilled workers and laborers did not get enough pay. Some 58 percent thought the government should aim at making people's wealth and incomes more nearly equal. About one in five said they "would like to see the government own and run the big industries of the country." Two-fifths favored strong labor unions with closed shops.[26]

Another study from the thirties investigated a related subject, attitudes toward property. This study was done in Akron, Ohio, a city that had experienced a sitdown strike in 1937, workers in all the major rubber companies having occupied and held the factories. The study presented eight brief stories involving rights of property (farmers preventing a mortgage foreclosure, unemployed miners appropriating coal during the winter, a sitdown strike, etc.) and asked whether respondents approved or disapproved. Respondents were scored on a scale ranging from 32 (absolute private property position) to zero (absolute social property view). The small merchants, of all major middle class occupations, fell closest to the latter end of the continuum with a mean score of 12.1. The only middle class groups more socially minded were ministers and W.P.A. (Works Progress Administration) white-collar workers. Small merchants also had the highest standard deviation (S.D. = 8.5) of thirteen occupational categories meaning that they had the least consensus of all these groups. "Business leaders" (managers), by comparison, had a mean of 29.1 and a standard deviation of 2.61. Their mean was approximately 10 points higher than the next middle class group, and the standard deviation was less than half that of the next group. In other words, managers showed a remarkable degree of conservatism on the subject of private property, and they had an extremely high consensus on the matter.[27]

There are, to be sure, a few studies that do offer support for the business conservatism hypothesis. There is, first of all, the work of Martin Trow, an investigation of reactions to the efforts of Senator Joseph McCarthy. The study was done in Bennington, Vermont, in 1954. His evidence shows that small businessmen in that community were *not* exceptionally conservative.[28] At the same time, however, when these small businessmen were asked about their attitudes toward McCarthy's methods, with education controlled, the opinions they expressed were consistently more favorable than those of salaried white-collar employees. Concerning big business and labor unions, these small businessmen were more likely to oppose both, and those who did so were called "nineteenth-century liberals." Small businessmen, it was found, expressed a relatively high level of approval for McCarthy's methods. An even higher level of support for McCarthy was found among the small businessmen who were nineteenth-century liberals. Lipset repeated this procedure with a larger study (N=9852) drawn from eleven states. His conclusion reads: "Efforts at partial replication of Trow's analysis with [these] data did not yield comparable results. . . . The hypothesis must be placed in the category of the not proven."[29]

Lipset has presented evidence from two studies of the period which allow a comparison of the independent businessmen with other segments of the population. A Roper study from 1952, before the strong revulsion to McCarthy's methods had appeared, showed small businessmen the most favorably disposed of all occupations. The difference was one of 17 percentage points vis-a-vis professionals and executives and 11 percentage points in the comparison with clerical and sales employees. The large study mentioned above found professionals and executives and managers to be strongly opposed. Otherwise the differences between independent businessmen and other occupations (especially the white-collar group and the supervisors and foremen) were very small, a matter of a few percentage points. One of the most persistent findings in these studies is a strong relationship with education, the less educated being more likely to approve McCarthy's activities. It seems likely that an education control would eliminate some or possibly all of this difference between the relatively well-educated professionals and managers and the less well-educated businessmen.[30]

The evidence from studies done during the depression, in short, does not support the assumption of either conservative or reactionary tendencies among independent businessmen. That evidence, to be sure, involves only two studies, one from Chicago and one from Akron. It is to be noted, however, that these studies do provide systematic evidence as opposed to impressions (or possibly mere arbitrary judgments) from the period.

The *evidence* in favor of the conventional hypothesis is very limited. Some supporting evidence comes from the study of Bennington, Vermont. That study, however, did not find independent businessmen to be more conservative than other middle class groups and also did not find them to be less tolerant of deviations from mainstream political orientations. The support for the conventional view appeared only in their approval of McCarthy's methods. The other support for the thesis is found in two studies reported by Lipset. They provided only limited support for the claim, however, the differences being rather small and possibly the result of educational rather than occupational determinants.

SMALL VERSUS NOT-SO-SMALL INDEPENDENTS

The assessment made thus far has dealt with the entire category of independents. Following the main line of tradition, however, one would expect the most serious strains, and presumably the most formidable reactions, to be found among small businessmen. It is possible, in other words, that the results as presented thus far hide support for the received thesis since they would average the responses of the marginal independents together with those of the well-off and affluent ones. To address this possibility, it is necessary to explore the differences *within* the independent business category.

The special focus on small businessmen has been made by numerous commentators. One such statement is that of A. A. Berle, co-author of a leading work on American corporations, author of numerous writings on the operation of the American economy, and at one time the honorary chairman of the Liberal party in the state of New York. He put the matter as follows:

> Small business almost invariably is more conservative than much of big business . . . they always were unchangeably against any Democrat—except . . . in the Solid South. . . . the several million votes of 'small business,' since they rarely, if ever, are detached from the Republican or (in the South) conservative column, will not produce any spectacular changes. They simply will be where they always were . . . The hardware stores in Des Moines, Iowa, or the little machine shops on the outskirts of Los Angeles are apt to be run by men who believe the country started down the primrose path to Gehenna when President Taft was defeated in 1912.[31]

This formulation predicts little more than a bland, sluggish, and unenlightened conservatism on the part of small businessmen. Other formulations suggest a much more alarming and dramatic potential.[32]

Again one may ask the question: Is it so?

The Berle claims are relatively easy to assess. One can compare the politics of small businessmen with those of "big business." Because that latter expression is not clarified, we have compared in two directions, with the more affluent independents (who, in general, would be "bigger" in terms of capital assets, sales, and employment) and with the more affluent managers (who are likely to be executives in larger firms). Berle, it will be noted, assumes near monolithic conservatism on the part of the small businessmen (i.e., "almost invariably"). Although he makes no specification of the quantities or the percentages, he does indicate the relative positions of these groups with his claim that "much of big business" is *less* conservative than this small business monolith.

Looking first at the 1964 party identifications of non-Southern independents, we find a very simple pattern: Republican sentiment increases with the level of income (Table 2.5). Looking at managers and officials, one finds no sharp differences associated with income: both levels of managers shown in the table are more Republican in their preferences than either lower or middle income independents. One concludes from this evidence that small

TABLE 2.5
PARTY IDENTIFICATIONS AND VOTING OF INDEPENDENTS AND MANAGERS BY INCOME: NON-SOUTH ONLY:
Married, Active Respondents

	Independent Business			Managers, Officials		
Family Income, 1964	To $5,999	$6,000 -9,999	$10,000 or more	To $5,999	$6,000 -9,999	$10,000 or more
Party Identification, 1964						
Democrat	64%	60%	42%	*	44%	47%
Republican	36	40	58		56	53
N=	(22)	(20)	(36)	(6)	(25)	(32)
1964 Vote**						
Democrat	71	59	50	*	64	45
Republican	29	41	50		36	55
N=	(21)	(22)	(34)	(5)	(25)	(33)
Family Income, 1968	To $7,999	$8,000- 14,999	$15,000 or more	To $7,999	$8,000- 14,999	$15,000 or more
Party Identification, 1968						
Democrat	61	62	41	*	60	38
Republican	39	38	59		40	63
N=	(23)	(29)	(17)	(5)	(25)	(16)
1968 Vote						
Democrat	50	46	30	*	33	27
Republican	45	46	61		55	53
Wallace	5	7	9		11	20
N=	(22)	(28)	(23)	(3)	(27)	(15)

* Too few cases.
** Includes also the preferences of the nonvoters.

businessmen are less conservative (or more liberal) than either more affluent independents or managers, regardless of the income level of the latter.

The 1964 voting pattern also provides no support for the received wisdom since, once again, among independents the level of Republican preference increases with income level. A similar pattern appears now among managers. The significant finding is the absence of support for the Berle hypothesis. Small business ranks provided the least support for Goldwater, the conservative Republican candidate. And conversely, the greatest support appeared among high income managers.

The 1968 study shows a similar pattern. There is, in this case, no difference in the party identifications of low and middle income independents: both groups show Democratic majorities in contrast to the Republican majority among more affluent businessmen. The comparison of businessmen with managers and officials this time shows very little difference between these occupational segments.

The pattern of 1968 voting shows Democratic preferences again to be inversely related to income. If the Wallace candidacy was purported to attract the "little man," it is not shown in this result since there is little variation by income level. What little variation exists is in the opposite direction, support for Wallace being positively rather than negatively related to income. Again, the comparison of the voting of small businessmen and managers shows no support for the Berle hypothesis.

Similar results appeared in the 1952 and 1956 Survey Research Center studies. The relationship, however, was not always linear. In the 1956 study, for example, the lowest income category had a somewhat higher Republican percentage than the middle income independents. Even in this case, however, the small businessmen did not present a monolith because they divided fifty-fifty between the parties, and that 50 percent level of Republicanism was still considerably lower than the figure among high income businessmen.[33] Independent businessmen, moreover, with only a few insignificant exceptions, had higher levels of Democratic identifications than equivalent managers. These differences were most pronounced at highest income levels where Republican sentiment among managers was very strong.

An examination of voting in 1952 and 1956 shows a considerable amount of shifting taking place: many marginal and middle income independents with Democratic identifications voted Republican in those years. The same tendency occurs among managers; but since the level of Republican identification was already rather high, the amount of shifting was necessarily somewhat smaller. One commentator, clearly within the received tradition, has spoken of the small businessman as "truly the marginal man in the industrialized society, and therefore . . . readily available for nihilistic mass movements."[34] It is difficult to make any comment on their disposition toward nihilistic mass movements. The evidence presented here shows that small independents avoided both the Goldwater and Wallace movements. The only "movement" for which they appear to have been "readily available" was the Eisenhower "crusade."

The lesson of these results is relatively simple. Small businessmen do not form a conservative monolith. They are not conservative absolutely, or, in comparison with managers or more affluent independents, relatively. The comparison of small businessmen with more affluent independents and with middle and high income managers shows them, on the contrary, to be more liberal than the latter groups, this being indicated by their party identifications and their candidate choices. The political reality, in short, is just the opposite of what has been claimed.

One might pursue the matter in some greater detail with the economic liberalism questions or, to test the notion of a scapegoating reaction, with the questions on civil rights. It would be cumbersome to present the data in all its detail. In summary, however it may be noted that these lines of investigation also showed no support for the assumption of a special conservatism among marginal businessmen. A majority of those in the lower income categories, for example, favored an extended medical care program while a majority of those in the highest category opposed it in both 1964 and 1968. Responses to the civil rights questions did not indicate support for a "reaction" hypothesis.

A similar examination of the pattern in the South is hampered by the small number of cases. The results, for what they may be worth, again indicate no serious support for the claim of a special reactionary propensity among small businessmen. Looking first at

1964 party identifications, one finds low income independent businessmen are overwhelmingly Democratic in orientation, and, by comparison, high income managerial ranks are the center of Republicanism. Although not constituting a majority, this is the only setting having a significant Republican concentration.

Looking at 1964 voting one does find a reaction in the small business ranks. Although they were overwhelmingly Democratic in identification (sixteen of eighteen respondents), they divided fifty-fifty in their voting. But once again, that does not make them special because managers and officials also divided in much the same proportions.[35]

In 1968 Southern small businessmen were again heavily Democratic in their party identifications. In their voting that year, one-half remained with the Democrats (seven of fourteen), which was a higher level than among the better-off businessmen or either group of managers. The number of cases is too small to make any major claims about the Wallace voting. Only three of the fourteen small businessmen supported Wallace. Low level managers were more likely to support Wallace (five of eight), but for the rest, Nixon was the big favorite.

One point touched on in passing in the initial discussion of the received line of theorizing was the notion of a tenacious attachment to one's "middle class" status or position. A principal source of desperation among economically threatened independents was the prospect of downward mobility, of being forced into the manual ranks. Given the strength of that attachment, it might be assumed that, when presented with the Survey Research Center's question on class identification, there would be near unanimous choice of the middle class option and, the inverse of that, an avoidance of the label "working class."

Here too the results show a quite different pattern (Table 2.6). Clear majorities of the poorest independents identified themselves as "working class." It appears that the thought of being linked with the working class does not provide a special source of alarm or concern for these marginal independents. Even in the middle income category, two-fifths of independent businessmen identified themselves as working class as did also approximately a quarter of those in the higher category. Once again something appears to be

TABLE 2.6
CLASS IDENTIFICATIONS OF THE INDEPENDENTS BY INCOME:
Married, Active Respondents

	Family Income		
	To $5,999	$6,000-9,999	$10,000 or more
SRC 1964			
Middle*	42%	59%	71%
Working	58	41	29
N=	(43)	(27)	(38)
	To $7,999	$8,000-14,999	$15,000 or more
SRC 1968			
Middle*	29	60	78
Working	71	40	22
N=	(42)	(40)	(32)

* Although they had the choice, none of the respondents described himself as upper or lower class.

amiss in the conventional line of theorizing about this occupational segment.[36]

SMALL BUSINESS OUTLOOKS—AN ALTERNATIVE EXPLANATION

This finding, together with Democratic preferences and liberal issue orientations, although surprising from the perspective of the received theorizing, is no surprise at all when seen from the group-bases perspective outlined in chapter 1. A large proportion of the independents come from working-class families. Many of the rest come from farm families, and a large percentage of both segments also identify themselves as "working class." In the received lines of theorizing, one assumes a *change* in their outlooks once they have "arrived," once they have "crossed over" from the manual ranks. This new outlook might best be characterized as "protective" or perhaps "defensive," the main concern being to hold on to the achievement at any cost.

This reading of the matter seems doubtful for a number of reasons. The most likely locations for *small* businesses are either small towns, or, if in a larger city, then in working-class neighborhoods. In general, the famous "mom and pop" grocery stores are in either one or the other of these locations, they being the only possibilities for those with limited capital. Given the location, it would seem likely that a majority of customers would be in working-class occupations. It also seems likely that the worker-turned-entrepreneur would maintain his links with his family, with lifelong friends in the neighborhood, with former co-workers, his former school friends, and so forth. For the farmer (or farmer's son) now turned storekeeper, a similar network of contacts also seems likely. Many people in his interpersonal network would have made the shift from marginal farming to factory work, now being manual workers.

If this is true, it would seem unlikely (not to mention unwise) to adopt a new and different political orientation, one that would be sharply opposed to those of friends, family, and customers. This is speaking only of the "tactics" of personal political orientations. There is also the reality to be considered. To the extent that one's customers (and family and friends, etc.) are in manual occupations and in unions, there would be little reason for these independents to oppose union efforts. Any wage increases gained by unions would be to their benefit. Because a really small businessman does not hire labor, those increases would not mean additional costs for him. So for reasons of personal ties and loyalties and personal interest, he has good cause to support rather than to oppose union activity. Something of the same might also be said for at least some welfare state developments, those that would increase sales volume for his shop. Even if he were making an employer's contribution for one, two, or three employees, the costs to him would be minimal as compared to what an increase in welfare benefits or coverage would mean for his business. This would be true especially in an area having many pensioners.[37]

The studies at hand do not allow direct exploration of these possibilities, that is, of social connections, personal influences, and assessment of union activity and the effects of social security. It is possible, however, to examine the attitudes of those independent businessmen of working-class or farm background and make comparison of their attitudes with those of businessmen from middle class backgrounds.

Most businessmen from working-class and farm backgrounds had relatively low earnings (Table 2.7). Most, in other words, were "small businessmen." From what has been indicated about this group, it is clear that their attitudes are not likely to be those of the *arriviste* nor are they likely to be "protective" or "defensive." A majority of those reporting that they came from working-class families still identify themselves as working class, and among the children of farm families two-thirds made the same identification. This is in striking contrast to the second generation middle class group, 85 percent of whom identified themselves as middle class.

Sizable majorities of ex-working class and ex-farm independents identified themselves as Democrats. The second generation middle class group, by comparison, divided fifty-fifty in their identifications. A small shift away from the conservative Republicanism of Goldwater was indicated among the second generation middle class group. A more marked reaction against Goldwater occurred

TABLE 2.7
FAMILY BACKGROUND AND SELECTED CHARACTERISTICS OF
INDEPENDENT BUSINESSMEN; Married, Active Respondents
(Survey Research Center, 1964)

	Father's Occupation		
	Nonmanual	Manual	Farm
Family Income			
To $9,999	42%	70%	80%
$10,000 or more	58	30	20
N=	(38)	(40)	(35)
Class Identification			
Middle class	85	45	32
Working class	15	55	68
N=	(40)	(42)	(34)
Party Identification			
Democratic	49	63	72
Republican	51	37	28
N=	(39)	(41)	(29)
1964 Vote*			
Democratic	54	73	56
Republican	46	27	44
N=	(37)	(40)	(32)

among the children of manual workers. There was, however, a strong shift toward Goldwater among the farm-reared. Almost all this shift, however, occurs within the South, that is, in Goldwater country. It is questionable whether this should be termed a reaction of independent businessmen. It would seem, given the geographical location, to be a result of regional rather than of the occupational factors.

In party identifications and in 1964 voting, businessmen who came from working-class families proved to be not too different from contemporary manual workers. Sixty-three percent, for example, identified themselves as Democrats, compared with a manual figure of 76 percent (shown in Table 2.2).[38]

Although rarely specified in detail, most discussions of "upward mobility" treat the "lower middle class" as a group with a separate location, as a collection of persons who have left the manual milieu behind and now live in a setting which is geographically closer to the upper middle class. In these "lower middle class" settings, so it is assumed, the newly arrived seek to avoid any sign of their previous "working-class" life and, at the same time, seek to emulate the attitudes and behaviors of the upper middle class. The present evidence *suggests* that the geographic assumption is not correct. The suggestion is that a large proportion of independents live in predominantly working-class neighborhoods. The evidence also suggests that they do not try to maintain a sense of separateness but rather identify and integrate themselves within those areas.

While on the subject of mobility, it proves useful to consider another assertion of Lipset's, namely his point about the *nouveau très riche*, those whose anxieties about holding onto their newly obtained wealth lead them to oppose the limited redistributive efforts associated with the contemporary welfare state. He contrasts those anxieties and attitudes of the new rich with the assurance felt by the old rich and links the former to Goldwater propensities (indicated, for example, in the voting of newly rich Los Angeles) and the latter to the limited support for that direction found in old rich San Francisco.

It is possible to make some assessment of this claim with the aid of the 1964 Survey Research Center study. Respondents were asked about the class of their families when they were growing up.

With this question one may classify independent businessmen into those reporting middle or upper class family backgrounds and those reporting working-class families.

Respondents may also be classified in terms of their current income. There are only a few cases of respondents who could be classified as *très riche* and for that reason we have had to settle for the categories relatively affluent versus not-so-affluent. If one takes those reporting a working-class background and who are now in the higher income categories as the new rich, one again comes up with a strikingly opposite finding. Two-thirds of these respondents identified as Democrats, and more than two-thirds, given the famous choice, chose Johnson over Goldwater.

By comparison, using the same general procedure, one could take those reporting middle or upper class family backgrounds and high current incomes as the "traditional" well-off populations. This procedure, to be sure, involves many hazards. One does not know for sure when they say "middle" or "upper" class that they were relatively well-off. And, the cutting line here is $10,000 which is not *riche* but only relatively so. But still, for what it may be worth, this group proves to be heavily Republican in party identification; and when faced with the 1964 choice, they remained Republican, nearly two-thirds of them favoring the Goldwater candidacy.[39]

A SUMMARY OF FINDINGS

The results of this inquiry may be summarized as follows:

1. Independent businessmen have a somewhat larger "marginal" subgroup than other middle class categories. That does not, however, mean that independent businessmen as a whole are marginal. It means simply that the minorities of those who have low earnings or who are not satisfied with their financial condition are somewhat larger than the equivalent minorities among other occupational segments.

2. There is a stronger tendency for independent businessmen to indicate feelings of powerlessness than is true with other middle class categories.

The differences with respect to both marginality and powerlessness are small. They do, however, run in the "right" direction, which is to say that the received claims do gain some support although the importance of these factors may be open to question. There is also a question of interpretation which may be raised, that is, whether the differences are due to their economic situation, to their position as independents, or to the relatively low education and/or relatively advanced age of independents. The available evidence suggests the latter.

3. An analysis of five national studies (including those of the especially innovative 1964 and 1968 elections) and of two community studies yielded no support for the assumption of independent business conservatism. This was based on comparisons of party identifications and votes of independents with three major white-collar groups, managers and officials, the salaried professionals, and clerical and sales employees.

4. An analysis of the same studies, this time looking at attitudes toward domestic economic issues, also found no systematic support for the standard claim. The best summary, as noted earlier, would stress the absence of significant differences between the major middle class segments. Fragmentary support for the conservatism claim did appear in some 1968 responses, but again the differences were relatively small. Some evidence from the 1956 study went in the opposite direction, that is, indicating independent business liberalism.

An analysis of questions from the 1948 Elmira study found a high level of conservatism on the part of the independents indicated with respect to the Taft-Hartley Law. That conservatism, however, was shared by managers and salaried professionals in that community; it was not distinctively a reaction of independents. In a number of other respects, attitudes toward price control, toward public housing, toward large corporations and labor unions, the result showed no independent distinctiveness and surprisingly high levels of approval.

5. A necessarily limited exploration of the correlates of inflationary or deflationary conditions also revealed no compelling evidence of a "reaction" developing under those circumstances. The best available evidence in support of the received thesis comes from the Trow Bennington study and from two studies reported by Lipset. The former study finds support for the thesis only with

respect to support for Senator Joseph McCarthy; with respect to economic conservatism and political tolerance, the conventional hypothesis was not supported. The differences indicated in the Lipset studies were relatively small and, conceivably, may have been due to education and age factors rather than to the economic situation of independents.

6. An exploration of the outlooks of *small* businessmen and a contrast with the more affluent independents and with managers (both those of middling income and those who were well-off) yielded no support for the claim of a special small business conservatism. The opposite was generally true: small businessmen were Democratic in their party orientations and liberal on economic issues. The affluent independents and managers tended, by comparison, to be Republican in identification and preferences and tended toward conservatism on issues.

In the South some small business "reaction" appeared in recent elections, but this tendency was not specific to businessmen but rather was part of a more general movement among all groups in Goldwater (or Wallace) country.

7. In contrast to assertions about the middle class attachments of small businessmen, the evidence reviewed here shows clear majorities among low income independents, given the choice of middle class or working class, identifying as working class.

This finding, seen from another perspective is not that surprising. Those who identify as working class also report coming from working-class or farm families. They also tend to be located in low (that is, marginal) income categories. It seems likely (although not proved with any evidence here) that many of these independents still live in working-class neighborhoods, that they maintain their interpersonal connections with those communities, and that the overwhelming majority of their clientele is working class. It also seems likely that their economic advantage would be enhanced by union gains and increased coverage and/or payments under government welfare programs.

The linkage of party preferences, issue orientations, and class identifications with one's origins, with one's original and contemporary "political socialization," points to the role and importance of interpersonal influences in determining attitudes and outlooks. The sizable differences in outlooks associated with family background, for example, stand in marked contrast to the very limited differences seen to be associated with independent versus depen- dent economic status. The political reaction observed in the South, which affected independents and white-collar groups alike, also suggests the importance of interpersonal factors within the region as opposed to an emphasis on the specific economic strains within independent business ranks. Another interpersonal factor of considerable importance involves what we may call the socio- religious affiliation.[40] White Protestants are Republican and con- servative on the economic issues. They also tend to be against government action to guarantee equal rights. All other groups— Catholics, Jews, Negroes—tend to be heavily Democratic and lib- eral in both economic and civil rights areas. This differentiation occurs within all occupational groups. The differences by socio- religious community are consistently greater than those associated with employment in old versus new middle class jobs. The heavy emphasis on this distinction, in short, would appear very much misplaced.

PERSISTENT ERROR—A SOCIOLOGY OF KNOWLEDGE

The evidence presented here, in sum, has shown that the major claims made about independent businessmen are, to say the least, very misleading. This raises a question as to the sources of this conventional misreading. Why have the political orientations of independents and particularly those of the small businessmen been so systematically misrepresented? A number of possible explana- tions may be suggested.

In part, the difficulty would appear to result from the "hold" or dominance of one particular theoretical tradition. The entire line of analysis appears to have been generated from some passing comments by Marx and to have been developed for some decades in Germany before being implanted in contemporary American social science. That particular line of argument converges and is consonant with native American social science perspectives. Many basic elements of the native American perspective were developed from small-town experience, and American small-town businessmen are, at least so it is thought, eminently conservative individuals.[41] Once a tradition is "implanted" and its claims meet with approval or assent on all sides, there is little incentive present to stimulate investigation of what appear to be established verities. Any such investigation would appear frivolous, a case of "testing the obvious."

The impressionistic evidence, in a number of ways, lends support for the major outlines of the traditional viewpoint. A useful illustration of the misleading impressionistic perception is provided by a study of one such small town. Called Valley City by the researchers, it contained about 2,000 adults. The study's field workers reported that "there was not a single Democrat on . . . Main street." The survey evidence in this community, nevertheless, showed that judgment to be far from correct. The authors report that, despite "the pervasive Republican climate on Main street, 47 percent of the businessmen and white-collar workers were self-identified Democrats."[42] The discrepancy was explained as largely a result of the fact that Republicans were well organized and Democrats had "almost no formal organization" there. In such a case, a "sensitive observer" would provide a mistaken judgment of "community" or "business" sentiment, a judgment according perfectly with the claims of the received tradition.

The Survey Research Center studies provide evidence suggesting that the basis for this misperception extends far beyond "Valley City." If one compares Democratic and Republican identifiers among the independent businessmen (in this case, in 1964), one finds that, although there is the same interest in the campaign, consistent differences appear in all other measures of public (and visible) political activities (Table 2.8). Considering, for example, attempts at convincing others to support one's candidate, it is clear that Democratic identifiers, on the whole, do not "talk politics" but that Republicans, by comparison, make considerable efforts to convince others. The data at hand do not indicate why this is so, that is, what factors inhibit activity by Democrats. The disproportionate public effort, however, would give rise to and sustain some "pluralistic ignorance," that is, misperception of the actual frequency distributions.

Another source of misrepresentation involves letter writing. A

TABLE 2.8

POLITICAL INVOLVEMENT OF DEMOCRATIC AND REPUBLICAN
BUSINESSMEN; Married, Active Non-South Respondents
(Survey Research Center, 1964)

	Party Identification	
	Democratic	Republican
Campaign interest		
Very much interested	44%	46%
Somewhat interested	34	32
Not much interested	22	22
N=	(41)	(37)
Tried to convince others in campaign	24	63
N=	(38)	(35)
Attended political meetings	13	20
N=	(38)	(35)
Worked for party or candidate	3	17
N=	(38)	(35)
Member of a political club	3	11
N=	(38)	(35)

majority of those who "have ever written to . . . public officials"
are Republican. Sixty-five percent (N=17) of the letter writers
identified themselves as Republican; whereas, only 30 percent
(N=105) of the nonwriters were so identified.[43] A legislator or
public official who judged "business" sentiment on the basis of his
mail would be seriously misled as to the state of actual opinion.
That result, moreover, states merely whether respondents have or
have not written and does not indicate *how many* letters they have
sent.[44]

Given the "bias" in the frequency of public discussion of
politics during a campaign or of public manifestations and support, it is not too surprising that all kinds of commentators,
intellectuals, and practical politicians have come to the conclusion
that business sentiment is basically conservative.

There are, in short, a large number of independent businessmen
who are essentially unseen and unheard. One might even refer to
them as the silent majority of the business ranks. Because they are
disproportionately small businessmen, it should come as no surprise that they are not seen. They are not likely to be in organi-

zations, not being able to get away from the shop or perhaps, in some instances, not being able to pay dues. It seems unlikely that small shopkeepers would be found in leading positions in local business organizations or that they would play any significant role in committees of such organizations.

Because small businessmen tend to be socially "invisible," the generalizations made about them are, in point of fact, based on experience with the somewhat more visible "middle-sized" businessmen. Many of the standard claims, it will be noted, do not apply to the very smallest units but only made sense in a discussion of those who are at least a step or two away from the margins. The very smallest businesses do not hire labor. They are either run by a single proprietor or, if any additional labor is enlisted, it is usually that of unpaid family members. In either case there would be no "threat" posed by labor unions and their wage demands made upon giant or middle-sized firms. There would also be no special source of complaint vis-a-vis "big government," about "red tape" and bureaucracy, let alone the employer's contributions to welfare programs. With no employees there would be no forms and no contributions. There is a question to be raised also about the impact of taxes on the small businessman. The very smallest businesses would not be subject to very much in the way of income taxes. They would be subject to the difficulties imposed on shopkeepers by sales taxes, but that kind of tax is not discriminatory vis-a-vis other firms. As for the effect of local land taxes, small units would be less likely to be touched *directly* because most of them are renters rather than owners. The direct touch of the land tax falls on a somewhat more affluent businessman, the "little man's" landlord.

Possibly the most important determinant of the systematic misrepresentation is the failure to undertake research in the area. To some extent this failure results from the character of the relevant census categories. The basic category is "Managers, Officials and Proprietors" which means that, unless there is a detailed presentation (that is, of its major components), the data given in official government publications will mix or "average" the results of two rather diverse groups, managers and proprietors. With rare exceptions, it is not possible to make the necessary separation so as to allow examination of the proprietors contained within that category (let alone those located elsewhere in the census listings). Because most surveys follow census categories, they too make the same combination of independents and managers and again prevent examination of the received hypotheses. It would be necessary to find studies containing a supplementary question, one asking about self-employment, before one could test these claims. To that extent, the lack of investigation in the area may be attributed to a fluke in the creation of the occupational categories, a fluke that, in effect, has stood in the way of relevant inquiry.

Another consideration involves the researchers themselves. It involves what one might call the social psychology of research. What may be operating is a special instance of the more general processes which focus (and limit) human perception, these being selective perception and selective retention.

Experimental studies have shown repeatedly that people do not "see" all the events before their eyes but rather tend to "sort out" those events they have been trained to see, those events that, in a sense, fit in with their trained understandings. Objects that do not fit in with those understandings are either not seen at all or, if perceived, tend to be forgotten. The "deviant" or "exceptional" fact is easily "lost" when there is no ready place for it within the standard framework of understanding. One can easily pick up a well-known and "recognized" fact, such as the conservative small businessman, and store it away in one's memory. But other facts, such as liberal or radical small businessmen, appear as oddities, as bizarre exceptions to the rule, as perhaps an aesthetic curiosity but never as a case with which to assess a going line of analysis, let alone as one requiring alteration of a going line or the creation of a new one.

Social scientists generally familiar with this subject know and remember the Trow article on the McCarthyite propensities of Bennington's "nineteenth-century Liberals," but at the same time they either forget or have never seen the report of a much more extensive study which failed to confirm that finding. There is a serious disproportion between the treatment of the confirmation and the disconfirmation. The former appeared originally in a Ph.D. dissertation and was published as an article in a professional journal, one that is repeatedly cited and has been frequently reprinted. The disconfirmation was reported in a brief three sentence account and has received practically no recognition (for example, in footnotes citing relevant literature). One finds the same propensity among student and professional researchers and among editors of social science journals: a confirmation of an accepted hypothesis is treated as noteworthy; whereas, disconfirmation of the same hypothesis is treated as little more than a curious exception. Where such a tendency persists, it clearly leads to a systematic bias.

The available evidence on the political orientations of American independent businessmen was reviewed in previous pages. An account of some European evidence also indicates the operation of what we might call "extra-scientific" factors, perceptual distortion, in other words. An early study in German electoral behavior pointed to and attempted to estimate the proportion of the Social Democratic party's vote which did *not* come from manual ranks. This study, based on aggregate voting statistics, estimated that one third of the party's vote came from white-collar or middle class ranks. That particular study did not make a further inquiry into the independent business versus salaried support for the party and hence must remain, as one says, only suggestive.[45] Another study, appearing a year later, this one by no less a figure than Robert Michels, also noted this seeming oddity and attempted to give an account both of the numbers and reasons for the presence of middle class groups within the Social Democracy. He made special note of the frequent presence of independent businessmen *because* of their socialist politics. Having been fired and blacklisted for political activities, the only course remaining open to them, short of emigration, was to open up some kind of establishment. Many of these independents ran public houses which served as meeting places for local party functions.[46]

A later account, this one reporting on voting in the 1930 German election, estimated "that 40 percent of the SPD voters were not manual workers, that the party was backed in that year by 25 percent of the white-collar workers, 33 percent of the self-employed in artisan shops and retail business." It seems likely that the proportion of businessmen favoring the Social Democrats would have been higher in the cities and lower in the countryside. If one assumes that a roughly equivalent percentage of independents were voting for the *Zentrum* and also that a small minority of them would have been supporting the Communists, it would appear that any casual description of independents as "conservative" would, to say the least, fail to do justice to the complexity of the situation.[47]

A study of British voting patterns in the early postwar years showed small businessmen, in 1945, to be relatively favorable toward the Labour party. They had the second highest percentage of Labour voters in the middle class, coming after the "lower office" group. The respective percentages were 27 and 30. In the years immediately following 1945, years of Labour government, there was a general decline in middle class support for the Labour party. Small business support fell to 15 percent in 1951, a level well below that of "lower professional" and "lower office" workers but similar to that of managers. It was higher than that of top or middle businessmen or of "higher professionals" or "higher office" workers. Small businessmen had shifted from what for the middle class was a relatively high level of labour support to a middling level. Again the picture does not add up to one of monolitic small business conservatism.[48]

An account of independent business politics would not be complete without a discussion of Poujadism. An examination of the voting in the 1956 French election showed that approximately one-fifth of the self-employed businessmen supported Poujade, a greater proportion than endorsed him from any other occupation.[49] But then, one might ask, who else would be inclined to vote for an organization calling itself the *Union de defénse des commerçants et artisans*? The other part of the picture, the aspect that is regularly neglected, shows that 7 percent of the businessmen voted Communist, 21 percent voted Socialist, and another 17 percent voted for the liberal *Mouvement republicain populaire*. Surveys in France regularly understate the Communist percentages: many Communist voters (for understandable reasons) do not wish to give information to unknown interviewers. It seems likely, therefore, that the above figure provides only a minimal estimate of the proportion of Communist businessmen.

The peculiarity of treatment given these European results is that the existence of liberal or left businessmen has been neglected completely, or else the evidence has been handled selectively with the discussion focusing only on the conservative portion of the distribution. The emphasis does not appear to be justified since the German and British studies, on the whole, indicate relatively small differences between the independents and other middle class groups. The French study does show a degree of independent business distinctiveness, largely it would seem because the movement in question made its appeal to independents and not to other middle class groups. Even then, the proportion of businessmen who were "available" and responded to Poujadist appeals was smaller than the proportion who admitted support for Communists and Socialists. It is also necessary to raise a question as to the sources of even these small differences. Was the shift away from the Labour Party, for example, due to the ineluctable strains suffered by small businessmen in the "modern" welfare state? Was the lower level of support for Social Democrats in the 1930 election due to the same cause? Or was the disaffection perhaps the result of Labour Party indifference toward independent businessmen? Some of the conservatism of German businessmen may well be the result of Social Democratic indifference to the plight of a segment that in any event was destined to "fall into" the proletariat. In addition to the lack of concern, there was also a "positive" contribution made by some party spokesmen; this took the form of denigrating, insulting comments, as for example, in the repeated references to the *kleinbürgerliche Elemente* ("petty bourgeois elements").[50]

Related to both the failure to undertake research and to the selective perception is another "procedure" which gives rise to mistaken judgments about independent businessmen. If one does not undertake direct research, the tendency is to fall back on second best or indirect procedures. Some of these we have already mentioned such as using one's personal impressions from casual conversations in business circles or assessing (sometimes with careful tabulation) sentiments expressed in letters to public officials. We have noted the biases in both cases, both of them tending to reinforce conventional understandings. Another "second best" or indirect procedure involves assessing pronouncements of business-men's associations. With rare exceptions these fall into the "well-known" pattern of conservatism and, with no further ado, it is assumed that those expressions represent the sentiment of the membership. Implicit in that procedure is a further assumption, namely, that the membership is also representative of the larger category which includes many nonmembers. These two "representative" assumptions, that the leadership of business organizations adequately represents the views of members and that both leaders and members together adequately represent the views of nonmembers once spelled out, are likely to engender some doubts. At that point one is likely to entertain some alternative possibilities. It is possible, especially in the light of the previous evidence on the different levels of political activity among Republican and Democratic businessmen, that the same disproportion might also carry over in the direction of business associations. In that case, one might again have a systematic bias in the public expressions made by the officers or spokesmen for those bodies. If we assume that the same relationship between affluence and organizational involvement obtains here as elsewhere, this would mean that less affluent businessmen (a majority of whom are Democratic identifiers) would not be in such organizations.

Unfortunately the surveys we have been analyzing do not allow a more detailed exploration of the question of memberships and involvements in business organizations. Some further comment is possible, however, on the question of the internal governance and representativeness of business organizations. This question is reviewed in chapter 7 in connection with the discussion of pluralism and voluntary associations. The finding there, not too surprisingly, is that the major small business organizations are eminently conservative in their public pronouncements. They also prove to be lacking even the most rudimentary forms of internal democracy. The lesson, in short, is that their utterances reflect another range of determinants—not small business sentiment.

The consequences of this misperception are relatively clear. Liberal and left commentators and activists define small business as being beyond the pale. There is no point in considering them. Because, as Berle put it, they are rarely "detached" from their conservative persuasions, they "will not produce any spectacular changes . . . [they] simply will be where they always were." That being true, there is no sense in making any appeal to them, in working out solutions which provide a role for them. In the extreme case, one which is typical of the "tough" left position, they are not even to be ignored; they are to be denounced. That practice, to the extent that is is appreciated, no doubt, plays some role in increasing the opposition to left initiatives. Both liberal and left readings involve overestimates of the strength of the "conservative enemy," estimates that contribute to either depression and disenchantment on the one hand, or a sensed need for more "spectacular" tactics on the other. It is unlikely that either of these reponses does anything to improve the human condition.

NOTES

1. Marx and Engels, in the *Manifesto of the Communist Party*, note that the "lower strata of the middle class—the small tradespeople, shopkeepers, and retired tradesmen generally, the handicraftsmen and peasants—all these sink gradually into the proletariat. . . ." Their discussion of the political orientations of this group is rather ambiguous. "The lower middle class," they say, "the small manufacturer, the shopkeeper, the artisan, the peasant, all these fight against the bourgeoisie, to save from extinction their existence as fractions of the middle class. They are therefore not revolutionary, but conservative. Nay more, they are reactionary, for they try to roll back the wheel of history." On the other hand they note that "If by chance they are revolutionary, they are so only in view of their impending transfer into the proletariat, they thus defend not their present, but their future interests, they desert their own standpoint to place themselves at that of the proletariat." From Karl Marx and Frederick Engels, *Selected Works* (Moscow: Foreign Languages Publishing House, 1951), vol. 1, pp. 39-40, 42.

A formulation from the 1930s, typical of many in the genre, is that of Harold Lasswell. It reads: ". . . Hitlerism is a desperation reaction of the lower middle classes. . . . Psychologically speaking . . . the lower middle class was increasingly overshadowed by the workers and the upper bourgeoisie, whose unions, cartels and parties took the centre of the stage. The psychological impoverishment of the lower middle class precipitated emotional insecurities within the personalities of its members, thus fertilizing the ground for the various movements of mass protest through which the middle classes might revenge themselves." From his "The Psychology of Hitlerism," Political Science Quarterly, 4 (1933) 374.

Similar formulations may be found in Lewis Corey, *The Crisis of the Middle Class* (New York: Covici-Friede, 1935), chaps. 6 and 7; in Erich Fromm, *Escape from Freedom* (New York: Rinehart, 1941); and in C. Wright Mills, *White Collar* (New York: Oxford University Press, 1951), chaps. 1-3. Mills's formulation actually involves a variation on the standard theme. The small businessmen in his view are hostile to government and labor, but they form an ambiguous alliance with big business. See also, for other statements of this position, S. M. Lipset, *Political Man* (Garden City, N.Y.: Doubleday, 1960), chap. 5.

2. From Seymour Martin Lipset and Earl Raab, *The Politics of Unreason: Right-Wing Extremism in America, 1790-1970* (New York: Harper and Row, 1970), p. 210. The statement originally appeared in Lipset, "The Sources of the 'Radical Right'—1955," pp. 259-312 in *The Radical Right,* edited by Daniel Bell (Garden City, N.Y.: Doubleday, 1963). The relevant passage is to be found on pages 281-282. The same formulation also appears in Lipset, "Beyond the Backlash," Encounter 22 (November 1964) 11-24 (there on pages 18 and 19). A condensed version of the Encounter article appears in Harper's 230 (January 1965) 56-63, the passage of concern being on page 59.

The quotation in the previous paragraph of the text is from Richard H. Hall, *Occupations and the Social Structure* (Englewood Cliffs, N.J.: Prentice-Hall, 1969) p. 164. Many of the themes outlined here are reviewed on pages 164-168.

3. The focus on husbands and wives makes the assumption that, in the majority of cases, husbands and wives will share the same political orientations and, moreover, that wives will follow the lead of their husbands in these matters. As far as can be ascertained from available evidence, these assumptions appear to be realistic. This is not to say, of course, that such an arrangement is desirable. Some discussion and relevant evidence appears in Richard F. Hamilton, *Affluence and the French Worker* (Princeton: Princeton University Press, 1967), Appendix B, and Juan J. Linz, "The Social Bases of West German Politics" (Ph.D. diss., Department of Sociology, Columbia University, 1959), chap. 7.

An examination of the Survey Research Center studies also showed a high correspondence in attitudes of husbands and wives in political matters. None of these studies (that is, the French, the German, or the American) is entirely appropriate for this purpose because the comparisons are of an aggregate of wives and an aggregate of husbands rather than of specific pairs. A work that is more useful for its detail (but less so for its scope) is Elihu Katz and Paul F. Lazarsfeld, *Personal Influence* (Glencoe: Free Press, 1955).

4. Most available work is focused on the economic problems of independent businessmen. This is very clearly (and understandably) the case with publications of the Senate and House Committees on Small Business and of the Small Business Administration. Most of the studies done by social scientists also focus on entry and exodus from the field, on mobility, success, and failure. See, for example, the following: Kurt Mayer, "Small Business as a Social Institution," Social Research 14 (September 1947) 332-349; Kurt Mayer, "Businss Enterprise: Traditional Symbol of Opportunity," British Journal of Sociology 4 (1953) 160-180; Kurt Mayer and Sidney Goldstein, The First Two Years: Problems of Small Firm Growth and Survival (Washington, D.C.: Small Business Administration, 1961); Eugene C. McKean, "The Persistence of Small Business: A Study of Unincorporated Enterprise" (Kalamazoo, Mich.: The W. E. Upjohn Institute for Community Research, 1958); Gordon F. Lewis, "A Comparison of some Aspects of the Backgrounds and Careers of Small Businessmen and American Business Leaders," American Journal of Sociology 65 (January 1960) 348-355; Gordon F. Lewis and C. Arnold Anderson, "Social Origins and Social Mobility of Businessmen in an American City," Transactions of the Third World Congress of Sociology, vol. 3 (1956); Alfred and Gertrude Oxenfeldt, "Determinants of Business Success in a Small Western City," Social Forces 30 (December 1951) 223-231; Edward B. Shils, "Small Business: Its Prospects and Problems," Current History 49 (July 1965) 36-44; Fred Sklar, "Franchises, Independence and Action: A Study in the Sociology of Entrepreneurship," (Davis, Ph.D. diss., University of California, 1973).

For studies of the British setting, see Frank Bechhofer and Brian Elliott, "An Approach to a Study of Small Shopkeepers and the Class Structure," European Journal of Sociology 9 (1968) 180-202; and Herman Levy, The Shops of Britain (London: Routledge and Kegan Paul, 1948).

A compendious work, now somewhat dated, is that of A. D. H. Kaplan, Small Business: Its Place and Problems (New York: McGraw-Hill, 1948).

Articles more directly connected with the political or at least with the motivational question are those of Joel I. Nelson, "Participation and Integration: The Case of the Small Businessman," American Sociological Review, 33 (June 1968) 427-438, and his "Anomie: Comparisons between the Old and New Middle Class," American Journal of Sociology 72 (September 1968) 184-192; and also Charles M. Bonjean, "Mass, Class, and the Industrial Community: A Comparative Analysis of Managers, Businessmen, and Workers," American Journal of Sociology 72 (September 1966) 149-162. The few studies of small business politics will be considered later in this chapter.

5. Technical details about the studies, together with the initial presentations of findings, may be found in: Angus Campbell, Gerald Gurin, and Warren E. Miller, The Voter Decides (Evanston, Ill.: Row, Peterson, 1954);

Angus Campbell, Philip E. Converse, Warren E. Miller, and Donald E. Stokes, *The American Voter* (New York: John Wiley, 1960); and, by the same authors, *Elections and the Political Order* (New York: John Wiley, 1966).

6. A detailed exploration of internal differentiation within the middle class may be found in Richard Hamilton, *Class and Politics in the United States* (New York: John Wiley, 1972), chaps. 4, 5, and 9. See also the discussion later in this chapter and in chapter 3.

7. Taking a different perspective, one may ask: Who are the marginal middle classes? (Table 2.1 asks, by contrast, what percentage of the various middle class segments are marginal, passably well-off, or very well-off?) If we take those 1964 middle class respondents who reported incomes of less than $6,000, we find that 43 percent of them (N=102) were independent businessmen and another 34 percent were in clerical or sales occupations. A clear majority of the "marginal middle class" was found in these two categories. Although one cannot say that most independents or clericals are marginal, one can say that most marginal middle class families are either independents or in clerical and sales occupations.

8. Unfortunately there was no similar satisfaction question in the 1968 study. There was such a question in the 1956 study. Although the income pattern was very similar to that in the 1964 and 1968 studies, there was *less* distinction in the pattern of satisfaction than in the 1964 responses. In 1956, 50 percent (N=131) of independents said they were pretty well satisfied with their current income. Among the, on average, much more affluent managers and officials, the equivalent percentage figure was 55 (N=103); and among the similarly affluent salaried professionals, it was only 42 (N=115). The clerical and sales group, despite relatively lower income, was little different from the salaried professional group; the percentage "pretty well satisfied" was 45 (N=119).

9. The 1956 study asked the same trend questions as the 1964 study. The results are generally very close to those indicated in Table 2.1. In 1956, smaller percentages of independent businessmen and of the clerical and sales employees said that things had been "getting better" over the past few years. The percentages saying things had stayed the same were proportionately higher.

10. Similar results were found in both the 1956 and the 1968 Survey Research Center studies.

The age relationship in 1964 is as follows. Looking first at the recent trend, we have the following percentages (of those with opinions) reporting their condition to be the same or worse: To 34 years, 29 percent (28); 35 to 44 years, 44 percent (34); 45 to 54 years, 58 percent (31); and 55 or more, 77 percent (35). Considering the expectations for the future, we have the following results for the same respective years: 18 percent (28), 55 percent (31), 46 percent (26), and 72 percent (32).

11. The percentages of those falling into the two lowest categories of political efficacy for independents, managers, salaried professionals, and clerical-sales groups, respectively, were 29, 25, 16, and 25. The percentages falling into the highest category were 15, 19, 25, and 14. There were larger differences in the middle categories; independents fall into the middle group, and the new middle class categories tended to be medium high. For question wordings, see the original Code Book, Deck 06, pp. 23-25.

12. For the 1968 question wordings, see the Code Book, Deck 06, pp. 67-68. The largest differences within the middle class were between independent businessmen and salaried professionals, the largest of these being a matter of 20 percentage points (the "can't understand" politics response).

A similar series in the 1952 Survey Research Center study also showed the same basic pattern of only marginal differences. It is impossible to present the evidence in support of these claims which, after all, are little more than asides at this point in the discussion. The relatively small differences are somewhat surprising in view of the low educational level of independent businessmen and in view of their higher average age. A control for education in the 1964 study eliminated the small differences in efficacy reported above. The lower sense of efficacy on the part of the independents, in short, is not a function of their occupational location but rather is a product of the lower educational level.

13. The party identification question reads: "Generally speaking, do you usually think of yourself as a Republican, a Democrat, an independent, or what?" (If Republican or Democrat) "Would you call yourself a strong (R) (D) or not a very strong (R) (D)?" (If independent or other) "Do you think of yourself as closer to the Republican or Democratic party?" Respondents fell into seven categories (exclusive of the small number of others, apoliticals, or "no answers"): Strong Democrats, Not Strong Democrats, Independent Democrats, Independents, Independent Republicans, Not Strong Republicans, and Strong Republicans. In all the presentations that follow, we have calculated the percentages of those with a political position, that is, excluding pure independents and the few other responses. Independent Democrats and Independent Republicans are counted as Democrats and Republicans. The excluded groups constitute 10 percent of the entire sample.

14. For a brief portrait of the man and the campaign, see Theodore H. White, *The Making of the President: 1964* (New York: Atheneum, 1965).

15. The questions: "Who did you vote for for President?" (If did not vote) "Who would you have voted for for President if you had voted?" The indicated votes have been combined with the indicated preferences of non-

voters. This procedure was adopted because the concern is with orientations or outlooks rather than with votes (or the expression of orientations).

16. Lipset makes this assertion ("Beyond the Backlash," op. cit., p. 19). "In recent decades," he says, "the control of large corporations by college-educated men and the scions of established wealth, rather than by the relatively less-educated founders of new firms, has created within the moderate wing of the Republican Party an alliance between economic power and traditional status, while small business and new independent wealth have tended to back the more conservative or *laissez-faire* faction of the Party. These differences were manifest in the fight for the 1964 nomination. . . ." But, as may be seen in Table 2.2, the managers in both the North and South gave greater support to Goldwater than did independent businessmen. Another question in the study asked about candidate preferences at the time of the convention. Among independent businessmen, 12.5 percent, and among managers and officials, 13 percent had favored the Goldwater candidacy.

17. Another way of assessing the received claims involves using party identifications as a kind of base point or anchorage, and calculating the percentage shift away from that "traditional" location. Contrasting independents with the managers and officials in the 1964 study, we find that 16 percent of the Democratic independent businessmen "defected" to Goldwater that year. Such a degree of "availability," however, must be seen in comparison with managers: some 23 percent of them "defected." There is also a countermovement that must be considered, the shift *to* the Democrats by Republican identifiers. Nearly a third of the independents (31 percent, N=42) voted or favored the Democrat in that election. By constrast, only 22 percent of the managers (N=41) defected in favor of the more "responsible" candidate. Democratic managers, in short, were more likely to be attracted to Goldwater and Republican managers were less likely to be repelled by Goldwater than was true of independents. It is difficult to reconcile these findings with Lipset's claim that "the backbone of 'moderate' Republicanism is located among the employees and executives of the large, urban-based corporations" ("Beyond the Backlash," op. cit., p. 21).

18. The data presented in Table 2.2. include Negroes. This does not seriously affect the comparison of middle class categories, however, because their numbers are so small: among the 1968 non-Southern respondents, there were three independent businessmen, one manager, and five clerical and sales employees. This problem is more serious in the South where the percentage of blacks, although still small, is greater than that found elsewhere. Five of 33 independent businessmen respondents in the South were black. But even when we took only whites in the region, there was still no support for the

received hypothesis. There was little difference in the new party identification figures.

There were even fewer middle class blacks in the 1964 study. There exists a much more serious problem if one compares the middle class groups with the manuals. In 1964, for example, 17 percent of the latter category consisted of blacks. For a comparison of the political orientations of white middle class and working-class respondents, see Hamilton, *Class and Politics . . . , op. cit., chap. 11.*

19. I wish to thank the National Opinion Research Center and the then director, Peter Rossi, for making their study no. 367 available to me. The Detroit area study was made available to Paul Eberts by Gerhart Lenski. The Elmira study was made available by the Bureau of Applied Social Research of Columbia University. For the original presentation of the Elmira findings, see Bernard Berelson, Paul F. Lazarsfeld, and William N. McPhee, *Voting: A Study of Opinion Formation in a Presidential Campaign* (Chicago: University of Chicago Press, 1954). I wish to express my appreciation to all those involved who made this secondary analysis of their materials possible.

There are a number of details needing examination. It will be remembered that "independent businessmen" consist of those found in the "managers, officials, and proprietors" category of the census *plus* those self-employed persons found in other categories. Most of these others are self-employed blue-collar workers, hence, for short, we have referred to them as artisans. A comparison of proprietors and artisans showed little difference between the two. Fifty-nine percent of the former (N=76) identified with the Democratic party in 1964 as did 61 percent of the artisans (N=36). The equivalent figures for non-Southern subgroups were 53 (N=60) and 54 (N=26). A similarity appeared also with respect to economic liberalism issues, the respective percentages of those favoring government supported medical care being 52 (N=67) and 58 (N=36).

20. The differences between independents and the three major new middle class groups with respect to father's occupation (percent who were farmers), the size of place where raised, and the size of place where now living are all very small, the largest one being a matter of 15 percentage points. The differences with respect to age, however, are somewhat more important. The percentages of those respondents who, in 1964, were 50 or over are: independent business, 41 (N=128); managers, officials, 30 (N=103); salaried professionals, 15 (N=105); and clerical, sales, 21 (N=99).

A separate examination of middle class groups within different sizes of community (taking large cities, middle-sized ones, and small towns) also failed to reveal support for the received hypothesis of independent business conservatism.

21. There was a prior screening question to each of these questions, one asking whether or not respondents were interested enough to have an opinion on the subject. The percentages given in the table are for those with opinions, that is, exclusive of those lacking interest in the subject. Of the four questions, this "government power" theme had the highest percentages indicating no interest. Twenty-seven percent (N=128) of the independent businessmen in 1964, for example, reported no interest in the area. The level of interest was somewhat (but not much) higher in 1968. At that time 21 percent (N=120) of the independents were not sufficiently moved by the subject to have an opinion. A sizable majority of this "not interested" group took a "liberal" position with respect to the government medical support question.

22. The 1956 study also contained a question on government tax cuts, one that asked whether the government should make cuts even if it meant reducing important services. This sounds like a standard conservative demand. As it turned out, however, those approving that suggestion were generally poor people who made very liberal choices with respect to the economic affairs questions. They appear to be saying that the government should cut *their* taxes and shift the burden to those better able to pay. See the discussion in *Class and Politics* . . . op. cit., chap. 3.

23. The combination of responses to the corporation question (that is, the combination of the full and the qualified approval) hides the fact that independent businessmen together with manual workers provided the highest levels of unqualified approval, 43 percent in both cases indicating that the corporations had "made America the kind of country it is today."

24. In Table 2.2 we have twelve rows of data summarizing various surveys on the question of party preferences. In each row there are five possible comparisons of independents with other middle class groups. In eight cases we did not present the data because of the small number of cases thus yielding a total of 52 comparisons. Assessing the statistical significance through the use of t-tests and taking the relatively undemanding standard of a .05 significance level yielded the following: Three significant differences in support of the hypothesis, seven in opposition to the hypothesis (that is, with the businessmen more liberal or Democratic), and 42 that were not significant.

The same assessment was made of the comparisons in Table 2.3. There, 40 comparisons were possible and only one of these was significant at the .05 level. That one difference showed the independent businessmen to be more liberal than the independent professionals.

In Table 2.4 (showing the Elmira data) fifteen comparisons were possible with other middle class groups. Three of these were significant, two in opposition to the business conservatism hypothesis and one, with respect to the Taft-Hartley question, in its support.

25. It should be clear that the conventional descriptions of candidate and party characteristics are in great measure accounts of appearances (that is, as opposed to realities). Harry S. Truman did campaign for civil rights even though he personally did not approve of the effort. His campaign strategist, Clark Clifford, had argued that a strong position in that area was a necessity in order to prevent defections to the Progressive party of Henry Wallace. Similarly the discussion of 1964 voting and its significance is based on the images or the appearances of the major candidates. The reality, especially in the case of Lyndon Johnson, was clearly of a markedly different character.

For a discussion of Truman and the civil rights question, see Irwin Ross, *The Loneliest Campaign: The Truman Victory of 1948* (New York: New American Library, 1968) pp. 124-126.

26. From Arthur W. Kornhauser, "Analysis of 'Class' Structure of Contemporary American Society—Psychological Bases of Class Divisions," pp. 199-264 in *Industrial Conflict: A Psychological Interpretation,* edited by George W. Hartmann and Theodore Newcomb (New York: The Cordon Company, 1940). The data appear on page 255.

Another study from the period, this one being of Santa Clara County in California, also does not support the claim of a monolithic business conservatism. The election in question was the 1934 gubernatorial in which the writer Upton Sinclair challenged conservative Republican orthodoxy. His attempt generated one of the most vicious opposition campaigns of the century. The county was Republican in its majority (57 percent), and there are indications of a very tight Republican control, almost all public officials (including librarians and school officials) being Republican in their vote. Nevertheless, in the 1934 campaign, 33 percent of the merchants voted Democratic, that is, for Sinclair, and 42 percent of the "service proprietors" did the same. See Dewey Anderson and Percy E. Davidson, *Ballots and the Democratic Class Struggle* (Stanford: Stanford University Press, 1943), p. 123.

27. Alfred Winslow Jones, *Life, Liberty, and Property* (Philadelphia: J. B. Lippincott, 1941), pp. 225-235, 378.

28. Martin Trow, "Small Businessmen, Political Tolerance, and Support for McCarthy," American Journal of Sociology 64 (November 1958) 270-280. It is worthwhile presenting Trow's summary of the matter (from footnote 10): ". . . it has been suggested that small businessmen, as a result of their economic experience and interests, tend to hold extremely conservative economic views and that these views led them into the radical right and support of McCarthy. A somewhat different hypothesis suggests that small

businessmen identify with, and tend to take over what they believe to be, the values of big business, which are also the values of the radical right. Neither of these hypotheses is supported by the Bennington data." The study also had a measure of "political tolerance" based on the responses to three questions about the right of free speech. The conclusion about small businessmen was that they "are no more politically intolerant than are salaried employees or manual workers of similar education" (p. 280).

Another study offering some support for the business conservatism hypothesis is that of Richard L. Nolan and Rodney E. Schneck, "Small Businessmen, Branch Managers, and their Relative Susceptibility to Right-Wing Extremism: An Empirical Test," Canadian Journal of Political Science 2 (March 1969) 89-102. This study was conducted in Wetaskiwin, Alberta, a community located 40 miles south of Edmonton and having a population of 6,000. A mail questionnaire was used with 134 small businessmen (out of 249) cooperating. The 121 usable responses were contrasted with those of 31 branch managers. Part of the support for their claim is dependent on an F-scale in which the "liberal" or nonauthoritarian response is the "disagree" option in all but one instance. An alienation scale has the same characteristic. This would indicate a likely problem with response set. The differences obtained following this procedure were not large, being significant only at the .10 level.

29. From his "Three Decades of the Radical Right: Coughlinites, McCarthyites, and Birchers–1962," pp. 313-377 in Daniel Bell, op. cit. The quotation is from pages 340-341. There is no mention of the Trow study in his later *Politics of Unreason.*

The original Trow dissertation contains much more detail including also a number of significant other themes not reported in the article. Native-born Benningtonians, for example, were more likely to approve of McCarthy's methods than were those coming from outside. The "outsiders" with relatively high education were particularly opposed to McCarthy's methods (p. 145). It seems likely that small businessmen would tend to be "natives" and salaried white-collar workers would be from the outside. If so, this would open up the question as to whether it was a peculiar concentration of local "nativism" which yielded this result. The linkage of McCarthy support with nineteenth-century liberalism is also strongest among the native-born although there is some connection even among those who came from outside Bennington (p. 148).

One might expect that the relatively well-educated Catholic businessmen would have come from outside. It is of interest to note that this group provided considerably less support for McCarthy than did the better-educated Protestant businessmen and also that the level of support in this group was essentially no different from that of better-educated Catholic white-collar employees. The percentages of McCarthy support among better-educated Catholic business and white-collar groups were 37 (N=27) and 36 (N=62), respectively (p. 117). See Martin A. Trow, "Right-Wing Radicalism and Political Intolerance: A Study of Support for McCarthy in a New England Town," (Ph.D. diss., Columbia University, 1957).

30. In this case the orientations of businessmen toward McCarthy would have been the result of their low average level of education and not of economic strains or pressures. The Lipset presentation is very limited. He gives a figure for the percentage difference between approvers and disapprovers but gives no indication of the absolute levels of support or of nonresponse rates. The relevant table appears on page 332 of the Daniel Bell volume and on page 227 of the Lipset-Raab work.

31. From A. A. Berle, "Is There a Business Vote? What is It?" New York Times Magazine, 26 October 1962, pp. 28 ff. The same kind of portrayal, big business as "liberal" and small business as backward-looking, is contained in the comments of Robert Heilbroner. See the account "Small-Business Men Called Obstacle to Reform" in the New York Times, 24 October 1968.

32. See, for example, the Lasswell quotation in note 1.

33. This slight irregularity in the pattern, moreover, does not necessarily indicate evidence for the received hypothesis. The poorest independent businessmen, as noted earlier, are located in small towns and also tend to be older. That "reaction" therefore appears to be a function of age, location, and political training associated with those factors rather than of occupational strains.

34. From William Kornhauser, The Politics of Mass Society (Glencoe: The Free Press, 1959), p. 202.

35. For a discussion of the 1964 development in the South, see Hamilton, Class and Politics . . . chap. 7.

36. Very similar results also appeared in the 1952 and 1956 studies.

37. Not all of these increases would go to small business. Families at all levels "commute" to shopping centers and supermarkets. In many instances local retailers get the "leftover" business, the purchases one forgot to make at the supermarket, perishables, extra milk (or beer), and purchases made on Sunday or after other businesses have closed. Local retailers also pick up business from those who find it inconvenient to travel to a distant shopping plaza or who, because they have no automobile (as is true of many retirees) cannot travel there. In all these instances increased wages or welfare benefits would still benefit small retailers, even if marginally.

Two detailed studies of small businessmen appear in Arthur B. Shostak and William Gomberg, eds., Blue-Collar World (Englewood Cliffs, N.J.:

Prentice-Hall, 1964).These are Kurt B. Mayer and Sidney Goldstein's "Manual Workers as Small Businessmen" (pp. 537-550) and Ivar Berg and David Roger's "Former Blue-Collarites in Small Business" (pp. 550-556). The latter presentation, because of its detailed discussion of satisfactions and dissatisfactions as well as political responses, is especially to be recommended.

The Anderson and Davidson work is the only one, to my knowledge, which has examined the politics of independent businessmen living in different occupational settings (p. 151). Retailers and wholesalers living in a working class district had a low Republican percentage (38), a figure similar to that of manual workers there. Unskilled workers in a rich precinct, by comparison, had a high level of Republicanism (71 percent), one similar to that district's retailer-wholesaler figure of 79 percent.

38. It would be easy, especially in the light of conventional readings, to take this difference as indicative of a *change*, that is, a shift toward Republicanism on the part of those who "arrived" in middle class. An examination of party identifications of fathers of these groups, however, indicated that upward mobiles came from families that were, on the whole, somewhat more Republican to begin with. This accords with the findings from Kenneth Thompson, "Upward Social Mobility and Political Orientation: A Re-Evaluation of the Evidence," American Sociological Review 36 (April 1971) 223-234.

39. The reported "class" of family has been used for this analysis rather than occupation of father so as to provide a larger number of cases for analysis. The result was very similar when we took the "new rich" whose fathers were manual workers; eight of the ten respondents favored Johnson. This compares with the "old rich" among whom eleven of twenty favored Goldwater.

For a discussion of the politics of the "downwardly mobile," of those who have fallen into the working class, see Hamilton, *Class and Politics . . . ,* op. cit., chap. 9.

40. See the discussion in chapter 3 of this work and also the discussion of independent business in Hamilton, Class and Politics . . . , op. cit., chap. 5.

41. See the discussion in C. Wright Mills, "The Professional Ideology of Social Pathologists," American Journal of Sociology 49 (September 1943) 165-180.

It is possible, of course, that at some time in the past independent businessmen were overwhelmingly conservative in their politics. Contemporary surveys do, in some cases, allow a limited assessment of this possibility. Where one has questions asked about both father's occupation and father's politics, one can examine the politics of occupational groups in previous generations. If one divides respondents by age, it is possible to "look back" two or three generations. While the procedure is hazardous and may be biased by unknown demographic factors (Republican small businessmen may have had small families while the Democratic businessmen may have been notably prolific), one can still get some glimmering of how things were.

Taking the findings "straight," the evidence offers no support for the thesis of a conservative monolith at any time in the past fifty to seventy-five years. Only the 1952 study finds businessmen in any period as having a Republican majority. That is indicated in the case of those respondents with businessman fathers who were themselves born prior to 1908. Even in this case, which would take us back to McKinley days, the division among the fathers was only sixty-forty in favor of the Republicans.

42. From Robert E. Agger and Daniel Goldrich, "Community Power Structures and Partisanship," American Sociological Review 23 (August 1958) 383-392.

43. Looked at from another perspective, we find that 10 percent (N=63) of the Democrats had written letters as against 26 percent (N=42) of the Republicans.

44. The figures in Table 2.8 probably understate the actual differences. They indicate, for example, only whether or not people had tried to convince others of their views, not how many attempts they had made. There was no direct question on the number but other evidence suggests disproportionate Republican effort. Democrats tended to have made efforts in a single context, that is, with family or friends or co-workers. Republicans were more likely to have tried with family and friends or with family and co-workers or in all three contexts. The number of cases is very small; but, again for what it may be worth, four of the five Democrats who had attended political meetings had attended only one. Five of the seven Republicans who went to meetings had been to two or more.

45. See Dr. R. Blank, "Die soziale Zusammensetzung der sozialdemokratischen Wahlerschaft Deutschlands," pp. 507-550 in the Archiv für Sozialwissenschaft und Sozialpolitik, vol. 20 (Tübingen: J. C. B. Mohr-Paul Siebeck, 1905).

46. Robert Michels, "Die deutsche Sozialdemokratie. I. Parteimitgliedschaft und soziale Zusammensetzung," pp. 471-556 in the Archiv für Sozialwissenschaft und Sozialpolitik, vol. 23 (1906).

47. The summary quoted in the text appears in S. M. Lipset, *Political Man* (Garden City, N.Y.: Doubleday, 1960), p. 149n. The summary is based on the work of Hans Neisser, "Sozialstatistischen Analyse des Wahlergebnisses," Die Arbeit 7 (1930) 654-659. See Also Linz, chapters 15 and 18, for more recent evidence.

Lipset also refers to "an excellent discussion of the reactionary politics of

upward mobile small business" in Robert Michels's "Psychologie der anti-
Kapitalistischen Massenbewegungen," Grundriss der Sozialökonomik, vol. 9,
no. 1, p. 249. This "excellent discussion" consists of three sentences, two of
them being simple assertions about the attitudes of workers toward the
proletarian turned "factory owner" and the other, a reference to sources on
the French and English experience.

48. The study in question is that of John Bonham, *The Middle Class Vote*
(London: Faber and Faber, 1954). The relevant data are to be found on page
129.

49. See Lipset, *Political Man*, op. cit., p. 225, and also Hamilton, *Affluence and the French Worker*, op. cit., pp. 42-44. Another study of a Poujadist
variety development must also be classified as one of those showing only very
small differences. See Maurice Pinard, *The Rise of a Third Party: A Study in
Crisis Politics* (Englewood Cliffs, N.J.: Prentice-Hall, 1971). The difference of
14 percentage points between the salaried lower middle class and the small
businessmen in their support for Quebec's *Créditistes* depends on three
respondents.

50. Kautsky referred to "parasitic small business" and went on to describe
it as a form of unemployment which was only somewhat more exalted than
begging (from Michels, op. cit., p. 503). See also Blank's discussion of the
Social Democrats' refusal to develop a farm program because that would not
accord with the principles of scientific socialism (p. 530). Small businessmen
certainly must have been charmed by the following expression of "support"
offered by a Social Democratic representative in 1869: "I am voting for the
abolition of guild restrictions on entry into a trade, not because I am
expecting blessings and happiness for our country and our society as a result
of this bill: quite to the contrary, I expect its implementation to cause the
loss of independent means of existence for thousands and tens of thousands
who will then join our ranks" (from L. D. Pesl, "Mittelstandsfragen," pp.
70-119 of *Grundriss der Sozialökonomik*, IX, I Tübingen: J. C. B. Mohr-Paul
Siebeck, 1926. The quotation appears on page 117, my translation).

CHAPTER 3

THE SALARIED MIDDLE CLASS:
SOME RECONSIDERATIONS

WHITE-COLLAR EMPLOYEES—THE RECEIVED CLAIMS

In this chapter the claims about differentiations within the salaried middle class will be examined. In particular, the claims about the motivational dynamics, about the sources of strain and the presumed political reactions, will be assessed in much the same manner as were the claims about the independent middle class in chapter 2.

A major theme in the discussions of the middle class is one holding that they have a very high level of concern with their position or status. Some of these formulations have been touched on in the preceding chapter as they applied to the independent middle class. The same claims have been made, with equal insistence, about the salaried or dependent middle class. Because it is generally felt that members of the "upper middle class" have some considerable grounds for assurance about their position in life, the major emphasis has been on the "lower middle class." "Traditionally . . . ," one author writes, "the white-collar worker has thought of himself as a member of the middle class, not of the working class." Another author, making a slightly different stress, speaks of the white-collar group's "well-known desire to set itself apart from the blue-collar group." Linked to this identification and this setting apart, the substance of the entire effort, is the assumption that there is a relatively sharp distinction between middle class and working-class values; the persistent claim in the literature is that "the white-collar worker has middle class values."[1]

The strain for the white-collar group, in particular for the lower middle class segment, results from some long-term social and economic developments. In one of the more renowned discussions of the subject, their problem is put as follows:

> Every basis on which the prestige claims of the bulk of the white-collar employees have historically rested has been declining in firmness and stability. [There has been a] leveling down of white-collar and [a] rising of wage-worker incomes. . . .

This loss of status gives rise to a "status panic." One result of such a "panic" is a tendency to "seize upon minute distinctions as bases for status." This behavior in turn operates "against any status solidarity among the mass of employees, often lead[s] to status estrangement from work associates, and to increased status competition. The employees are thus further alienated from work, for, in striving for the next rank, they come to anticipate identification with it, so that now they are not *really* in their places."[2]

As for the positive political choices, the options would be support for some "middle class" party, or, in time of acute strain, because of the threats to their status and the even more alarming "ultimate" threat, falling into the proletariat, there is the possibility that this group, like the independent businessmen, would also provide mass support for fascist movements, for movements promising somehow or other to preserve their faltering position.[3] One such formulation, that of Sigmund Neumann, reads as follows:

> It was in this stratum [i.e., among the salaried classes] that emerging National Socialism found its most ardent recruits.
>
> The extraordinary quantitative growth of the white-collar man in modern industrial society led also to a qualitative change in his social prestige. His had become a static class position, if not a castlelike predicament. At the same time, the discrepancy between his actual status and his now unfulfilled traditional aspirations of eventual independence and individual security made this group the frustrated class par excellence. This fate was re-emphasized in Germany by the specific

experiences of a military defeat, money inflation, and radical economic depression, all of which hit the salaried employees the hardest. Thus a total crisis revolutionized this stratum. . . .

National Socialism seemed to offer a satisfactory answer, with its simple solution of world conquest by the "masterrace" which channeled desperate personal perplexities into outer drives of nationalist expansion. It satisfied emotional hungers, historical traditions, and activists' escapism from the bad dream of reality into the no man's land of utopia. This easy victory of demagoguery . . . was possible for a drifting middle class which was unprepared for daily public responsibilities and thus accepted short cuts of grandiose schemes.[4]

The first major attempt to "import" the theory into the United States was in the work of Lewis Corey in 1935. The exiles from Nazi Germany also made some transplantations when they, from time to time, undertook analyses of the American scene. For all practical purposes, however, the importation of the theoretical framework was not successful, that is, did not gain wide currency in the social sciences, until the publication in 1951 of C. Wright Mills's *White Collar*. Even so, what has been accomplished was the implantation of the main outlines of the theory through a series of *assertions* that the various American occupational groups behaved in much the same manner as had been claimed about Germany by Lederer, Kracauer, Mannheim, Speier, and other German commentators. Very little evidence has been offered to support those assertions.

The German materials were reworked in some of the later American formulations. In the more optimistic variants, the ominous import of the Weimar position disappears completely. Rather than a "leveling down" of white-collar incomes, there was a stress (based on the same limited evidence showing income compression) on the disproportionate increase of working-class incomes. The working class was in the process of achieving a wholesome middle class existence and, since the middle class too was improving its position in terms of real income, there was no special concern with "strains" and "anxieties." At the same time, the rapid expansion of "middle class" jobs made possible a considerable amount of upward mobility. Because, as a result of the expansion, there was no equivalent downward mobility, there were many gainers and only few losers. The entire trend was toward the development of an affluent, middle class society. As in the famous fairy tale, they all lived happily ever after.[5]

In another variant, one that is not quite so cheery, the same strains exist for the lower middle class as in the original formulation. But in this variant the upper and upper middle classes are transformed. They are no longer portrayed as a grasping, profit-oriented bourgeoisie. They are now secure in their wealth, educated, and sensitive to their responsibilities. They come to be portrayed as the defenders of those values that any intelligent and decent person would wish to see protected.

Again it is useful to raise a simple question as to the validity of the claims. Essentially we are asking: Is it so?

THE "LOWER MIDDLE CLASS"—DEFINITIONS

A fairly widespread procedure in the contemporary social sciences involves the taking of two "middle class" census categories, "managers, officials and proprietors" and "professional, technical and kindred" and labeling them "upper middle class" and then taking two others, "clerical and kindred" and "sales," and counting them as "lower middle class." This method gives rise to some misleading conclusions.

The procedure is intended to yield categories that are differentiated in terms of "life chances," in terms of income, education, and prestige. The actual picture, however, is one of considerable overlap. (For the income distributions see Table 2.1). The largest percentages of low income middle class persons, as has already been noted, are to be found among the proprietors and among the clerical and sales employees. Small minorities among both managers and professionals also fall into the lower income categories. And some proprietors and some clerical and sales employees fall into the high income categories.

This overlap is not all so surprising when one recognizes the wide range of occupations actually contained within these categories. When thinking of "managers," one envisions presidents and vice-presidents of firms, executive suites, high education and much on-the-job training, high salaries, and high prestige. In fact, however, the category includes a wide range of occupations from much further down the chain of command. There were in 1960, for example, 185,000 store buyers and department heads. There were 72,000 public administration inspectors. When one thinks "managers" or even "officials," one ordinarily would not have railroad conductors in mind, but 45,000 of them were included. And similarly, one does not think of the department store floormen, but they too, 6,000 of them, have been placed in the category.

The professional category presents similar problems. When one thinks of professionals, the tendency is to think "doctor" and "lawyer"; but in point of fact, physicians and surgeons made up only 215,000 of the 4.5 million male professionals of 1960, and the lawyers and judges numbered only 202,000. As against these high paid and high status professionals, there are many groups that are unlikely to be either highly paid or accorded very much status. There were 142,000 elementary school teachers and 276,000 secondary school teachers. There were 46,000 photographers, 27,000 radio operators, 86,000 musicians and music teachers, 52,000 sports instructors and officials, 206,000 draftsmen, 35,000 funeral directors and embalmers, 53,000 medical and dental technicians, and last but not least, 196,000 clergymen.

The clerical jobs are generally low paid, have relatively low educational requirements, and probably do not yield much prestige for job holders. This category includes agents, bank tellers, bookkeepers, cashiers, dispatchers and starters, mail carriers, office machine operators, postal clerks, shipping and receiving clerks, stock clerks and storekeepers, and ticket agents. The sales category is somewhat more heterogeneous. On the one hand, it includes a large number of sales clerks and salesmen, as well as 191,000 newsboys. On the other hand, there were large numbers of advertising agents and salesmen, insurance agents, brokers and underwriters, stock and bond salesmen, and real estate agents and brokers.[6]

If in fact there were significant differences in outlook and behavior associated with upper middle and lower middle class existence, the use of this conventional procedure based on census categories would tend to obscure that reality. When, in other words, one compares categories that are only modestly differentiated in terms of incomes and life-styles and then finds that, for example, the political differences between them are rather small, that finding does not constitute much of a contribution to the understanding of the situation. If, on the basis of that kind of result, it is concluded that the entire direction of research is fruitless, the effort may, on balance, have a negative impact. It may mislead other researchers and their readers for years and may also direct them into less important lines of endeavor.[7]

An examination of Table 2.2 does show very little difference in the political outlooks of the various middle class categories; but, as has been shown elsewhere, when these categories were divided by income into "lower" and "upper" subgroups, fair-sized differences appeared. In fact, the differences between the upper middle and lower middle classes proved more important than the difference between manuals and nonmanuals.[8]

THE CLASS IDENTIFICATION QUESTION

It is not possible to consider all of the assertions touched upon here. Only a few of the major themes, the key assumptions, may be addressed. The first of those to be considered is the question of the identification of salaried employees with the middle class.

The Survey Research Center studies all contain class identification questions. These vary somewhat in their specific formulation, but they all yield a choice between two basic labels, that is, "middle class" or "working class." In some years there were specifications into "upper" and "average" subgroups of the middle and working class. A choice of either upper or lower class labels was also possible; but since it was rare that more than a handful of respondents chose either of these options, we have taken only two major categories for the following analysis.[9]

It would be a mistake to make too much of these responses. Other studies have indicated that changes in the question wordings, especially changes in the number and kinds of options offered, can yield sizable differences in the result.[10] It seems unreasonable, therefore, to take these responses as indications of a basic or fundamental "class consciousness," that is, one that might have world historical consequences. For present purposes, however these questions do allow an assessment of the claims about class identification. If it were true that the white-collar worker thinks of himself as middle class and desires to set himself apart from the blue-collar group, that ought to be indicated in the response to these questions. If the basic claim were correct. they could all, or nearly all of them, respond by saying they were middle class.

None of the salaried groups have that kind of monolithic identification with the middle class (or avoidance of the working-class label). The highest level of middle class identification is found among the salaried professionals. Eighty percent of this group has, in recent years, identified with the middle class. At the same time, a fair-sized minority, one-fifth of them, have chosen the working-class label. Again in recent years, that is in the studies from 1956 to 1968, approximately three-tenths of the managers and officials group have identified with the working class. And, perhaps most remarkable of all, in the studies from 1952 through to 1968, approximately half of the clerical and sales group have chosen to identify themselves with the label "working class." The distribution of choices in the manual category is more or less constant throughout the period. The percentage identifying as working class has varied between 74 and 79 percent with no trend indicated (Table 3.1).

Except for the change between 1952 and 1956 in the managers and professional categories, the remarkable thing about the results shown in Table 3.1 is their constancy. Aside from those differences, the picture is one of no change. This is true even though there were large increases in real living standards occurring during the years in question. In a period when commentators of all persuasions were talking about the acquisition by previously deprived groups of "middle class" living standards, the individuals themselves, at least in this limited symbolic aspect, in the choice of a label, remained unchanged in their orientations.

Because these responses, as they stand, prove to be somewhat

TABLE 3.1
OCCUPATION AND CLASS IDENTIFICATION;
Married, Economically Active Respondents

	Occupation			
Class Identification	Managers, Officials	Salaried Professionals	Clerical Sales	Manuals
SRC 1952				
Middle*	60%	72%	48%	21%
Working	40	28	52	79
N=	(89)	(72)	(120)	(579)
SRC 1956				
Middle	72	78	48	22
Working	28	22	52	78
N=	(102)	(114)	(117)	(599)
SRC 1964				
Middle	70	80	53	26
Working	30	20	47	74
N=	(101)	(104)	(94)	(417)
SRC 1968				
Middle	73	80	51	22
Working	27	20	49	78
N=	(73)	(129)	(77)	(348)

* See footnote 9 for question wordings.

enigmatic, it is useful to make some exploration of the matter so as to obtain an understanding of what these identifications are likely to mean to the respondents.

The responses are correlated with income, those in the higher income category (shown in Table 3.2) being consistently more likely than those in the lower income category to identify with the middle class. The relationship between the three major middle class groups holds at both income levels, the salaried professionals being the most heavily identified with the middle class and the clerical and sales group, of the middle class groups, tending to be somewhat less identified.

In the high income category, the manual workers prove to be an exception to the pattern of majority middle class identification. Clear majorities in both years identified with the working class. These workers, it will be noted, constitute the "affluent" segment

TABLE 3.2
CLASS IDENTIFICATION BY OCCUPATION AND INCOME;
Married, Economically Active Respondents

Family Income and Class Identification	Occupation			
	Managers, Officials	Salaried Professionals	Clerical, Sales	Manuals
SRC 1964				
High Income*				
Middle	80%	85%	76%	37%
Working	20	15	24	62
N=	(51)	(48)	(21)	(56)
Lower Income				
Middle	60	72	47	25
Working	40	28	53	75
N=	(48)	(54)	(72)	(354)
SRC 1968				
High Income*				
Middle	81	87	75	35
Working	19	13	25	65
N=	(36)	(64)	(16)	(48)
Lower Income				
Middle	64	73	44	24
Working	36	27	56	76
N=	(36)	(63)	(59)	(294)

*High income means in 1964 $10,000 or more. Lower income means $9,999 or less. In 1968 the cutting line was $12,000.

of the blue-collar rank, the much discussed "labor aristocrats," the "bourgeoisified" workers. Despite their "arrival" in this advanced state of well-being, they tend to be remarkably persistent in their choice of a "traditional" label. It appears that for them occupation is the decisive factor, one that far outweighs the fact of "affluence."[11]

Significant minorities of the lower income, salaried white-collar groups identify themselves as working class: this amounts to roughly two-fifths of the managers, a quarter of the salaried professionals, and just over half of the clerical and sales category. The conventional description, in short, would appear to be appropriate for only a part of this "lower middle class." For the others, a different basic line of analysis is necessary.

The class identifications are also linked to family backgrounds. Those lower income white-collar workers who come from middle class families are more likely to identify with the middle class than are those who come from either working-class or farm backgrounds. One could explore this matter directly, but it proves more fruitful to take up the question of background in conjunction with the subject of education. Because educational attainment is very strongly associated with age, it is necessary to explore the background-class identification relationship within different age categories. As a basis for this exploration, a preliminary discussion of the question of "class" and age follows.

CAREER DIFFERENCES WITHIN THE LOWER MIDDLE CLASS

The division of the white-collar group into an "upper" and "lower" middle class on the basis of income, while more appropriate than the division by census categories, still leaves difficulties in that again some families are "misplaced." An upper middle class career, especially in recent times, begins with a considerable amount of educational outfitting. One then, characteristically, begins work in a large bureaucratic organization. As Max Weber put it, one's career in such an organization is conceived as following a planned movement from one position to another, gradually working up in the hierarchy, to jobs of ever greater responsibility and remuneration. That means that many persons from upper middle class backgrounds are going to begin their careers with the firm at relatively low levels in the hierarchy. They are, in a sense, temporarily declassed. But, given their background and training, and given the clarity of the career line planned for them, they are not likely to see themselves as permanent or lifetime members of the "lower middle class." It seems likely that these "temporary" lower middle class persons (as defined by the arbitrary income division) would be strongly identified with the middle class since they are thinking in terms of their futures rather than of their present circumstances.

The "other" case would be that of the person engaged in routine white-collar work, in the kind of job that is not planned to be a step in a sequence leading ever higher. It seems likely that railroad conductors (classed as managers) and draftsmen (professionals) hold this kind of job, the kind that does not, in the ordinary course of events, lead to more desirable positions. Holders of this kind of job would, in all likelihood, form the permanent lower middle class.

The Survey Research Center studies show some evidence of these different career lines and the differences in outlook associated with them. Unfortunately there was no way to separate out those respondents of *upper* middle class backgrounds. The best that was possible was an analysis based on middle class respondents coming from middle class families and those from manual or farm families. We have taken those younger than 35 years as the category in which most of the "temporaries" or "misplaced" persons would be found. Ninety-four percent (N=31) of those persons coming from middle class backgrounds had received an education which took them beyond high school. Among those of working-class and farm backgrounds, by comparison, only 53 percent (N=45) had had the same educational advantage. Even this understates the differences since, if we take those who have gone beyond high school, we find that those from middle class families are more likely to have completed college than those from working-class and farm families. The percentages were 45 (N=29) and 21 (N=24), respectively.

The segment of the lower middle class that is of middle class background and has gone beyond high school, those who are likely to be only temporarily "lower middle," do in fact have a very high level of middle class identification (Table 3.3). The same holds true of those persons of working-class and farm background who have achieved an education beyond the high school level. But those of working-class and farm background who never went beyond high school, those who are not likely to be going on to "better things," have a sharply opposed pattern of identifications. The respective percentages of the three groups who identified with the middle class were 79, 76, and 26.

Turning to the lower middle class group who were 35 years or more, one finds a similar pattern although with some anticipated variations. Many of the "temporaries" have presumably made their

TABLE 3.3

CLASS IDENTIFICATION, INCOME, AND SATISFACTION WITH INCOME OF LOWER-INCOME SALARIEDS: BY AGE, FATHER'S OCCUPATION, AND EDUCATION; Married, Economically Active (Survey Research Center, 1964)

Respondent's Education	Father Middle Class		Father Manual or Farm	
	Beyond High School	To High School	Beyond High School	To High School
TO 35				
Percentage Identifying as				
Middle Class	79%		76%	26%
N=	(28)	(2)	(23)	(19)
Family Income				
To $5,999	38		38	49
$6,000-$7,499	35		33	19
$7,500 to $9,999	28		29	33
N=	(29)	(2)	(24)	(21)
Financial Satisfaction				
Pretty well satisfied	31		25	33
More or less satisfied	41		67	48
Not satisfied	28		8	19
N=	(29)	(2)	(24)	(21)
35 OR MORE				
Percentage Identifying as				
Middle Class	71	63	84	28
N=	(17)	(19)	(19)	(36)
Family Income				
To $5,999	11	21	11	42
$6,000-$7,499	28	16	37	32
$7,500-$9,999	61	63	53	26
N=	(18)	(19)	(19)	(38)
Financial Satisfaction				
Pretty well satisfied	44	47	32	45
More or less satisfied	56	42	63	47
Not satisfied	—	11	5	8
N=	(18)	(19)	(19)	(38)

*Too few cases.

transition by this age, that is, would be located in the higher income categories. This older segment does, accordingly, have somewhat larger proportion of persons from working-class and farm backgrounds and of limited educations, that is, those who are likely to be part of the "permanent" lower middle class. An examination of the income distributions of the various segments shown in Table 3.3 indicates that the first three, those who are heavily identified with the middle class, also tend to be in the highest of the lower middle class income categories, that is, in the $7,500 to $9,999 category.[12] A sizable majority of the fourth segment, the permanent lower middle class, fell below that level of income.

Roughly half of the second generation middle class group had achieved some advanced education, and that group, as would be expected, is heavily identified with the middle class. The less-well-educated "half" of the second generation group is also heavily identified with the middle class. Their relative lack of education was apparently no special hindrance to their careers since, as noted, they still have achieved relatively high incomes. Those from working-class and farm backgrounds who had achieved some education beyond high school also tend to be middle class identi-fiers. The majority working class identification is to be found within that segment, 40 percent of this age category, which came from working-class or farm backgrounds and had not achieved much education. They also provide the overwhelming majority of the lower income families in this age group.

The choice of a "middle class" identification in response to the options posed by the Survey Research Center's questions appears to be closely linked to the *upper* middle class condition. Those persons who identify themselves as middle class, in summary, tend to be in nonmanual occupations *and* to be in the higher paid income categories or to have some reasonable expectation of coming into the higher income categories. A majority of those who are in blue-collar occupations identify with the working class, even those at the very highest income levels. A majority of those who are in the genuinely lower middle class jobs, those with no "great expectations" for the future, also identify themselves as working class.

The important point to be noted about the "lower middle class" as defined by income is that it will contain persons with markedly different careers. For that reason it does not make sense to talk about *the* lower middle class or about the strains *they* suffer. There will be differences in the ways in which they assess current situations depending on their backgrounds and career lines. The famous comparison—between the earnings of white-collar and skilled manual workers—is going to have markedly different significance depending on those career lines. Persons with "great expectations" are soon going to leave the skilled workers far behind. Those who currently fall below the income levels of the skilled and have no expectation of ever catching up *may* suffer the strains that Mills and others talked about. On the other hand, because they clearly differ from the expectations of Mills and others in one respect, in the overwhelming percentage who identify with the working-class rather than the middle class, there is a strong likelihood that they would not suffer the strains and anxieties about their status that have been attributed to them. The lessons may be summarized somewhat elliptically with two statements: those members of the lower middle class who identify themselves as middle class are either not marginal or not likely to remain marginal; and, those who are economically marginal (and are likely to remain so) do not identify themselves as middle class.

If the received line of theorizing were adequate, one ought to find a considerable amount of dissatisfaction with the current level of income expressed within the lower middle class ranks. If they were concerned, to the point of anguish and panic, about the leveling down of white-collar incomes and the rising of wage-worker incomes, that should be indicated in their responses to the income satisfaction question.

The result (also shown in Table 3.3) does not accord with this expectation. A majority in all categories report that they are either pretty well satisfied or more-or-less satisfied with their financial condition.

A closer examination of the responses yields some important specifications. The highest level of outright dissatisfaction is found in the younger subgroup among those who came from middle class backgrounds and had achieved education beyond high school. It seems unlikely that their dissatisfaction would be linked to a leveling down of incomes. More likely would be the possibility of inadequate or too slow advance. This kind of strain stems from the peculiarities of the upper middle class career rather than from the dynamics of class relations in advanced capitalist societies. Such strain would also be both limited in extent and, in the ordinary case, temporary. Only three-tenths of those in the category report outright dissatisfaction, and 86 percent (N=29) expect financial improvement in the future.

A generally higher level of satisfaction was indicated among those who were 35 years of age or more. Of some importance in this context is the finding that those of manual and farm backgrounds and with limited education, those with the lowest incomes, have approximately the same distribution of satisfactions as the other groups. Put somewhat differently, the group that, in objective terms, is the most deprived, that is the most economically marginal segment of the age group, is not characterized by the intense frustration so often asserted.

It would appear that there are different patterns of expectation associated with the differences in background and, a further correlate, it would appear that there are also different sources of frustration or satisfaction. Some persons, of middle class background appear to have high aspirations and early frustrations as the pace of advance proves to be slow and the expectations not immediately fulfilled; they seem unable to defer gratification.[13] The other major tendency involves those of working-class and farm backgrounds who did not receive very much in the way of education and who have relatively low incomes. They tend to identify themselves as working class and to indicate satisfaction with their incomes.[14]

PARTY PREFERENCES AND POLITICAL ATTITUDES

A second major claim made about the salaried white-collar workers is that they have "middle class values." Exploration of this topic is hindered by the failure to specify precisely what is meant by that expression. If it means that they identify with those above them in the social hierarchy and adopt their political outlooks, then support for the Republican party and its candidates may be taken as evidence bearing on that claim.

Looking first at party identifications, one finds that all three of the younger segments of the non-South lower middle class are heavily identified with the Democratic party (Table 3.4). In the older age category, three of the segments have heavy Democratic majorities. The one exception to this pattern occurs in the case of the well-educated, second generation middle class segment which proved to be very heavily identified with the Republican party. It will be noted that the groups from working-class and farm backgrounds who had achieved education beyond high school and who largely had identified with the middle class were still, nevertheless, heavily aligned with the Democrats. This suggests, once again, that the choice of the class label by itself, has limited political significance.

It is possible, of course, that the "real" or "underlying" senti-

TABLE 3.4
PARTY IDENTIFICATION AND VOTING OF LOWER INCOME, NON-SOUTH SALARIEDS: BY AGE, FATHER'S OCCUPATION AND EDUCATION; Married, Economically Active (Survey Research Center, 1964)

	Father Middle Class		Father Manual or Farm	
Respondent's Education	Beyond High School	To High School	Beyond High School	To High School
TO 35				
Party Identification				
Democrat	67%		72%	79%
Republican	33		28	21
N=	(18)	(1)	(18)	(14)
1964 Vote*				
Democratic	63		76	77
Republican	37		24	23
N=	(19)	(1)	(17)	(13)
35 OR MORE				
Party Identification				
Democrat	21	73	72	70
Republican	79	27	29	30
N=	(14)	(11)	(14)	(23)
1964 Vote*				
Democratic	43	82	58	60
Republican	57	18	42	20
N=	(14)	(11)	(12)	(20)

* The results include also the indicated preferences of nonvoters.

ments of the lower middle class would not be manifested until such time as a candidate appeared to make the appropriate appeals, one who played on their problems and alerted or catalyzed their anxieties. If their strains and frustrations would somehow lead them to support rightist candidates, those who, in the terms of Lipset and Raab, "strike the preservatist nerve," one might find that indicated in the support for Goldwater in 1964. Here again there was no widespread, across-the-board approval indicated. The educated, second generation middle class segment had the highest Goldwater percentage to be found among the younger segments, although even that was still a minority. In the older age category it was again the second generation middle class group, specifically the educated segment of that group, that gave Goldwater a majority. All other lower middle class groups provided very sizable Democratic majorities.[15]

Conventional economic conservative orientations would constitute another indication of "middle class" values and hence a test of the received claim. The heaviest conservatism appeared within the older, educated, second generation middle class category. They were strongly opposed to federal government support for education, strongly opposed to government supported medical care programs, and strongly opposed to a government guarantee of jobs and living standards. They also had a relatively high concern with something called "government power." A similar pattern, although not as pronounced, appeared among the equivalent younger group. The economically marginal groups, the poorly educated segments coming from working-class and farm backgrounds, tended to have an opposite, liberal position on the same issues. The "middle class" position, in short, the strongly individualistic, antigovernment orientation, proves to be characteristic only of a small segment of the entire lower middle class category, those who happen to have come from middle class families and who have received advanced education.

The white-collar worker, it will be remembered, is supposed to be opposed to unionization, this aversion being linked to his fear of "proletarianization" and to the fear of status loss. The picture as far as actual memberships are concerned is quite simple. The "traditional" middle class segment has the lowest level of union involvement, and the less well-educated group from working class and farm background has the highest level of membership. The other two categories fall in between.[16]

It has sometimes been claimed that the upper class constitutes a special repository of virtue when it comes to civil rights. The available evidence does not support that position. The responses to a wide variety of questions showed the non-South lower middle class to be either as supportive of civil rights as the upper middle class or, in some cases, more supportive. In the South the picture was mixed. Some comparisons did show support for the conventional hypothesis, some showed no difference, and some showed small reversals of the conventional expectation. The basic picture then was one of no clear and consistent support for that hypothesis. The best that could be offered in support of that claim was some scattered evidence from the South.[17]

It ought to be clear by now that the conventional claims made about the "lower middle class," about the stresses and strains to which it is subject, about its nervous and anxious character, and its conservative political thrust—those claims are not supported by the evidence reviewed here. The entire focus is seriously misleading in that the stress on "class" leads one to avoid or to overlook other considerations of greater importance such as social backgrounds and subsequent careers.

THE GROUP-BASES QUESTION

One such consideration involves what has been called the socioreligious factor. Political orientations, the frameworks for analysis, tend to be passed on within family and community networks. Different outlooks are found within various religious, ethnic, and racial communities, and these subcommunity influences appear to outweigh "class" as a determinant of outlooks. It seems unlikely that the decisive factor operating within the subcommunities is a specifically ethnic or religious ethic. It seems more likely that each major group, in the course of its settlement and subsequent experience in the country, has made political arrangements and developed political loyalties which are then passed on and maintained within the interpersonal networks, this as a part of growing up in the various Catholic, Jewish, Negro, or white Protestant subcommunities. Because the religious factor is adventitious, it providing merely a convenient boundary line for defining a group rather than providing any serious political determination, the term socioreligious has been chosen so as to emphasize the interpersonal considerations.[18]

Unfortunately, the number of Catholics, Negroes, and Jews in the ordinary representative sample of the U.S. population is so small as not to allow inquiry into the orientations of each specific segment. This is particularly difficult when working with a subdivision of the entire sample, as in this case with the salaried upper and lower middle classes. For this reason it has been necessary to combine the Catholics, Negroes, and Jews in the following discussion. It must suffice at this point to note that all three groups are considerably more likely to be Democrats, to be more liberal in economic matters, and to be more supportive of government guarantees of civil rights than are their class peers among the white Protestants.

The political orientations of the non-Southern socioreligious and class segments may be seen in Table 3.5. Beginning with the 1964 party identifications, one finds that the lower middle class white Protestants divide in half in their party loyalties while the other groups are overwhelmingly Democratic. The difference between them is a matter of nearly 40 percentage points. Both of the upper middle class segments are more Republican than their lower middle class socioreligious equivalents. Again there is a division following the "communal bases," the Protestants having a Republican majority and the others having a Democratic majority.

There was some shift away from those party loyalties indicated in the 1964 vote. The most noteworthy instance is the movement within the "other" upper middle class. A fair-sized defection of Republican party identifiers occurred there while the equivalent white Protestants maintained their basic pattern. That shift meant a difference of approximately 30 percentage points between the socioreligious communities at both class levels. At the same time, the differences between the upper and lower middles within each of these communities was roughly 10 percentage points. The

TABLE 3.5

PARTY IDENTIFICATIONS AND VOTING OF MIDDLE CLASS
SALARIEDS: NON-SOUTH WHITE PROTESTANTS AND OTHERS,
1964 AND 1968; Married, Economically Active

	Lower Middle*		Upper Middle	
	White Protestants	All Others	White Protestants	All Others
NON-SOUTH				
1964 Party Identification				
Democratic	47%	85%	41%	57%
Republican	53	15	58	43
N=	(62)	(54)	(41)	(30)
1964 Vote**				
Democratic	53	85	45	74
Republican	47	15	55	26
N=	(60)	(55)	(40)	(31)
1968 Party Identification				
Democratic	44	80	22	71
Republican	56	20	78	29
N=	(64)	(41)	(45)	(38)
1968 Vote**				
Democratic	27	61	17	72
Republican	67	25	71	22
Wallace	7	14	12	6
N=	(60)	(36)	(42)	(36)
SOUTH				
1964 Party Identification				
Democratic	65	100	54	76
Republican	35	—	46	24
N=	(43)	(8)	(24)	(17)
1964 Vote**				
Democratic	45	89	52	71
Republican	55	11	48	29
N=	(44)	(9)	(27)	(17)
1968 Party Identification				
Democratic	55	75	52	***
Republican	45	25	48	
N=	(36)	(8)	(21)	(5)
1968 Vote**				
Democratic	18	50	14	***
Republican	56	37	82	
Wallace	26	13	5	
N=	(34)	(8)	(22)	(3)

* The cutting line was $10,000 in 1964 and $12,000 in 1968.
** The results include also the indicated preferences of nonvoters.
*** Too few cases.

socioreligious fact, in short, was of considerably greater importance than the class fact.

The pattern of non-Southern lower middle class identifications in 1968 was very similar to that found in 1964. There was some difference, however, in that the upper middle class white Protestants were much more heavily Republican than in 1964 and the "others" were more heavily Democratic. The differences in party identification between the socioreligious groups in 1968 then were roughly 35 to 50 percentage points at the lower middle and upper middle levels, respectively. The differences in the voting of the socioreligious groups in 1968 were of approximately the same magnitude.

The 1968 data also allow an assessment of the Wallace candidacy and of its success in appealing to lower middle class resentments. The comparison of the identifications and the 1968 choices makes clear that there was a considerable disaffection of lower middle class Democrats in that year, that shift occurring in both the white Protestant and the "other" segment. Most of the defection, however, was to the Republicans rather than to the third party. The Wallace sentiment moreover, was not a peculiarly lower middle class phenomenon. There was fair-sized Wallace support found among the lower middle class "others." An equivalent level of support, however, appeared among the upper middle class white Protestants. It appears that neither class nor socioreligious community provides much help in accounting for the non-Southern Wallace support.[19]

One other observation about these results deserves special emphasis. The findings presented prior to the present discussion involve *averages* of the very diverse orientations found within each class level. Where there are differences of 35 and 50 percentage points between component segments, it does not make much sense to talk about the orientations of *the* upper middle or *the* lower middle class. Any such formulation would be seriously misleading. It would hide an important source of division within the society, and it would encourage a focus on a factor of considerably lesser importance. It should also be clear that, when discussing middle class categories, it is necessary to ask: Which lower middle class? or, Which upper middle class?

The discussion of the socioreligious segments in the South is complicated by the problem of small numbers. For this reason it only makes sense to discuss the white Protestant groups. The evidence in this case does show a "reaction" on the part of the lower middle class. Although somewhat more Democratic in their identifications in both 1964 and 1968 than the upper middles, there were important defections indicated in both years when it came time to vote. In 1968 the rejection of the Democratic candidate in both class levels is especially noteworthy: the lower middles shifted, to the greater extent, to Wallace while the upper middles shifted overwhelmingly to the Republicans. This reaction is discussed in more detail in chapter 4. This Southern reaction provides the only evidence to be discovered in this entire investigation which could be counted as substantial support for the received hypothesis.

THE "NEW WORKING CLASS"

Much of the evidence that has been presented here has relevance to contemporary discussions of the "new working class." This refers to the rapidly increasing numbers of technical and scientific workers, the key persons, presumably, in the operation of a modern economy. Such persons find themselves in a position where their knowledge "comes into conflict with the limits imposed on [their] autonomy by the hierarchial organization of work and society." The technician, so it is said, "is trained for work of a broad scope . . . but finds himself rendered both powerless and confined within outmoded relations of production." Where in times past technicians have been closely linked to the owners and managers of the established social order, they now are increasingly "alienated" and will more and more tend to ally themselves with those groups in the society which favor radical reorganization of the existing arrangements. This contemporary discussion revives an idea first put forward by Thorstein Veblen in the *Engineers and the Price System* some fifty years ago.[20]

The "new working class" groups are most likely to be found within the salaried professional category. The questions at hand do not approach directly the matter of their job strains and the possibility of their alienation and disaffection. The evidence shown in Table 3.1 indicates a remarkable steadfastness in their identification of themselves as middle class, a fact that does not suggest new or wavering loyalties.

The examination of the political sentiments of the salaried professionals also does not suggest the presence of special progressive sentiments within the category. They were not particularly distinguished in the 1964 study by their party identifications or their voting, either within the South or outside it (see Table 2.2). In 1968, however, with one minor exception, the salaried professionals had the highest Republican percentage of all the middle class groups. Even this understates the tendency since, it one were to exclude the notoriously liberal and Democratic teachers and professors, the conservative propensities of the remaining salaried professionals would be even more impressive.[21]

The positions of the salaried professionals on the economic liberalism issues also do not promise significant new progressive directions. If, moreover, one were to take the differences between the 1964 and 1968 results (in Tables 2.3 and 2.4) as indicative of a trend, then that trend is unfavorable; it does not accord with the expectations of "new working class" theorizing. There is little shift indicated in the responses toward three of the economic liberalism issues. In the response to the fourth, the question on "government power," the professionals show increased alarm and concern.

This limited evidence, in short, does not suggest any significant progressive movement among the salaried professionals. It would appear that they too are largely following in familial or subcommunity political traditions. They are probably aided in this by being located in relatively conservative settings both on and off the job. They are also, on the whole, relatively well rewarded. It is difficult to assess the importance of the various factors operating in their lives; the available evidence suggests that the influences of family tradition and contemporary milieu outweigh the impact of any special "alienation" they might feel in the course of their work.[22]

The support for "liberal" and more radical economic innovations in the United States is found largely within blue-collar and lower middle class ranks. Within any given class segment, but especially within the middle class, support for these liberal innovations is greater among Catholics, Jews, and Negroes than among white Protestants. All of this indicates that an adequate assessment of contemporary opinion must take account of both class and socioreligious dimensions.

Although it is always possible that the future holds a decidedly different distribution of opinion and behavior, that prediction involves the action of factors that are not yet operative. Put somewhat differently, this analysis places the roots of contemporary outlooks in the combination of existential circumstances and the various mediations of social structure rather than in what is sometimes referred to as the more "fundamental" developments of the "class relations within the production process." While the latter might be "fundamental" in explaining developments in the future, it offers little aid in understanding current mass outlooks. If the "fundamental" developments were forcing a transition in the outlooks of key groups, that *change* in outlook, an empirical fact, ought to be evidenced in contemporary studies of the groups in question. If it is not, then there ought to be some reconsideration of what is and what is not "fundamental."

The major conclusions may be summarized as follows:

The focus on the "middle classness" of white-collar workers is mistaken, at least in the emphasis. A sizable minority of the marginal white-collar workers identify themselves as working class. This rather stable fact indicates that for this large minority the claims about the "middle class" self-conception and the desire to set themselves apart from blue-collar workers are dubious ones.

It is somewhat more difficult to assess the claim about their having "middle class values." On the basis of their party identifications and their voting behavior, they prove to be similar to blue-collar workers and rather unlike the more conservative upper middle class.[23]

The related assumptions of strain and tension as a fundamental feature of white-collar existence, of status panic, and of a potentially very dangerous reaction all appear open to serious question. The "traditional" middle class does not appear to be suffering "proletarianization." They are the principal recipients of the high quality advanced education offered in the country. Although temporarily, that is, at the beginnings of their careers, they may suffer low earnings, they are destined to progress rapidly into the higher income categories. The nontraditional "middle class," those of working-class and farm backgrounds, those located in jobs that do not "lead anywhere," are the ones who identify themselves as working class, who hold liberal positions in economic affairs, support the Democrats, and are more likely to be members of unions.

The middle class is also differentiated on another dimension, that is, in terms of the socioreligious or communal background. Basically that means that white Protestants at any given class level are more conservative than are equivalent Catholics, Jews, or Negroes. In general, this factor proved to be of greater importance in explaining the observed political differences than whether one was "upper" or "lower" middle class.

As for the penchant of the lower middle class for "rightist" candidates, here too, the received theory appears to be in error, at least in the all-embracing sweep of the claims. Outside the South, that is to say, for three-fourths of the nation, there was no clear evidence of special or disproportionate lower middle class support for either Goldwater or Wallace. There was, however, support for that claim indicated among the white Protestant lower middle class in the South. They gave disproportionate support to both Goldwater and Wallace, that is, more than the upper middles. This was the only context in which the received line of theorizing has received any clear support.

According to the received line of theorizing, the lower middle class constitutes a specially dangerous collection of individuals, ones who, if aroused, would do immense damage to the functioning of democratic societies. The appropriate strategy in the face of such a threat, in one view of the matter, is a kind of withdrawal: one should avoid policies that would "stir them up." Given the portrayal of the sources of their tensions, this quietism means sacrificing liberal or left options, foregoing moves toward an improved welfare state, and avoiding moves toward equalitarianism.

In another, more "modern" reading, the appropriate strategy is for all liberal elements in the society to make common cause with the educated and responsible upper middle class. The idea here is to build an alliance against the "threat from below," against the angry and threatened lower middle class. The evidence reviewed here casts doubt on both claims, that is, the assumptions of a "dangerous" lower middle class and of a peculiarly responsible "upper middle class." Members of the latter group, particularly the white Protestant segment thereof, prove to be eminently conservative in their choice of party identifications and in their choice of candidates. They are the most conservative on the economic liberalism issues. And, they tend to be unenthusiastic about the use of the federal government powers so as to guarantee equal job opportunities and equal schooling for blacks. This line of theorizing, in short, reaches conclusions that are the reverse of the reality indicated in these studies; it claims the relatively liberal lower middle classes to be illiberal and the relatively illiberal upper middle classes to be friends of liberal virtue.

SOCIAL INFLUENCE—FURTHER ELABORATIONS

The above findings clearly do not accord with the conventional, handed-down readings of the character and behavior of white-collar workers. From that perspective the findings prove rather paradoxical. From another perspective, however, they present no paradox at all, the difficulty stemming from the use of an inappropriate framework for analysis of the group.

There is a tendency when discussing white-collar workers to focus on the "downtown", or central office of the firm, on the largest banks or insurance companies and on the largest of the department stores. While dramatic and spectacular, that focus misrepresents things in much the same way as does the focus on the giant automobile assembly plant, that is to say, it misrepresents the frequency distributions. There are thousands of middle-sized office units and tens of thousands of smaller ones which, when taken together, employ more people than the giant firms. The front office focus is misleading also in its suggestion that the administration and paper work occurs only at that point in the firm. In point of fact, "administration" involves connections or linkages of center and periphery within those units and that in turn means that much "office work" will be "decentralized." It will, in other words, be located in the offices next to the factories or even, in some cases, will take place within the factories. The performance reports, quality controls, evaluations, and the like, all originate from within the factories. A fair amount of "white-collar" work is found in railroad yards where men work all shifts keeping a record of the movement of cars (fulls and empties) from one line to another and pass the billing along to the appropriate recipients. In truck yards too there is a fair amount of paper work to be done by dispatchers and billing clerks.

It seems likely that the employees in the downtown or main offices would tend to be of middle class background. Those doing the clerical and administrative tasks in the factory office or in the rail yards, those working as dispatchers for the trucking companies or keeping records in the warehouses, on the other hand, would tend to come from working-class or farm backgrounds. If that is true, then the kinds of daily contacts, the substance of daily conversations on economics, politics, national affairs, and so on, as well as the development of appropriate life-styles, would probably be very different depending on the office, whether it is at the "center" or at the periphery of the firm.

Many of the white-collar workers of manual background are likely to have life histories similar to those of the independent businessmen discussed in the preceding chapter. Many of them would have been raised in working-class neighborhoods; they would have gone to school with other working-class children; they would, many of them, still live in working-class neighborhoods; and it seems likely that they would maintain contacts with these friends, neighbors, and kinsmen. The idea of maintaining "distance from" blue-collar workers would probably appear rather curious to these persons, as pretentious and somewhat ridiculous.

Much of the speculation about the lower white-collar workers assumes that they *can* maintain distance from the manual workers. Implicit in this judgment is the assumption of separate territory, of separate home communities. While there are, to be sure, fine gradations in the social levels of the middle class suburbs surrounding major cities, it seems likely that only a small proportion of the economically marginal white-collar workers would be living there. It seems more likely that they live scattered in the working-class neighborhoods of the central city or else in working-class suburbs. They would constitute an occupational minority in those locations, but probably would not be socially separated from their neighbors.[24]

It seems unlikely that these white-collar workers would feel a "status panic" when faced with the fact that skilled workers, some of them, earn more than they do. That would be a fact of existence, easily recognizable from the earliest discussion of jobs, of the good ones and the not-so-good ones. It is possible that the white-collar job is viewed as a "soft touch". For that benefit, one must accept some concomitant loss, in this case, a loss of some income. But again on the credit side, the white-collar job involves steady indoor work, frequently with controlled temperature and atmosphere. Those advantages have to be compared with, in one frequent example, high paid skilled work in construction where employment is irregular and seasonal and is done in all kinds of weather, in heat, rain, cold, and snow.

Some white-collar workers are likely to have been "upwardly mobile" in the course of their careers. In some firms, after putting in most of a lifetime as an operative, it is necessary to change jobs as one's physical capacity declines. Faced with the choice of an unskilled cleanup job, or where seniority and job bidding allows, an opportunity to work in a soft clerical job, the latter, even if low paid, comes as a very welcome alternative. Again, status panic appears as an unlikely response. In all these instances, the identification as "working class" would seem more appropriate than the rather distant conception or self-image, "middle class."

Those in middle class origins would be likely to settle in middle class communities. Quite possibly some of those who came from working-class families and who had achieved higher education would also come to be located in these middle class communities. They might be subject to considerable social pressure with respect to their political orientations if they happened to come into communities with markedly different outlooks, that is, with heavy Republican dominance. If, however, the upward mobility were within the socioreligious community, that is, if one moved, say, from an Italian working-class community into an Italian middle-class community, that might result in a shift of class identification but allow a persistance of the basic political orientation. If they did come into a position of conflict, if they were liberal Democrats with continuing loyalties and concerns with their community of origin but happened to locate in a conservative Republican community, the solution to their interpersonal situation might be to not talk politics, that is, to hide one's political "difference." That might, in part, account for the phenomenon of the silent Democrats noted elsewhere.[25] That silence, in turn, has lead many observers, unwittingly, to misrepresent the actual distribution of sentiment within the middle class.

It cannot be stressed too much that this account of the sources of differentiation within the white-collar ranks is hypothetical; while plausible, the supporting empirical studies are lacking. Essentially what has been shown in this chapter is the connection existing between the social origins and education of the various groups and some aspects of their outlooks, that is, their class identifications, satisfaction with incomes, political orientations, and so forth. The lines of explanation offered in the previous paragraphs involve social structures and influences which intervene in time between their origins and early training and their contemporary outlooks. Unfortunately, contemporary social science research has tended to avoid inquiry into the details of the social structure. The main direction of effort has shifted to "larger" social structural developments or, alternatively, to all-embracing "cultural" explanations.[26]

PERSISTENT MISREPRESENTATION—SOME EXPLANATION

There is, once again, a question to be raised as to why commentators have so persistently misread the situation of the salaried workers. One difficulty stems from the failure of the commentators either to read or else to appreciate the evidence that has been available. There has, for example, been evidence on class identifications available for some decades now. The first of the studies making use of a class identification question similar to those used here, that of Richard Centers, was done in July 1945, the results being published in 1949. This study found that 35 percent of the white-collar group identified themselves as working or as lower class.[27] A study done in September and October of 1948 found 57 percent of the "clerks" identifying as working class. This same study, a comparative one involving nine nations, also found 58 percent of British clerks identifying with the working class. Roughly half of the clerks in Australia, France, Mexico, the Netherlands, and Norway identified as working class. The significant exceptions to this general pattern are to be found in West Germany (in what was then the British Zone) and Italy. In these countries the percentages of working-class identifiers among the clerks were 25 and 22, respectively.[28]

The study of the Chicago population in the 1930s discussed in the preceding chapter included a detailed presentation of the responses of "office employees" who were divided into those with low, medium, and high positions. Those findings also were not in accord with the conventional understandings. Approximately four out of five, for example, agreed that businessmen had too much influence in running the affairs of the nation. This level of agreement did not vary significantly by the job level of the respondent. Asked about the pay of unskilled workers and laborers (whether they were getting too much, not enough, or about right), approximately two out of three said not enough, a response that suggests concern and generosity as opposed to the grasping, panic-stricken, and anxiety-ridden white-collar worker portrayed in the literature.

A key theme in the basic line of theorizing is the presumed hostility toward the trade unions. The study asked: "Are you in favor of strong labor unions to which almost all workers would belong?" For a group that supposedly is opposed to or disdainful of this kind of "proletarian" solution, the responses are somewhat unexpected. Fifty-six percent of those in "low" office positions thought that a good idea as did 40 percent of those in "medium" positions and 31 percent of those in the higher ranks.

For a group that presumably identifies with those "above" them in the bureaucratic hierarchies, they again give unexpected responses. Nearly seven out of ten of the office workers said that business leaders and executives "get too much" pay. One would expect a group that is so concerned with status and with the minute signs of rank to oppose any equalizing tendencies. Their sentiments about the pay of laborers and executives, however, would suggest the opposite. A direct question was asked on this subject: Do you believe the government should aim at making people's wealth and incomes more nearly equal?" The respective percentages of the high, medium, and low categories who thought that to be a good suggestion were 55, 47, and 60.[29]

This study did not find a sharp differentiation between the outlooks of the "middle class" and the "working class." It is useful to cite the summary of their findings:

> The largest gap is . . . between the business groups together with the associated professions of engineering and law, on the one hand, and the worker groups composed of manual laborers and the lower levels of white-collar employees, on the other.
>
> The spread of attitudes among the several professions and among the several levels of office workers is noteworthy. They illustrate the divergences running through the "middle class." The professional and higher office workers who are most closely associated with business interests tend to resemble the owner and executive groups most; the more "social" professions and the mass of lower salaried office workers lean farther away from the businessman's viewpoint. . . . That more independent and detached professional groups like college professors. public school teachers, and clergymen have swung much farther away from the prevalent attitudes of those who exercise economic power is a fact of no small importance. The marked tendency of lower level white-collar workers in the same direction is perhaps no less noteworthy. . . . From the point of view of class lines, these observations re-enforce the conclusion that while no sharp divisions occur, the extreme groups of well-to-do businessmen and of manual workers (and their union officials) constitute the clearest opposed "classes" and that the "middle" groups tend to lean one way or the other depending upon their income level and the intimacy of their absorption into upper business circles.[30]

It is clear that the commentators, somehow or other, have failed to appreciate this evidence. If they were aware of those studies, the knowledge of them has not been incorporated in their writings. In most cases these works have not even been cited. One might, to be sure, have considered the 35 percent who identified themselves as working class (in Centers's study) to be a peculiar "exception" to the persistent generalization about the white-collar group. It would still, however, have been necessary to reckon with the findings of the Buchanan and Cantril comparative studies.

One other point deserving attention in connection with the Buchanan-Cantril study is the distinctiveness of the West German and Italian cases. The German case is of particular importance since this line of theorizing was originally developed there and since this fragment of evidence suggests that Germany might be different. If that were so, it would pose some difficulty when the theoretical orientation was transplanted into another context. This would be especially problematic when the transplantation was accomplished without the presentation of supporting evidence or where there was no subsequent generation of the necessary evidence.

This points, once again, to a difficulty with much of contemporary intellectual life, the ready acceptance of handed-down lines of theorizing. What occurred, it would seem, is that the dominant theoretical orientation of the German intelligentsia was read into the American experience. This reading in and the ready acceptance of the reading by contemporary American commentators amounts to a special variation on what the scholastics once referred to as the argument by common consent, although in this instance, because the groups in question are of such limited number, this might be considered an argument by uncommon consent. The basic problem with arguments by consent, whether common or uncommon, is that a widespread acceptance of a claim, by itself, says nothing at all about the state of the relevant evidence. And the basic practical intellectual problem that follows from such procedure is that a widespread consensus discourages independent inquiry.

Another difficulty with handed-down theorizing is that the outlines of the theory come to dominate even in the face of contrary evidence. For example, the conventional analyses suggest a high degree of stability within the rank, that being the only way in which some elements of the theory make sense. This is particularly true with respect to the claims involving a remembrance of "how things were," that being a prerequisite to the unfavorable judgment of the present. One German study, however, showed the heavy recruitment of the white-collar rank from working-class and farm backgrounds and indicated how their orientations, particularly toward unions, were carried over into their new employment. Those findings nevertheless, have been neglected or else have been treated peripherally in subsequent discussion. Mills, for example, did not treat origins and mobility until four-fifths of the way into his book and even then he did not draw any important lessons from that development nor did that recognition lead to any serious revision in his basic discussion of the white-collar group. The new arrivals from working-class origins were treated as eager *arrivistes,* more than willing to adopt the values of the traditional middle class, and anxious to hold onto their newly acquired advantage, to maintain their distinctiveness. It would appear that the traditional line of theorizing had led him to erase the evidence of the few studies that were available.[31] The evidence, it will be noted, is adjusted to fit the received theory rather than the theory giving way to fit or handle a range of new experience. That direction of influence, clearly, is most likely to occur in a context where little research is done or where a large proportion of the intellectual commentators are compulsively hostile to research.

In addition to what we may call the "social psychological" sources of misperception, there are also to be sure, some "realistic" factors that give rise to the conventional misreadings. Although there was roughly equivalent interest in the 1964 campaign on the part of Republican and Democratic identifiers, for example, there were systematic differences indicated in the level of political activity with the former being considerably more active in all measures of political affairs (Table 3.6). This finding, it will be noted, parallels the experience already discussed among the independent businessmen. A more detailed examination of the evidence, moreover, suggested that the figures given in Table 3.6 underestimate the actual differences between the groups. The Republicans who tried to convince others were active in more contexts than the equivalent Democrats; the Republicans, for example, attended more meetings than did Democrats. Again, if there were no systematic evidence available to the analyst-

TABLE 3.6
POLITICAL INVOLVEMENT OF NON-SOUTH SALARIEDS BY
INCOME AND PARTY IDENTIFICATION
(Survey Research Center, 1964)

| | Family Income | | | |
| | To $9,999 | | $10,000 or More | |
Party Identification	Democratic	Republican	Democratic	Republican
Campaign interest				
Very much interested	46%	51%	53%	51%
Somewhat interested	39	41	35	46
Not much interested	15	7	12	3
N=	(74)	(41)	(34)	(37)
Tried to convince others in campaign	33	61	25	61
N=	(70)	(39)	(32)	(36)
Attended political meeting	4	15	16	33
N=	(70)	(39)	(32)	(36)
Worked for party or candidate	3	13	12	26
N=	(70)	(39)	(32)	(35)
Member of a political club	4	10	7	14
N=	(70)	(39)	(32)	(36)
Wrote letters	21	29	26	46
N=	(70)	(39)	(32)	(36)

commentator and if one were, as a result, to go by personal impressions, by one's "feel" for the data, this difference in the visibility of the orientations would lead to serious errors of judgment.

Another major difficulty with handed-down theorizing, especially where there is no correction made in the course of subsequent work, is that initial errors will be passed along to later generations of scholars and students. In the course of time they take on the appearance of indubitable truths. It is useful to consider some of the more fundamental, axiomatic assumptions of the received position. As a case in point, Mills reported that the "average income of the salaried employee in 1890 was roughly double that of the average wage-worker." An extended depression kept wages relatively low during the following decades. "In the early twentieth century," Mills says, "the salaried employee's advantage over the wage-worker was solidly based on economic facts." Beginning with World War I, however, some income compression occurred, that is, white-collar and blue-collar incomes began to converge, thus giving rise to one of the strains so central to Mills's analysis.[32]

During the period, however, there also occurred a sizable increase in the numbers and the proportion of women in the labor force. Of special relevance to the point in question here, it was also a period of considerable growth of women's employment in the white-collar ranks. This would mean that a comparison of wages and salaries which did not take account of the changing male-female composition of the categories could well yield a comment on sex-related discrimination rather than on the dynamics of class and the class-related strains. The leading analysis of incomes for this period, that of Paul Douglas (the major source used by Mills), does not make separate consideration of the incomes of men and women; in fact, he notes the extreme difficulty of doing so with the available data. Douglas's evidence does suggest that the greatest relative decline of white-collar income occurred in those fields having the greatest changes in the sex composition of employees as, for example, government employment. In basic manufacturing the trend was in the opposite direction, some decline in the proportion of women occurring there. It is possible too that the reduction in child employment would also give the appearance of a general rapid rise in manufacturing wage rates.[33]

On the whole, given this difficulty with the income data for the period, it would appear that the claim of income compression, of relative loss for the white-collar workers, must be put into the category of the not yet proved. It is possible that, with the coming of women into office employment, there actually was an increase in the income differences between male blue-collar and white-collar workers. Many men in offices would be promoted from clerks to supervisors as women were assigned the more routine processing tasks.

Still another difficulty in the assessment of the income trends is posed by economic cycles. In general there is income compression in good times and expansion in bad times; where there is full employment and a high demand for labor of all kinds, manual workers tend to do relatively well, but where there is widespread unemployment, blue-collar workers do poorly. That means one must take care about the beginning and end points of any time series. If one were to begin a series in the thirties and end it in the late forties or early fifties, it would ordinarily suggest a trend toward compression simply as a result of the choice of upswing phase. If one began in the twenties and ended in the thirties, it would suggest the opposite. In general, the income compression claims have rested on the former experience. The period covered by Douglas begins with the recession of the nineties and ends with the "good years" of the war and the relative boom conditions of the early twenties. The war itself also contributed to wage compression, the manual workers making their first serious gains in real income of the century while, at the same time, clerical workers and teachers were suffering very serious losses of real income. The arguments of income compression in the post-World War II period are also based on the same phase of the cycle. In a sense, the relative rise of blue-collar incomes in that period constituted a return to the "normal" state rather than the occurrence of "something new" on the scene.

The received accounts seriously misrepresent the situation of the white-collar group as it is affected by depressions. Some evidence of their real situation is revealed in a study of teaching salaries covering the period from 1904 to 1960. This series gives both the money income and a correction for inflation and deflation. Considering first the university teachers, the basic finding is that their highest real earnings for the entire 56 year period were achieved in 1932, near the bottom point of the depression. There was some subsequent loss in purchasing power in the later years of the decade, but at no point did the real earnings of any rank of professors fall below what it had been in 1930. Similar results appeared in the case of primary and secondary school teachers. In some instances the highest real earnings occurred in the late fifties. Prior to that late upswing, however, the peak earnings for the century were achieved during the thirties. Even though many teachers took pay cuts in the early depression years, the fall in price levels was such that they still came out ahead of where they had been in the previous decades. In short, for this segment of the white-collar ranks, it may be said that "they never had it so good" as during that decade.[34]

This leads one to raise the question as to whether the German experience might not have been the subject of a similar misreading. One series on the subject does in fact show the identical finding in that country: there was a *rise* in the real incomes of white-collar workers as the depression worsened. This means that Sigmund Neumann's assertion about salaried employees being hit "the hardest" such that the "total crisis revolutionized this stratum . . ." is in error. It might be true that they were hit "the hardest" by military defeat and money inflation, but the workings of a depression are in many ways directly opposite of an inflationary crisis.[35]

The assumption that white-collar workers were drawn in overwhelming numbers to the National Socialists as a consequence of their personal economic deprivations is therefore open to some question. The previously cited study of the German election of 1930, in which the National Socialists drew 18 percent of the vote, estimated that one-quarter of the white-collar workers and one-third of the civil servants supported the Social Democratic party. Most of that support for the SPD must have been "lower" rather than upper middle class. In the larger cities the percentage of the lower middle class voting for the Socialists must have been considerably greater, possibly approximating one-half. One must also add onto the SPD share the vote for the Catholic *Zentrum* which would have been greater in the lower than in the upper middle class.

The fact that, in later elections, the vote for both of these parties was relatively stable (except for some defection of blue-collar workers from the SPD to the Communists), would indicate that a large percentage of the urban lower middle class voters, probably a majority of them, resisted the Nazi blandishments up to the end of the free elections. The tendency of the National Socialist vote to vary inversely with the size of community, to be heavily concentrated in the small towns and rural areas, also argues against the assumption of a peculiar susceptibility of white-collar workers since their proportion tends to decrease in the smaller communities.[36]

The failure of the Socialists to make even heavier gains within the white-collar ranks may have its roots in their own theoretical and practical limitations. Much of the struggle over "revisionism" involved the question of party appeals to this particular group. Because white-collar employees were not thought to be true proletarians, because of the assumption (or definition) of them as prestige seekers, as trying to maintain both distance and "appearances," they were as often the target of attacks as of appeals. In one formulation they were the *Stehkragenproletariat* (roughly translated, "the stiff collar proletariat") and in another they were the *Unteroffiziere des Kapitals* (" the noncommissioned officers of capital").

A related difficulty with the received line of theorizing involves the interpretative or explanatory assumptions. The going preference assumes that "social structures" have direct and immediate, unavoidable impacts. One's location in certain positions produces "strains" which in turn lead to specified responses. It is possible, however, that social structures, by themselves, do not have any such closely constraining or limiting effects. Opinion leaders, political parties, pressure groups, and so forth may operate within any given scene and may provide alternative frameworks for interpretation and alternative programs or solutions for given existential problems. It is possible, in short, that within any given structure one might have a variety of responses emerging, the specific outcome depending on the character and capacities of the "social forces" which operate, guide, or direct within a given milieu.

It is also within the realm of possibility that the agents of change may stand in the way of their own success. Where they are freighted with outmoded or irrelevant intellectual baggage, they may be led to the use of inappropriate or detrimental strategies. In the instances cited above (as well as in the case of the small businessmen discussed in chapter 2), they offered insults rather than appeals. The definition of a group as hopelessly conservative or as "potentially" reactionary may well have played a role in making some of them conservative or reactionary. Even then, despite the insults, a fair-sized minority of both the independent and salaried middle classes of Germany came to support the party.

Something of this sort may have been operating in the United States during the same period. There may have been in other words, an American variant on the German theme wherein the self-defeating strategy yields evidence to support one's own "original" and erroneous judgment. For many years the commonplace judgment was that white-collar workers were "unorganizable." The proof of that proposition was to be found in the fact that so few of them had been organized. There are some indications, however, of leadership inadequacies in the white-collar unions. Some white-collar union leaders were timorous and hesitant in face of the organizing task, preferring to hold and administer the limited achievement rather than to extend their influence. The major opposition within a number of American white-collar unions was provided by Communist groups. Their tactical innovations were frequently of such a bizarre character as to discourage the support of any reasonable person. Much of the effort of both union establishment and opposition was directed into the factional struggle and diverted from the organizational task. In many instances, it will be noted, it was the union and the opposition leaders who put forth the self-serving conclusion (based on "experience") that white-collar workers could not be organized.[37]

Mills indicated that "the political directions . . . of the new middle class may be sorted out into four major possibilities."[38] These were:

1. Their development into a politically independent class destined, because of their "performance of the pivotal functions required to run modern society," to be "the next ruling class." This might be described as the "managerial revolution" thesis.

2. They will not rise to independent power but will constitute a moderating, interstitial, buffer group between labor and capital. By virtue of their growing numbers the parties of right and left would have to moderate their positions and make appeals to this new, third group. This view is central to liberal analyses of the contemporary scene.

3. They are "really bourgeoisie" and will remain so. They "will form, as in Nazi Germany, prime human materials for conservative, for reactionary, and even for fascist, movements. They are natural allies and shock troops of the larger capitalist drive."

4. They "will become homogeneous in all important respects with the proletariat and will come over to their socialist policy."

For the moment, that reaction has been delayed, but with the "intensification of the class struggle" they will be "swept into the proletarian ranks." A "thin, upper layer may go over to the bourgeoisie, but it will not count in numbers or in power."

There is little evidence available to suggest support for the first of these claims, for the independence or autonomy of the entire class. Although the second view is frequently put forward by liberal spokesmen, as far as the outlooks of the populations themselves go, it would seem a questionable description. The available evidence is most clear with respect to the third option. They are, on the whole not conservative and not reactionary. Outside the South, they were less likely to support the conservative Goldwater than were the upper middle classes. And they were, again outside the South, no more attracted to the innovative "populist" George Wallace than were other segments of the society.

The fourth of these options appears to be the most realistic, at least to the extent that it recognizes a key distinction within the ranks of the salaried, with the upper ranks being the conservatives and the lower middle classes, the more liberal. On the recent American scene, the division is one of Republicanism and conservatism on the issues versus Democratic sentiments and generally liberal positions as opposed to support for "socialist policy."

The division follows closely along the lines of social origins (and possibly also of current social and economic condition). It seems likely that that has been true for some decades. It has not taken an intensification of the class struggle to sweep the lower middle class salaried employees into "the proletarian ranks." The "normal" processes operating within the society "recruit" them from the "proletarian" ranks but also provide for the maintaining of the social connections with those ranks.

It would be beyond the scope of this chapter to consider the impact of future crises, stability, steady growth, or continued inflation. The main effort has been to assess the usefulness of the received theoretical claims as far as they help to understand the current situation and development. In that respect the received theories prove, to say the least, rather misleading. One of the most serious difficulties of the received theorizing is the near exclusive focus on the "larger" structual development and the presumed impact of the "more fundamental" economic factors. Those stresses have led to the overlooking of the role of political activists and what one may call, more generally, the social organizational factor. It seems likely that the key to any future change in the situation as outlined here would depend on the combination of those two factors, the economic and the social organizational. The most important of the difficulties with the received theorizing is the failure of its "bearers" to generate the relevant supporting research or to alter their views in the light of research materials already available.

NOTES

1. The first quotation is from Douglas Dowd. "The White Collar Worker," pp. 125-32 in *American Labor in Midpassage*, edited by Bert Cochran (New York: Monthly Review Press, 1959). The second is from Robert Presthus, *Men at the Top: A Study in Community Power* (New York: Oxford University Press, 1964), p. 304. The "middle class values" quotation is also from Dowd, p. 131. For an earlier discussion of the themes considered in this chapter, see Richard Hamilton, "The Marginal Middle Class: A Reconsideration," American Sociological Review, 31 (April 1966) 192-199.

2. C. Wright Mills, *White Collar: The American Middle Classes* (New York: Oxford University Press, 1951), pp. 249, 254. See also Erich Fromm, *Escape from Freedom* (New York: Rinehart, 1941), pp. 291 ff.

3. Most of the major works in this tradition are cited by Mills in his acknowledgments, pp. 357-358. The best recent summary of the discussions of the middle classes is to be found in the work of Juan Linz, "The Social Bases of West German Politics" (Ph.D. diss., Department of Sociology, Columbia University, 1959). Chapters 14-19 all bear on various aspects of middle class politics. Chapter 15, "The Politics of the Old and New Middle Classes" (pp. 504-525), reviews the received theories. The Linz work is one of the few *empirical* investigations available of the outlooks of the various middle class segments. Other recent works of some interest are the following: Fritz Croner, *Soziologie der Angestellten* (Köln: Kiepenheuer & Witsch, 1962); Ludwig Neundorfer, *Die Angestellten: Neuer Versuch einer Standortbestimmung* (Stuttgart: Ferdinand Enke Verlag, 1961); Siegfried Braun, *Zur Soziologie der Angestellten* (Frankfurt a.M.: Europäische Verlagsanstalt, 1964); and David Lockwood, *The Blackcoated Worker: A Study in Class*

Consciousness (London: George Allen and Unwin, 1958). A predecessor of the Mills's work is that of Lewis Corey, *The Crisis of the Middle Class* (New York: Covici Friede, 1935).

4. Sigmund Neumann, *Modern Political Parties* (Chicago: University of Chicago Press, 1956), pp. 366-367.

5. A work of this persuasion which had considerable influence in the fifties was that of Frederick Lewis Allen, *The Big Change* (New York: Harper, 1952). Also having considerable impact was a work by the editors of Fortune (magazine), *The Changing American Market* (Garden City: Hanover House, 1955). Many of the observations and conclusions of this work later made their way into sociology textbooks. For additional references on the subject, see Gabriel Kolko, *Wealth and Power in America* (New York: Praeger, 1962), and Richard Hamilton, *Affluence and the French Worker* (Princeton: Princeton University Press, 1967), pp. 70-71.

6. This discussion is based on U.S. Bureau of the Census, *U.S. Census of Population, 1960, Subject Reports, Occupational Characteristics,* Final Report P.C. (2)-7A (Washington, D.C.: U.S. Government Printing Office, 1963), Table 1. The information presented in these paragraphs is for males only.

7. It means all studies which follow that procedure and which have concluded that the differences between the lower middle and upper middle class are small or nonexistent are suspect. They are very likely to be understating the actual differences. To be sure, not all studies follow that procedure and make that mistake.

8. See Richard Hamilton, *Class and Politics in the United States* (New York: John Wiley, 1972), chaps. 5 and 9.

9. The few upper class identifiers have been counted with the middle class and the few lower class identifiers with the working class group. The procedures used here are the same as those outlined in chapter 2. The focus is on married respondents with wives classified by the occupation of the husband. Most of the results presented in the following are based on those with opinions only.

The following subjective social class questions were asked in the four SRC Election Studies:

1952: There's quite a bit of talk these days about four different social classes. If you were asked to use one of these four names for your social class, which would you say you belonged in, the middle class, lower class, working class, or upper class?

1956: There's quite a bit of talk these days about different social classes. Most people say they belong either to the middle class or to the working class. Do you ever think of yourself as being in one of these classes? (If yes) Which class? Would you say that you are about an average (class selected) person or that you are in the upper part of the (class selected)?

1964: There's quite a bit of talk these days about different social classes. Most people say they belong either to the middle class or to the working class. Do you ever think of yourself as being in one of these classes? (If yes) Which one? (If no) Well, if you had to make a choice, would you call yourself middle class or working class?

1968: There's been some talk these days about different social classes. Most people say they belong either to the middle class or to the working class. Do you ever think of yourself as belonging to one of these classes? (If yes) Which class? (If no) Well, if you had to make a choice, would you call yourself middle class or working class?

(If middle class) Would you say you are about average middle class, or that you are in the upper part of the middle class?

(If working class) Would you say that you are about average working class, or that you are in the upper part of the working class?

10. See the early discussion by Richard Centers, *The Psychology of Social Classes* (Princeton: Princeton University Press, 1949), chaps. 3 and 4. See also the discussion in Hamilton, *Class and Politics* ... op. cit, chap. 3, and that by E. M. Schreiber and G. T. Nygreen, "Subjective Social Class in America: 1945-68," Social Forces 48 (March 1970) 348-356.

11. This may be seen in the following detailed presentation (SRC 1964):

PERCENT IDENTIFYING AS WORKING CLASS
(Married, Economically Active Respondents)

Family Income, dollars	Nonmanuals, percent	N	Manuals, percent	N
To 4,999	70	(54)	84	(104)
5,000-5,999	57	(51)	86	(58)
6,000-7,499	44	(59)	77	(107)
7,500-9,999	27	(103)	55	(85)
10,000 or more	22	(179)	62	(56)

In part, at least, this peculiarity appears to be linked to some aspects of working-class careers. High income working-class families are ones with second and third earners, and that usually means that the high earnings are temporary. The income of middle class families, with much greater frequency, is due to the effort on a single earner, and their earnings tend to increase throughout the career. See Hamilton, *Class and Politics* ... chap. 10 on this point. Some indication of this difference appears in the assessment of their future earnings. In 1964, 64 percent (N=120) of the high income middle class groups shown in Table 3.2 anticipated future improvement of their financial condition. The equivalent figure among the high income blue-collar group was 42 percent (N=55).

12. One of the difficulties involved in the use of an arbitrary income division is that this procedure also misplaces some persons. The same income may have different meaning depending on the community context: a given income, for example, might be viewed as relatively high in smaller communities but as average or even low in a large city. Many of those who have been defined as "lower middle class" by the procedure used here are located in middle-sized communities and smaller towns and may possibly consider themselves to be among the "upper middles" of those settings.

13. Seven out of the eight such respondents expected economic improvement in the future. Their dissatisfaction does not appear to be due to imminent "proletarianization" or to the "threat" of permanent lower middle class status.

14. At a given level of income, their satisfaction is greater than that of the other groups. Again the lesson is that the "traditional" middle class is not being "proletarianized," and the permanent low income middle class does not stand in desperate fear of that fate.

THE DATA: SRC 1964

	Income Level, dollars	
	6,000-7,449	7,500-9,999
Category:	Percent pretty well satisfied with current income	
Father middle class, or father worker or farmer and respondent went beyond high school	24%	46%
N =	(33)	(48)
Father worker or farmer and respondent did not go beyond high school	44	61
N =	(16)	(18)

15. There were only four lower middle class blacks contained in Table 3.4. The results would have been much the same had one taken only white respondents.

16. Taking the lower income non-South salarieds, one finds 14 percent (N=35) of the traditional middle class group to be unionized as against 27 percent (N=37) of the middle class segment of working-class or farm background and with no advanced education. The situation, it should be noted, is undergoing some change. The percentage of non-South clerical and sales families containing a union member, for example, increased from 26 percent (N=93) in 1952 to 35 percent (N=62) in 1968. See also the discussion of white-collar unionism later in the text.

17. See Hamilton, *Class and Politics . . .* , op. cit., chap. 11, Table 11.2, and chapter 4 of the present work.

18. See *Class and Politics . . .* , chap. 5.

19. The number of cases is small, but, for what it may be worth, an examination of the vote of independent businessmen by income and socio-religious group also did not indicate a lower middle class reaction. The highest Wallace support was found within the upper middle class subgroups, among both the white Protestants and the "others."

20. The qoutations are from Stanley Aronowitz, "Does the United States Have a New Working Class?" pp. 188-216 in *The Revival of American Socialism,* edited by George Fischer (New York: Oxford University Press, 1971). See also Serge Mallet, *La Nouvelle Classe ouvrière* (rev. ed.; Paris: Anthropos, 1969); and Bogdan Denitch, "Is There a New Working Class?" Dissent, 17 (July-August 1970) 351-355.

21. The same division by socioreligious category is found among the salaried professionals. Taking the higher income group of 1968, both Southern and non-Southern, one finds 72 percent (N=40) of the white Protestants identified as Republicans as opposed to only 24 percent (N=25) of the "other" category.

22. Some suggestion of the conservatism of the settings in which the salaried professionals find themselves is indicated by the shifts away from the father's political position. Some 40 percent (N=58) of the 1968 salaried professionals with Democratic fathers identified themselves as Republicans. A study of University of Wisconsin students indicated that this shift comes relatively early in the "professional" or "technical" career. One of the few indications of *conservatizing* influence was found among those students of working-class backgrounds who were studying engineering and related subjects. See Dario Longhi, "Higher Education and Student Politics: The Wisconsin Experience," (M.S. thesis, Department of Sociology, University of Wisconsin, 1969).

23. The comparison with the blue-collar workers appears in Hamilton, *Class and Politics . . .* , op. cit., chap. 5.

24. On the location of white-collar workers in one major city, Milwaukee, see ibid., chap. 4. There are some differences in the location and current situation of those white-collar workers of farm background. They are more likely to be in middle-sized communities or smaller towns. Insofar as they failed to gain the educational qualification necessary for the better paying jobs, it seems likely that they too would come to be located in working-class neighborhoods.

25. See chapter 2 for the discussion of this phenomenon among independent businessmen. The same development among salaried employees is taken

up in the pages that follow. See Table 3.6 See also Hamilton, *Class and Politics* . . . op. cit., chap. 6.

26. The leading work exploring the social pressures and the channels of influence was that of Bernard Berelson, Paul F. Lazarsfeld, and William McPhee, *Voting* (Chicago: University of Chicago Press, 1954). In the same tradition and showing the same sensitivity to the social determinants of outlooks and changes in outlook were the early works of Seymour Martin Lipset, notably his *Agrarian Socialism* (Berkeley: University of California Press, 1950) and, together with Martin Trow and James S. Coleman, his *Union Democracy* (Glencoe: The Free Press, 1956). This focus is almost completely absent from his later works.

27. Centers, op. cit., p. 86. His study did not include Negroes. Examination of the class identifications of middle class blacks in the 1964 and 1968 studies indicated that the overwhelming majority of them identified themselves as working class. This may account for the *relatively* low level of working class identification in Centers's study.

28. From William Buchanan and Hadley Cantril, *How Nations See Each Other* (Urbana: University of Illinois Press, 1953), Appendix D. The data are also reproduced in Hamilton, "The Marginal Middle Class: A Reconsideration," op. cit., p. 197.

29. Arthur W. Kornhauser, "Analysis of 'Class' Structure of Contemporary American Society—Psychological Bases of Class Divisions," chap. 11 in George W. Hartmann and Theodore Newcomb, eds., *Industrial Conflict: A Psychological Interpretation* (New York: Cordon, 1939), especially p. 255. Similar findings are reported for other middle class groups, school teachers, college professors, clergymen.

30. Ibid., pp. 254-256.

31. The recruitment from working-class ranks was already noted in the Weimar literature. It was also noted that they behaved differently from the "traditional" middle class, for example, in their joining of the socialist Zentralverband der Angestellten as opposed to the very "traditional" Deutschnationale Handlungsgehilfen-Verband. See Hans Speier, "The Salaried Employee in Modern Society," Social Research 1 (February 1934) 111-133. This article is reprinted as chapter 6 of his *Social Order and the Risks of War: Papers in Political Sociology* (New York: George W. Stewart, 1952).

32. Mills, op. cit., p. 279. He is citing the leading work on the subject, that of Paul H. Douglas, *Real Wages in the United States: 1890-1926* (New York: August M. Kelley, 1966), pp. 246, 364-365. This work was originally published in 1930.

33. For data on the trends in the labor force showing the shift in the location of employed women during this century, see Hamilton, *Class and Politics* . . . op. cit., chap. 4. In effect what occurred was a shift of a low paid

group, women, from manual to nonmanual employment. By itself, this would suggest compression. It is possible, as a consequence, that the disparity in the earnings of male manuals and nonmanuals has been constant or possibly has even increased. Another difficulty mentioned (but not solved) by Douglas is that the salaried and clerical category includes superintendents and managers and salaried officers of corporations (p. 359). See also his discussion of the shifting sex composition of the clerical rank (p. 366, especially note 1).

The situation as of 1890 was somewhat more complex than the straight-forward manual-nonmanual comparison would suggest. The 1890 income of clericals was given as $848, and that was nearly double the figure for all those in manufacturing industry, $434. There was, however, considerable variation within manufacturing, the figure being lower in those industries employing large numbers of women (for example, in textiles, $320) and higher in the industries where the employees were mostly men (in the iron and steel industry, $556). In a sector that has been largely overlooked by most commentators, teaching, it appears that incomes were well below those of manufacturing, the 1890 average annual earnings being only $256.

34. See Sidney G. Tickton, *Teaching Salaries: Then and Now* (New York: Fund for the Advancement of Education, 1961). A study by the Canadian Teachers' Federation found a similar result, 1933 being the peak year for real income in the period 1910 to 1940. See their *Teachers Salaries: Trends and Comparisons* (Ottawa, 1964).

35. For data on the real incomes of German workers, employees, and civil servants for the period 1929 to 1952, see J. Heinz Müller, *Nivellierung und Differenzierung der Arbeitseinkommen in Deutschland seit 1925* (Berlin: Duncker und Humblot, 1954), p. 140. The basic table is reproduced in Richard Hamilton, "Einkommen und Klassenstruktur: Der Fall der Bundes-republik," *Kolner Zeitschrift für Soziologie und Sozialpsychologie* 20:2 (1968) 250-287. With 1929 = 100, the real income of workers had fallen to 93 in 1932. At that time the real income of employees had increased to 113 and that of civil servants, who had suffered some cuts, was 102. It might be true, as Neuman states, that money inflation hits the salaried employees the hardest, but then again, it might not be. It is remarkable that intellectuals stress the point that the middle classes lost their savings during the inflation but fail to point out that the working classes also lost theirs. The impact of lost savings in the working class is probably much more formidable than it would ever be for the better-off middle classes who have many more oppor-tunities to recoup.

36. In the larger communities it would appear that the lower middle class was not overwhelmingly attracted to the National Socialists. In the small towns and rural areas, particularly those that were heavily Protestant, all groups (with the occasional exception of working-class Socialist voters) sup-

ported the National Socialists. See, for example, the detailed account by Rudolf Heberle, *From Democracy to Nazism: A Regional Case Study on Political Parties in Germany* (Baton Rouge: Louisiana State University Press, 1945). All of the empirical studies of Germany make clear that religion was very strongly associated with support for the National Socialists. Again this point is omitted from the arguments of those who simply talk about the propensities of *the* lower middle class.

37. By now it should be clear that this is not true. For a useful review see Adolf Sturmthal, ed., *White Collar Trade Unions: Contemporary Developments in Industrial Countries* (Urbana: University of Illinois Press, 1966).

The Communist involvement in white-collar trade unions (in the State, County and Municipal Workers of America, The United Federal Workers, and the United Public Workers) is touched on in Nathan Glazer, *The Social Basis of American Communism* (New York: Harcourt, Brace and World, 1961) p. 138. They were also active in the American Federation of Teachers. For a discussion of the rather staid leadership and their Communist opponents, see Robert W. Iversen, *The Communists and the Schools* (New York: Harcourt, Brace, 1959), chaps. 1 and 2, and Stephen Cole, *The Unionization of Teachers: A Case Study of the UFT* (New York: Praeger, 1969), chaps. 1-3. Cole, incidentally, is one of the few authors who has picked up the fact of the increases in real living standards on the part of employed teachers during the depression. He quotes one teacher, describing his depression period earnings, as follows: ". . . a teacher on maximum . . . was a prince or a princess. Nobody earned that sort of money. . . . There were no taxes. It was a great deal of money. I didn't know anybody at that time earning that kind of money" (p. 25). Iversen mentions the pay cuts but failed to note the increase in real incomes thereby suggesting the opposite. Where many commentators have suggested that depression and widespread white-collar unemployment would "radicalize" and lead to new forms of trade union and political party activity, Cole notes that in many ways the impact of the depression was just the opposite. Those who were employed, even though they had many nonsalary grievances, were not about to endanger their position by engaging in new styles of militancy. Rather than creating "unity" (or revolutionizing the entire "stratum"), the depression gave rise to very sharp differences of interest between employed and unemployed teachers.

38. These too derive from German originals. Emil Lederer and Jakob Marschak laid out three of the following possibilities in their article "Der neue Mittelstand," in *Grundriss der Sozialökonomik,* IX. Abteilung, I. Teil, pp. 120-141. The four alternatives appear in Theodor Geiger's important article, "Panik im Mittelstand," Die Arbeit 7: 10 (1930) 637-654. The notion of the status panic also derives from this source.

CHAPTER 4

BLACK DEMANDS AND WHITE REACTIONS

THE LIBERAL WORLD VIEW

Liberal social scientists, those in the centrist tradition, have portrayed the American scene as one fraught with imminent danger of backlash. The black population, no longer accommodating and quiescent, has been demanding equality and, even more, compensation for past crimes against their people. The whites in the power structures have reacted by yielding to these demands as well as they are able, by paying off here, passing special legislation there, by some highly visible appointments to fend off one thrust, by creating jobs in response to another, and by unusual judicial leniency so as to forestall still another.

In the liberal litany, these responses are undertaken by enlightened and fundamentally decent upper and upper middle class populations. They are secure in their social positions, affluent enough to have all their basic needs more than satisfied and with enough left over to provide for a wide range of amenities. These groups are also the recipients of advanced education, and, as all the world knows, education creates open, more tolerant outlooks.

And so, after years of neglect, the confident and tolerant upper and upper middle classes yield to the black demands. Their willingness to make amends was limited by the minor inconvenience of a costly war (together with sundry additional "commitments" to "world affairs") which prevented the diversion of resources toward this new end.

The thrust and response do not occur in a vacuum. Mute observers of this scene, the white lower middle class and the white workers, have watched and waited. They have received no special benefits, no special reparations. In many instances, they have "paid the costs" of the upper and upper middle class generosity. It is, after all, the white lower middle class and working-class neighborhoods that are being integrated. It is the schools in those neighborhoods that are affected by busing. It is their jobs that are "threatened" by fair employment practices, by the Philadelphia plan, and so forth.[1]

As opposed to the openness and tolerance of the upper middle class, these latter groups, so it is said, show diametrically opposed traits. Their lives are not characterized by security and affluence. Although no longer living on the margins of existence, what they have is a recent achievement. The "threat" of integrated neighborhoods, the fear of depreciating home values and a move to another, more expensive neighborhood make easy acceptance of the black initiatives, to say the least, rather difficult.

One is, moreover, speaking of white ethnic minorities, of those who have just barely "made it" and who are not about to give up hard won gains of position and status. One is also speaking of groups who do not have the benefit of all those years of formal education. As a consequence, they have never learned the tolerant outlooks, the need for "give and take," and the respect for the "rules of the game."

Possibly the key ingredient in this complex of events is the struggle for jobs. White skilled workers will attempt to hold onto theirs and to preserve new openings for their children. The white operatives, laborers and service workers, lacking the "sure thing" of the skilled workers, will be exposed to a fierce competition for this scarce and valuable resource—jobs.

The basic dynamic of the contemporary situation, then, puts the poorest, the least secure, least educated, and least tolerant whites in close physical proximity to blacks. It is in this context that struggle, resistance, or "backlash" is likely. Black moderates, to be sure, are allied and working with the white upper and upper middle classes. Together they are working for "responsible" social change. The black militants, on the other hand, are making extreme and, in the short run, unrealizable demands. Their protests, their marches and demonstrations, and their violence or threat of violence have paved the way for the reaction from white "middle America."

The Viet Nam War added further complications and strains. The effects of the war were more serious for white "middle America" than for the upper middle class. The war took the sons of "middle America" and returned dead and wounded. War-induced inflation eroded incomes, and counterinflationary policy created unemployment. Mixed into this already tense and explosive situation one saw increasingly bizarre and unfathomable protests on the part of white radicals, protests that appeared to challenge everything white "middle America" ever learned or stood for. These developments also served to "bring things to the boiling point." They too contributed to the welling reaction.[2]

After the customary references to the tragedy of Weimar, one then turns to the lesson, the need for "responsible" leaders to let up on the demands and, at least for the moment, to take some of the pressure off the white workers and the white lower middle class. In the long run, with the liquidation of the Viet Nam enterprise and with stable economic growth in the future, there will be enough of everything to satisfy all groups. In the short run however, the imminent threat of civil war can be averted only by following the strategy of present restraint and gradual change.

It would be impossible to comment on all of the claims of this world view. Key to the assumed dynamic, however, is the judgment that intolerance is greatest among the poorer working class whites and that tolerance is greatest in the upper middle and upper classes.

Rather than take this on faith, it would seem worthwhile to examine some relevant evidence.

Much of the evidence presented in support of this claim is anecdotal, depending on flagrant instances of brutality as for example, the instance of the open housing marches in Chicago and Cicero in the Summer of 1966, or Father Groppi's marches to the south side of Milwaukee in the Summer of 1967, or, in the Viet Nam context, the action of the Hard Hats in the Wall Street area in May of 1970. Such scenes can misrepresent things. The ugly scenes on the south side of Milwaukee involved a maximum of 8,000 persons, most of them spectators. The area within a radius of fifteen or so blocks contained a population of more than 150,000. The number of counterdemonstrators, in short, constituted only a very small minority of the area's population. Going by the arrest records, a large proportion of the counterdemonstrators were not even from the area. Moreover, a small study done at that time by the Milwaukee *Journal* found a majority of the area's residents in favor of open housing.[3]

There is a fair amount of survey evidence available which allows a more accurate assessment of the sentiment within the various class segments. The evidence, as we shall see, provides some surprises.[4]

It ought to be noted, before examining the data, that the attitudes of the general population do not cluster in the same ways as do those of intellectuals, academics, and those others who are members of ideologically attuned liberal or conservative communities. Within such communities there is a high degree of consistency in outlooks with "liberals," for example, taking "liberal" positions on all issues of concern and, *mutatis mutandis,* a parallel clustering appearing among conservatives. Within the general population, however, there is much less of a tendency for attitudes to cluster in these ways. Rather than there being, for example, tolerance or equalitarianism (or their opposites) in the responses to all questions, one finds, with fair frequency, equalitarian responses in the answers to some questions and the opposite in the responses to others. There is, moreover, some evidence of shifts occurring over time in *opposite* directions, greater tolerance being found in one area of concern and less in another. Rather than viewing these attitude changes as "irrational" or "confused" or "uncrystallized," it makes some sense to view them as responses of the general population to their existential conditions, to their formal and informal educational experiences. That is to say that these attitude "clusters" make some sense relative to that experience and training; these clusters are only "irrational" or "confused" relative to the rather restricted experiences of the intellectual communities. This is not to say that certain clusterings of attitudes are good or bad; it is merely to suggest something about

their sources and to indicate the error one might make by interpreting the attitudes of the general public from the conventional
perspectives of upper middle class intelligentsia.

CLASS AND CIVIL RIGHTS

Two previous reviews of national evidence in this area showed
only fragmentary support for the standard claims. Most of the
evidence in fact showed no difference in the distribution of
attitudes of white manuals and nonmanuals toward the rights of
blacks. This was true in a review of Survey Research Center
questions up to and including the 1964 election study and in a
series of Gallup questions posed in 1965.[5] The second review
covered the same subject matter using the Survey Research Center's 1968 election study.[6] Among the non-South whites there was
again no difference in the attitudes by class level. The attitudes of
the less skilled manual workers (operatives, laborers, and service
workers) were very similar to those of the upper middle class. The
pattern was more complicated in the South, but even there little
support was to be found for the conventional lines of analysis.

A second lesson of some importance is that the 1964-1968
comparison did not indicate the occurrence of any massive or
across-the-board backlash. In most instances the trend was positive, that is, in the direction of greater tolerance. Only in respect
to a government role in school integration was there a reverse
tendency: skilled workers reacted, but so did the lower and upper
middle classes. On the other hand, the less skilled blue-collar
workers shifted in a positive direction. The trend in the South was
also very irregular. One thing was clear, however: no support was
found for the belief that a massive backlash was occurring.

Before proceeding further with the Survey Research Center
studies, some additional evidence and insight may be gained from
consideration of some studies done by the National Opinion
Research Center. A study from December 1963 probed into a
number of areas not covered in previous surveys. Another study
done by the same organization in April 1968 and using many of
the same questions provides additional evidence and again allows

an assessment of the trends.[7] The comparison has been restricted to manuals and nonmanuals.

There are essentially no class differences in the responses of non-South whites to seven of the eleven questions. These asked about schools, public transport, neighborhoods, Negro intelligence, jobs, parks and restaurants, and voting. In the responses to six of these questions, the level of pro-integration or "liberal" sentiment runs between 80 and 90 percent. The level is somewhat lower for neighborhood integration, running to only 70 percent (Table 4.1).

The questions discussed up to this point (both here and in the previous reviews) have involved events or facilities which, in a sense, are open or public. In general, the closer or the more intimate the degree of contact involved, the greater the opposition to integration. The Survey Research Center evidence, for example, showed less support for neighborhood integration than for integration of schools, parks, or public transport. When it was a question of bringing a Negro home to dinner, as shown in this NORC study, the level of approval declined still further. When it was a question of intermarriage laws, the "liberal" sentiment was still lower. In these latter instances, moreover, some class differences did appear. Only 40 percent of the blue-collar workers were opposed to laws against intermarriage in contrast to 58 percent of the white-collar group.

Some of the responses appear to be contradictory. Some 70 or so percent said it would not make any difference were a Negro with the same income and education to move into the neighborhood. And yet only about 50 percent *dis*agreed with the notion that whites have a right to keep Negroes out of their neighborhoods. Some 20 percent of the non-South whites apparently were liberal in the one response and illiberal in the other. The positions, strictly speaking, are not contradictory. It would not make any difference to those respondents personally but, at the same time,

TABLE 4.1

CLASS, REGION, AND ATTITUDES TOWARD BLACKS;
Married, Economically Active Whites (NORC Study No. 330, 1963)

	Non-South		South	
	Manuals	Nonmanuals	Manuals	Nonmanuals

Percent "liberal" (of those with opinions)

A. "Do you think white students and Negro students should go to the same schools, or to separate schools?"

	Manuals	Nonmanuals	Manuals	Nonmanuals
% same	79	81	21	49
N=	(358)	(275)	(141)	(86)

B. "Generally speaking, do you think there should be separate sections for Negroes in street cars and buses?"

	Manuals	Nonmanuals	Manuals	Nonmanuals
% no	87	93	41	67
N=	(367)	(278)	(140)	(92)

C. "If a Negro with the same income and education as you moved into your block, would it make any difference to you?"

	Manuals	Nonmanuals	Manuals	Nonmanuals
% no	72	71	40	66
N=	(362)	(272)	(141)	(90)

D. "In general, do you think Negroes are as intelligent as white people, that is, can they learn things just as well if they are given the same education and training?"

	Manuals	Nonmanuals	Manuals	Nonmanuals
% yes	86	77	60	62
N=	(359)	(273)	(139)	(89)

E. "Do you think Negroes should have as good a chance as white people to get any kind of job, or do you think white people should have the first chance at any kind of job?"

	Manuals	Nonmanuals	Manuals	Nonmanuals
% same	87	91	72	87
N=	(359)	(277)	(139)	(90)

F. "Do you think Negroes should have the right to use the same parks, restaurants and hotels as white people?"

	Manuals	Nonmanuals	Manuals	Nonmanuals
% same	85	89	31	62
N=	(359)	(273)	(140)	(90)

G. "Do you think it should be made easier than it is now for Negroes to vote in the South?"

	Manuals	Nonmanuals	Manuals	Nonmanuals
% yes	93	92	61	80
N=	(335)	(247)	(127)	(90)

H. "How strongly would you object if a member of your family wanted to bring a Negro friend home to dinner?"

	Manuals	Nonmanuals	Manuals	Nonmanuals
% not at all	57	66	20	32
N=	(354)	(278)	(140)	(91)

I. "White people have a right to keep Negroes out of their neighborhoods if they want to, and Negroes should respect that right."

	Manuals	Nonmanuals	Manuals	Nonmanuals
% disagreeing	45	52	13	37
N=	(364)	(294)	(140)	(96)

J. "Do you think there should be laws against marriages between Negroes and whites?"

	Manuals	Nonmanuals	Manuals	Nonmanuals
% no	40	58	12	38
N=	(355)	(286)	(141)	(93)

K. "Negroes shouldn't push themselves where they're not wanted."

	Manuals	Nonmanuals	Manuals	Nonmanuals
% disagreeing	23	30	6	23
N=	(365)	(292)	(142)	(96)

they would approve a "right" of other whites to keep out blacks. It would be a mistake to label this kind of position "racist" because it is quite different from committed opposition to equality. At best, one could fault it as a kind of blind laissez-faire position, one that is indifferent to the human lives and feelings involved.[8]

The final question in this 1963 series, the one about Negroes not pushing themselves where they are not wanted, may also involve this same kind of laissez-faire orientation. It is clear that much of the approval for this statement must come from the same majority of respondents who approved of equal rights for blacks in a wide range of "public" areas. It seems likely that behind these alternative orientations is an all-too-familiar attitude of "why make trouble." It is important to note that the wish to "avoid trouble" has rather conservative implications. Had blacks and whites in the late fifties and early sixties followed that advice, there would have been no sit-ins, no bus boycott, no school integration struggle, and also, there would have been no change.

A second National Opinion Research Center study, this one from April 1968, provides additional evidence on the subject. It shows, once again, a high level of tolerance with respect to schools and jobs (Table 4.2). More than four-fifths of the non-South respondents say that the native intelligence of Negroes and whites is the same. More than four-fifths say that a Negro of the same income and education in the block would make no difference. With respect to these questions, the maximum manual-nonmanual difference was 9 percentage points, and in the responses to the job question (where approval was highest), there was even a slight reversal.

Once again, a different pattern appears when one considers closer social relations. The right-to-keep-Negroes-out question again shows a lower level of approval and also shows a larger class difference, one of 18 percentage points. A similar class difference appears with respect to the question about pushing-where-not-wanted. Here again, the responses to these questions stand in sharp contrast to the high level of tolerance indicated with respect to the question about the Negro of the same income and education moving in. The same explanation seems likely, namely, that the

TABLE 4.2

CLASS, REGION, AND ATTITUDES TOWARD BLACKS;
Married, Economically Active Whites (NORC Study No. 4050, April 1968)

	Non-South		South	
	Manuals	Nonmanuals	Manuals	Nonmanuals

Percent "liberal" (of those with opinions)

A. "Do you think white students and Negro students should go to the same schools, or to separate schools?"

	Manuals	Nonmanuals	Manuals	Nonmanuals
% same	80	89	35	64
N=	(285)	(226)	(96)	(80)

C. "If a Negro with the same income and education as you have moved into your block, would it make any difference to you?"

% no	83	88	55	63
N=	(288)	(227)	(100)	(84)

D. "In general, do you think Negroes are as intelligent as white people, that is, can they learn things just as well if they are given the same education and training?"

% yes	81	89	64	54
N=	(277)	(225)	(91)	(80)

I. "White people have a right to keep Negroes out of their neighborhoods if they want to, and Negroes should respect that right."

% disagreeing	45	63	20	34
N=	(289)	(230)	(96)	(83)

J. "Do you think there should be laws against marriages between Negroes and Whites?"

% no	42	71	8	36
N=	(286)	(224)	(98)	(83)

K. "Here are some opinions other people have expressed in connection with Negro-White relations. Which statement on the card comes closest to how you yourself feel?" "Negroes shouldn't push themselves where they're not wanted."

% disagreeing	16	35	6	20
N=	(290)	(228)	(100)	(84)

L. "How do you feel about fair employment laws, that is, laws that make white people hire qualified Negroes, so that Negroes can get any job they are qualified for? Do you favor or oppose such laws?"

% favoring	89	88	79	77
N=	(292)	(231)	(99)	(85)

M. "How do you feel about open occupancy laws, that is, laws that make white people sell or rent to qualified Negroes, so that Negroes can move into any homes or apartments they can afford? Do you favor or oppose such open occupancy laws?"

% favoring	49	60	22	31
N=	(286)	(225)	(97)	(81)

N. "Which factor do you believe accounts most for the failure of the Negro to achieve equality, a lack of initiative and drive or the restrictions imposed by a white society?"

% restrictions	36	56	25	29
N=	(249)	(214)	(88)	(75)

O. "All in all, do you think Negro groups are asking for too much, too little or just about what they should be asking for?"

% "too little" or "what they should"	36	56	25	29
N=	(249)	(214)	(88)	(75)

TABLE 4.2 (Continued)

	Manuals	Nonmanuals	Manuals	Nonmanuals
P. "If you were referred to a Negro doctor, would you go to him?"				
% yes	76	81	43	61
N=	(282)	(224)	(97)	(81)
Q. "What would your reaction be if a teenager of yours wanted to date a Negro boy or girl? Would you object strongly, mildly, or not at all?"				
% not at all	6	13	0	5
N=	(295)	(225)	(101)	(86)
R. "How do you yourself feel about the actions Negroes have taken to get things they want? Do you generally approve of them or generally disapprove of them?"				
% approve	9	25	5	12
N=	(292)	(222)	(96)	(77)

one response represents a personal position and the other a laissez-faire attitude with respect to what others do or have in mind.

There is a still larger class difference in this study in the responses to the laws-against-intermarriage question, this being the largest difference for the non-South to be found in any of the studies reviewed thus far (29 percentage points).

Six of the seven NORC questions reported on thus far are exact repeats of those used in the 1963 study. In the nonmanual ranks the shift in responses to all six questions was toward increased tolerance. In the manual rank the pattern was not as clear. There were some increases in tolerance, most notably in the response to the question about the Negro moving into the neighborhood, but in other cases there is either little change, or in two instances, slight declines, the latter with respect to Negro intelligence and the pushing-where-not-wanted question.

One point is unambiguous about these NORC results; there is no evidence in these studies showing a *massive* reaction. In response to only two of the questions is there any suggestion of a "reaction." Both of these occur in the manual ranks, one change amounting to 5 percentage points and the other to 7. Otherwise the pattern is one of either immobility or improvement in outlook. Both manuals and nonmanuals in these studies showed increases in the percentages agreeing that whites and Negro students should go to the same schools. If there were a "reaction" of the size and the importance discussed in the alarmist literature, it certainly ought to be indicated in surveys such as these. There should be large and consistent changes in attitudes indicated in all, or at least many, of the areas touched on by these questions. It is possible, to be sure, that *the* reaction had not yet developed at that point.[9]

The 1968 study contained a range of additional questions which are also of some interest. The reduced tolerance in close or intimate relations is very strikingly indicated by the responses to a question about a teenaged son or daughter dating a Negro. Only 6 percent of the blue-collar respondents said they would *not* object. The level of equalitarian sentiment is not much different in the middle class ranks: there, only 13 percent would *not* object.

THE SOUTHERN EXPERIENCE

The evidence of the NORC 1963 study shows clear and, with a single exception, consistent support for the working-class authoritarianism hypothesis. The same tendency was evidenced in the NORC 1968 study, although in this case there were more instances of "no difference" than in 1963. The evidence for the southern states presented here does tend to support the received hypothesis about blue-collar intolerance. As for the 1963-1968 trends, the responses to the six questions contained in both NORC studies indicate only feeble support for the backlash hypothesis and a fair amount of evidence of increased tolerance.

CLASS AND CIVIL RIGHTS: A SUMMARY

The following conclusions appear to be in order:
Outside the South there is
1) No clear evidence of class differences in the areas of public concern and controversy, that is, on questions about jobs and public facilities.

2) Some·tendency for class differences to appear in response to questions involving closer contacts and private social life.

3) No clear and consistent evidence in suport of the backlash thesis. Most of the evidence points rather in the opposite direction, toward increased tolerance.[10]

Without going into the details, among Southern whites there is

4) Some evidence of class differences in the areas of public concern and controversy. A few comparisons show no class differences and two even show greater tolerance among blue-collar workers. The evidence here, in short, is not entirely consistent. There is, however, unlike in non-South regions, some support for the received hypothesis.

5) Evidence of class differences of great consistency in response to those questions about closer social contacts. The largest and most consistent class differences appear in the responses to questions in this area.

6) No clear and consistent evidence in support of the backlash thesis. There is, once again, more evidence pointing in the opposite direction.

CLASS AND THE VOTE: THE 1964 AND 1968 ELECTIONS

Attitudes are one thing, so it is said, and behavior another. In this connection the aphorism means that when "the chips are down," the "real" or "underlying" predispositions of the blue-collar workers will come through. As will be remembered, the catering to "subterranean impulses" with "code words" which was characteristic of the 1964 election was supposed to generate the backlash. Even though none of the polls indicated its coming, it was a season of disbelief. And even at a very late date, after much evidence had been published and made available, a prominent commentator claimed that the "disturbance of spirit" felt by white working men "had been absorbed in the Goldwater vote."[11]

The evidence is sharply opposed to that claim (Table 4.3). The Goldwater sentiment increased with class level in both the South and the non-South regions. Outside the South all four groups showed significant defections from the "normal" level of Republicanism as indicated by the party identifications. It cannot be stressed too much, especially given the propensity to assume the opposite, that the highest level of Goldwater support was to be

TABLE 4.3

CLASS AND SUPPORT FOR GOLDWATER: BY REGION;
Married, White Respondents, Head Economically Active
(Survey Research Center, 1964)

	Class			
	Operatives Laborer, Service	Skilled	Lower Middles	Upper Middles
	Percent for Goldwater*			
Non-South	23%	16%	35%	51%
N=	(150)	(98)	(160)	(114)
South	21	33	45	44
N=	(38)	(21)	(44)	(50)

* Figure includes both those who voted for Goldwater and those who were nonvoters but preferred Goldwater.

found in the upper middle class. Among the blue-collar workers there was a decided reaction against the Goldwater candidacy. Given the "choice," they preferred the "echo."[12]

The 51 percent for Goldwater in the non-South upper middle class hides an important source of differentiation. Catholics and Jews tend to identify with and vote for the Democrats; white Protestants identify with and vote for the Republicans. In this case 70 percent (N=64) of the non-South, upper middle class, white Protestant voters chose Goldwater. It would be a mistake to write these voters off as untutored *arrivistes.* Twenty-two percent of these Goldwater voters had had at least some college and another 42 percent had finished college or gone on for a higher degree. This finding of a sharp division along religious lines again makes clear that it is unrealistic to talk about *the* upper middle class.[13]

There is a question as to whether or not this is "racism" in the upper middle class. Some of that response was undoubtedly a genuine, real choice. Economic conservatives are concentrated in the upper middle class; and they did, for the first time in years, have a candidate who, ideologically at least, was to their liking. Some of that vote was probably tactical, that is, some Republican identifiers did not want to see their party wiped out because of a poor choice of candidate. The other side of the coin is that the demagogic appeals which "should have" picked up massive working-class support did not do so, either in the North or in the South.

But that was 1964. The backlash had not developed as it presumably did in the next four year period. Goldwater was a conservative and, of course, so one says in retrospect, could not be expected to generate working-class votes. In 1968, however, there was the Wallace candidacy. And Wallace spoke clearly and directly in a language that would be readily understood and appreciated by the increasingly uneasy blue-collar workers. And, so one is told, they voted for the racist demagogue, George Wallace. The point has been made by the eminent commentator quoted earlier who has summarized the matter as follows:

> ... George Wallace in 1968 was different. His vote [unlike that for Dixiecrat Strom Thurmond in 1948] was *not* a sectional vote. . . . No less than 4.1 million [of his 9.9 million] votes came from the Northern and Western states: and these were, overwhelmingly, white workingman votes. Despite all the influences of the media, all the pressure of their labor leaders, all the blunders and incompetence of the Wallace campaign, they had voted racist.[14]

Once again, it is useful to raise a simple question: Is it true? And once again it is useful to turn to the available evidence. While the Wallace vote did have greater territorial spread than Strom Thurmond's, it was still very much a sectional accomplishment. Over half of his vote came from the eleven states of the Confederacy, states that provided only a quarter of the 1968 votes. Another 9 percent of his vote came from border states where historically there has been considerable Southern influence. For this reason, we have once again examined the results separately by region.

Was it the white workingman who voted for Wallace? Outside the South the basic result, as indicated by the Survey Research Center study, was as follows: the Wallace percentage among the non-South blue-collar workers was 9 percent (N=149); among the white-collar workers, it was 8 percent (N=250). There was, in short, essentially no difference between the two groups.[15]

The study also asked the nonvoters which of the candidates they preferred, that is, who they would have voted for had they chosen to participate. A recalculation so as to include the nonvoter preferences makes little difference in the result. Ten percent of the blue-collar workers favored Wallace as against 9 percent of the white-collar workers. These results, it will be noted, prove to be remarkably consistent with the evidence on attitudes: outside the South there was no clear difference between manuals and nonmanuals either in attitude or in the vote for Wallace.[16]

To maximize the number of cases for analysis, the following discussion includes the responses of the voters and of the non-voters who reported a preference for one of the three presidential candidates. A more detailed look at the result, using the four categories delineated earlier, shows only slight differentiation within the blue-collar rank, the Wallace percentage being some-what greater among the less skilled workers (Table 4.4). One would anticipate differentiation in the white-collar rank: it would seem likely, given the going assumptions, that the white-collar Wallace sentiment "must be" lower middle class. The present evidence, however, indicates that the upper middle class was just as susceptible to the Wallace appeals as the lower middle category.

The pattern in the South is more in keeping with conventional expectations. There Wallace had the support of nearly half of the skilled workers. A third of the less skilled and of the lower middle class supported him. The upper middle class turned out to be very moderate, or at least, so it would appear. Most of the Southern white upper middle class voted for Nixon in 1968. A majority of these Republican voters took intolerant positions with respect to two of the four civil rights questions, that is, with respect to

TABLE 4.4
CLASS AND SUPPORT FOR WALLACE: BY REGION;
Married, White Respondents, Head Economically Active
(Survey Research Center, 1968)

	Class			
	Operation, Laborers, Service	Skilled	Lower Middles	Upper Middles
	Percent for Wallace*			
Non-South	12%	7%	9%	9%
N=	(86)	(94)	(158)	(128)
South	33	48	32	13
N=	(42)	(33)	(44)	(54)

* Figure includes both those who voted for Wallace and those who were nonvoters but preferred Wallace.

government intervention to guarantee job equality and school integration. A majority took a tolerant position with respect to integration of public facilities and with respect to the open housing option.[17]

A partial explanation of the orientations in the South may be offered. Taking only the "indigenous" white population, those reared in the South, one finds that the intolerant attitudes are strongly centered in the small towns and rural areas. The tolerant response to the integrated public facilities question, for example, goes from 24 in the small towns, to 48 in the middle-sized communities, to 60 percent in the large cities. The tolerant responses to the housing question show a similar pattern, the respective percentages here being 38, 56, and 60. The Wallace vote also happens to be centered in the smaller communities, although the pattern is not as clear as it is for attitudes. Wallace was favored by 37 percent of those in the small towns, 40 percent of those in the middle-sized cities, but only 18 percent of those in the large cities.[18]

It is impossible with the materials at hand to say why the Southern small towns have the outlooks they do. It might be the influence of backward fundamentalist sects preaching the inferiority of the sons of Ham. It might be a result of competition and exploitation in that particular context. The standard image has blacks and poor whites competing for jobs. While no doubt true in many instances, it should also be noted that in general the rural blacks were located in different areas from the majority of the rural whites, thus making direct continuous competition difficult. Blacks were located in the lowland plantation areas, Whites in the uplands and the hill country.

Regardless of its sources, the intolerance does appear to originate in small-town and rural locations. The white manual population of the South is very disproportionately found in these areas: over half of those in the 1968 study, for example, were living in communities of less than 2,500 persons. The same is true of the lower middle class, a result which stems in part from the way they have been defined. The upper middle class is disproportionately located in the large and in the middle-sized cities.

The above paragraphs describe the "indigenous" Southern white populations. The migrants to the South, who are considerably more tolerant than the indigenous groups, come to be located, overwhelmingly, in the middle class ranks of the large and of the middle-sized cities. Ten of thirty-three cases fall within the large city upper middle class. Twenty-one of the thirty-three fall within the middle class of the large and the middle-sized cities. It is possible that their influence in those contexts serves to erode some of the original southern hostilities.

An indication of erosion of the indigenous racial hostilities appears in examination of the attitudes of small towners who are now located in larger communities. Taking those who grew up in small towns and separating them into those still located in small towns, those in middle-sized communities, and those in large cities, we find the tolerant percentages with respect to integrated public facilities to be 20 (N=59), 39 (N=33), and 74 (N=19). A similar pattern appears with respect to the housing question, the respective percentages being 38 (N=61), 53 (N=34), and 65 (N=20). There is, to be sure, another possibility, that the tolerant small towners move out and the intolerant ones stay. Although there may be some tendency in this direction, it seems unlikely that such self-selection would entirely explain this result.

If we take the small-town-reared group who are still living in the small towns and divide them into manual and nonmanuals, we find that 41 percent of both categories supported George Wallace in 1968. There was some original class difference in the pattern of Wallace support in the small towns. That difference was due to the limited enthusiasm for Wallace on the part of middle class persons raised in larger communities but who had migrated to the small-town and rural areas.[19]

THE 1968 ELECTION: THE GALLUP POLLS

Because the evidence presented thus far with respect to the Wallace support goes so much against the received claims on the subject, it proves useful to consider some additional evidence. The discussion in the following pages, therefore, is based on Gallup polls, those of September, October, and November 1968. The latter was a postelection study. In addition, the Gallup studies from December 1968 and January 1969 were also reanalyzed.[20] The results, as we shall see, parallel closely the findings of the Survey Research Center's national study that we have just reviewed. The procedure to be followed is the same as that used in the previous discussion. We are considering only the white respondents. They have been classified as manual or nonmanual according to the occupation of the main earner in the family. We are also, once again, considering the patterns in the South and elsewhere separately.

The results for the non-Southern states, as shown in Table 4.5, indicate considerable initial Wallace support in both manual (20 percent) and nonmanual (11 percent) ranks as of September. By November the support in both ranks had fallen off. Most of the shift, it would appear, was to the Democratic candidate, Hubert Humphrey.

The results with respect to the key question being considered

TABLE 4.5
PARTY CHOICES OF WHITE MANUALS AND NONMANUALS
BY REGION (Gallup Studies, 1968)

| | Percent Favoring | | | |
	Humphrey	Nixon	Wallace	N
NON-SOUTH				
Manuals				
September	32	48	20	(330)
October	40	39	22	(351)
November	48	43	9	(304)
Nonmanuals				
September	29	59	11	(322)
October	37	54	9	(393)
November	43	53	5	(317)
SOUTH				
Manuals				
September	10	39	51	(124)
October	17	31	52	(116)
November	14	33	53	(70)
Nonmanuals				
September	12	44	44	(104)
October	18	53	29	(122)
November	20	57	22	(98)

here, that of the class differences, prove to be rather strikingly at variance with the received claim. The difference was 9 percentage points in September and 13 in October. As of the election, the difference was a mere 4 percentage points, a result which is very close to that of the Survey Research Center's 1968 election study which revealed a difference of only a single percentage point. The examination of the Gallup studies from December 1968 and January 1969 showed differences of 4 and 3 percentage points, respectively.

For the non-Southern population, in short, the emphasis on working-class susceptibilities and on a contrasting middle class "responsibility" constitutes a gross distortion of the actual result.

A different pattern appears once again in the South. There was, first of all, no clear trend indicated among the Southern manuals. Just over half of the white workers in this region favored the Wallace candidacy throughout the campaign. Within the Southern nonmanual ranks, however, there was a defection from Wallace. In contrast to the pattern elsewhere, this shifting appears to have gone disproportionately to Nixon.

This difference in the Southern development means that the pattern of the class differences also varies. There was a 7 percentage point disparity in manual and nonmanual Wallace support in the South as of September. This increased to 23 in October and finally to 31 in November. A similar end result appeared in the Survey Research Center study.

The basic findings then may be summarized as follows: Outside the South, there was a small initial class difference in the support for Wallace. In the course of the campaign, this dwindled to a minuscule difference. In the South, by comparison, there was a small initial difference and, in the course of the campaign, there was a considerable increase in the disparity. The result in short, cannot be summarized with a single statement about class-specific propensities. There are two separate and distinct patterns in evidence.

CLASS AND THE VOTE: A SUMMARY

The lessons would appear to be simple: the white working-class population, that part of it which is located outside the South, is not as illiberal as some have portrayed it. They were considerably less responsive to the Goldwater appeals than the presumedly virtuous upper middle class. And they were no more responsive to the Wallace appeal than the middle class populations. In short, this part, the overwhelming majority of the working class, did not fall for the appeals put forth by two rather different kinds of dema-gogic candidates.

In the South the situation is different. The appeals of one of the candidates were decisively rejected; the appeal of the other ac-cepted. Even here, in this one clear instance of support for the received theorizing, the matter proved to be somewhat more complicated. The "reaction" occurs, for the most part, in the small towns and rural areas. The Southern white working class is more likely than other nonfarm categories to be located in or to have issued from those settings. In short the "reaction" appears to have its origins in the special heritage of small towns of the South and not in the contemporary dynamics of black-white relations. The greater tolerance of the small-town workers who have moved to the cities suggests the orientations are not fixed, that they are capable of being reformed.

SOME POSSIBLE EXPLANATIONS

Many commentators take survey results as indicating immovable constellations of attitudes. When a poll indicates, for example, that 70 percent of the population opposes a given policy, it is assumed that nothing more is to be said on the subject: that provides the framework, the limits for policy considerations. Some commentators also operate on the assumption that attitudes are self-generated: they issue out of the general population according to some peculiarly inscrutable principles. Public opinion "sways," going this way and that; the "pendulum" swings, so it is said. No serious attempt is made to discover reasons for the sway or origins of the swing. Public opinion is treated as an "uncaused cause."

Most people are not aware of the historical sources of the intolerance in the American population largely because that his-tory has never been taught. Prior to the Civil War, at a point when less than one percent of the population outside the South was black, the question of black-white relations dominated the political scene. Politicians and political newspapers continuously stressed the threat of free blacks to the jobs and living standards of white workers. Much of the anti-slavery sentiment was not predicated on equalitarian sentiment, but just the opposite. It was assumed, or hoped, by Abraham Lincoln for example, that the black population would be returned to Africa or colonized in Latin America on the occasion of gaining their freedom. Francis Scott Key, author of a famous poem (". . . land of the free . . . home of the brave"), was a member of the most important of the colonization societies.

Much of the discussion before the war focused on the reasons blacks would not care to migrate out of the South, why abolition would not present a "threat" to white working men. During the war, the masses of freedmen posed an immense political problem, the threat being once again that they would "overwhelm" the northern cities, take the jobs of white workers, and undercut the living standards of whites.

From the perspective of public opinion as the uncaused cause, the widespread concern is viewed as the "source" of the politicians' (and the newspapers') behavior. They, honorable men all, were forced to respond to what they discovered to be a mass concern. It is, on the other hand, extremely difficult to find examples of consistent "responsibility" on the part of politicians of the period. This suggests another alternative reading of the events—that the politicians and the party newspapers stimulated the hostile attitudes. They generated the fears as a useful tactic, at least so they thought, for getting votes.[21] Such orientations persisted into the postwar decades.

A little-known feature of the period beginning with the turn of the century is the contribution to attitudinal racism and racial violence made by the Hearst newspapers. The Hearst entry in Atlanta played some role in stimulating a race riot there. It seems likely, following their usual "competitive" tactics, that they forced other newspapers to follow their lead, one theme of which was eminently intolerant portrayals of the black population.

It is easy to overlook the changes that have taken place. Many people who are old enough to remember the special contributions of American newspapers to the heritage of racism have forgotten how it was. Few people read old newspapers and few have retained the details from the previous age. It would, for example, be difficult to find a contemporary equivalent to the following description of a murder suspect, a description that appeared in the "world's greatest newspaper" in June of 1938:

> He has none of the charm of speech or manner that is characteristic of so many southern darkies. That charm is a mark of civilization and so far as manner and appearance go, civilization has left [the suspect] practically untouched. His hunched shoulders and long, sinewy arms that dangle almost to his knees; and his outthrust head and catlike tread all suggest the animal. He is very black—almost pure Negro. His physical characteristics suggest an earlier link in the species. Mississippi river steamboat mates . . . would classify [him] as a jungle Negro. They would hire him only if they . . . needed rousters. And they would keep close watch on him. This type is known to be ferocious and relentless in a fight. Though docile enough under ordinary circumstances they are easily aroused. And when this happens the veneer of civilization disappears. [22]

Not only have journals changed the "tone" of their reporting, but other media also, in particular the movies and television, have altered their typical presentations. There has been a shift from the clownish walk-on role to serious adult roles. Not twenty years ago the eyerolling, dialect-talking Negro was still a favorite in Hollywood productions. In place of the comic, the regular television fare now includes Negro secretaries and school teachers, Negro policemen and cowboys, Negro CIA agents and electronic technicians. [23]

An important correlate of the disappearance of the virulent journalism and the ridicule has been a significant change in attitudes in recent decades. This has been shown in an impressive summary of studies which asked identical questions in 1942, 1956, and 1963. As far as that study is concerned, there was, with minuscule and fragmentary exceptions, an immense and continuous shift toward more favorable attitudes. Another study, with evidence through to 1965, found the same trend. The comparison made above of the responses to NORC questions from 1963 and the same questions in 1968 showed the same result. A more recent study with evidence up to 1970 also shows the trend continuing.[24]

Another source of this trend, one that for the moment can only be the subject of speculation, involves the so-called American dilemma, the opposition of two strongly held values, one being individual advancement and the other being the equality value. Most of the theorizing that has been discussed here, it will be noted, is built upon a near-exclusive focus on the former value. That emphasis, which is widespread in the social sciences as well as in the more popular, journalistic contributions of liberal intelligentsia, leads to the portrayal of the working and lower middle classes as fierce strivers, competitive and ruthless, willing to step on anybody to get ahead. The avoidance of the more humane concern with equality makes possible the grim, bleak, Hobbesian view that predominates in their formulations.

But if that were a satisfactory portrayal, it would not be possible to account for the attitudes indicated in the previous review of the evidence. It would not be possible to account for the long-term trend. And it would not be possible to account for the repeated victories of civil rights liberals over racist conservatives. It would, for example, have been impossible for someone like the late Estes Kefauver to survive politically in Tennessee—and yet he managed to beat back all contenders. His support came from blacks and from poor whites with the upper middle classes being very strong in their support for his conservative and racist opponents.

The key to the trend, possibly, lies in facing up to the implications of this "second pole" of the dilemma. That was certainly the key to Kefauver's success, namely his forthright defense of equal rights and his refusal to back away from or hedge on his support for civil rights legislation. When the idea of equality is brought into the public discussion and its relevance to contemporary issues pointed out, the initiative is changed and it is then the racist candidate who finds himself hedging and on the defensive, unable to come out and say directly just what his position is with respect to that value.

It seems likely that the changes in media content have also

played a role in making clear just how the equality value had been sacrificed and for how long. And that too, in a sense, has helped to unmake the dilemma. For poor people and those not too well-off, the equality value is a highly prized possession, one they cannot easily give up. The upper middle class, by comparison, raised on notions of their special talents and of the just and proper rewards for their contributions (in older times, social darwinist notions buttressed these outlooks), are less concerned with equality and do not see its importance for those elsewhere in the society. From their distance (aided by the equally "removed" contributions of various intellectuals), they read in their images of competition and strife and of unrelenting hostility.

THE SOURCES OF THE MISREADING

A question deserving some attention is generated by this discrepancy between the evidence presented here and the productions of liberal intellectuals. One might sum it up with a modification of a recent slogan: they are "telling it like it isn't." And the question is: How does that come about?

The liberal alarmism has a number of sources, the most important of which, possibly, is a rather striking misperception of the frequencies of tolerant and intolerant attitudes. This misperception is shared by the population in general. Respondents were asked whether they favored segregation, integration, or something in between. Outside the South approximately one respondent in ten was in favor of pure segregation, a ratio which was roughly the same in all four class segments (Table 4.6). The respondents were also asked how they thought most people "in this area" felt on the subject.[25] Roughly two-fifths of the respondents thought that most or all of the people in the area favored strict segregation. The responses, for a number of reasons, are not entirely comparable. It is clear, nevertheless, that the amount of segregationist sentiment is wildly exaggerated, not by a matter of a few percentage points, but rather by a few hundred percent. Some exaggeration, not quite so extreme, also exists in the south.

It is likely that these distortions have some rather important

TABLE 4.6

ATTITUDE TOWARD SEGREGATION AND PERCEPTION OF
ATTITUDES BY CLASS AND REGION; Married, White Respondents,
Head Economically Active (Survey Research Center, 1968)

	Class			
	Semiskilled Laborers, Service	Skilled	Lower Middles	Upper Middles
NON-SOUTH				
% personally favoring strict segregation	10	13	10	8
N=	(100)	(100)	(186)	(141)
% thinking most or all people in area favor strict segregation	47	44	42	41
N=	(88)	(93)	(161)	(136)
SOUTH				
% personally favoring strict segregation	35	42	27	7
N=	(45)	(48)	(49)	(59)
% thinking most or all people in area favor strict segregation	66	63	53	50
N=	(47)	(46)	(49)	(64)

consequences. Those who support segregation would be considerably more outspoken and aggressive in the presentation of their claims, feeling that they speak for a large portion of the white population. The opposite would also be true: the opponents of segregation would feel intimidated and hesitant to speak out, being convinced of enormous opposition to their position. As long as political leaders thought there was considerable and possibly growing segregationist sentiment in the population, they would be hesitant to take the lead against those institutions. Also, those leaders who were not averse to the use of such appeals would feel encouraged to continue their play with "code words" and "Southern strategies."[26]

There are a number of processes operating to contribute to this misreading, some of which were touched on above. Most of the Gallup presentations published during the 1968 presidential campaign made no separation by region, thereby averaging two divergent patterns. The Southern pattern would come through in the nationwide figure and thus suggest general, across-the-board confirmation for the "working-class authoritarianism" thesis.

Another tendency involves the magnification of small percentage differences. The Gallup results throughout the campaign showed the manual workers to be only a few percentage points ahead of the nonmanual categories in their level of Wallace support. The relationships indicated in the monthly polls were somewhat erratic, and in some cases the manual percentage even fell below that of some of the nonmanual groups. Despite this, the formulations tended to be categorical: it was the racist workers and the virtuous (or "moderate") middle class.

There was also selectivity involved in the treatment of the evidence said to show the Wallace working-class support. Much was made of the endorsements of Wallace from union locals. That evidence was usually taken at face value and the standard racist lesson was read in. It was a rare commentator who considered any other possibility. Joseph Kraft was one of these, and he pointed out that many workers in Flint, where the Buick local of the United Auto Workers had made a Wallace endorsement, resented the union leadership. As he put it, "the Wallace noises are probably being exaggerated by internal union considerations." "A large number of those now talking Wallace to spit in the eye of the union," he wrote, "will probably not vote for him on Election Day." The selectivity in attention appears in the treatment given a subsequent event, when Local 599 reversed itself and recommended for Hubert Humphrey. One other face that received only rare attention in the alarmist literature was the point that many of these polls of union locals had "been rigged by Wallace supporters."[27]

Some data presentations make use of attitude scales. In such cases, a range of questions would be used, some having high, some middling and some low tolerance response levels. They would then be combined so that the result would, typically, be single scale scores rather than a number of percentages for each of the separate questions. This allows some methodological gains and a considerable degree of economy in the presentation of findings. In the case of the NORC studies reported here, it would mean combining the questions on jobs, housing, and schooling (which showed either small or no class differences) with the questions on more intimate contacts (which did show class differences). The overall result, mixing as it does two diverse orientations, would hide the lack of difference in those areas of greatest public concern. In this case the conventional wisdom would gain some support even if there were a separate presentation by region.

Some presentations have shown tolerance and intolerance by educational level (presumably a surrogate or close equivalent to occupation). These presentations characteristically show a very strong relationship, and one is invited to translate the result back to the "obvious" implications for the poorly educated and the well-educated occupational groups. But it is a poor surrogate for occupation for the simple reason that education is very strongly related to age. And much of what one is showing in the education-tolerance relationship is that older people are less tolerant than younger people. Put somewhat differently, it means that older, small-town or rural (and poorly educated) Southern women are less tolerant than young urban non-Southern (and college edu-cated) men. Put still another way, this means that there are a lot of other factors operating besides education to yield those hand-some distributions.

The evidence presented here is not entirely new. Similar results have appeared from time to time, but, because they did not fit in with the dominant preconceptions, they have generally been ig-nored. More than ten years ago Charles Herbert Stember reviewed a large number of national studies in his book *Education and Attitude Change* and found that many of the conventional judg-ments were unfounded or at least were not as clearly and unambig-uously supported as some have thought. His summary conclusion reads as follows: "Socio-economic status has no uniform effect of its own on attitudes toward the rights of Negroes." Regretably, his work has not gained the attention it deserves. And so, one result is that the conventional wisdom persists. One study that reviewed evidence challenging the conventional wisdom was treated as fol-lows by two sociologists: "There is just too much independent evidence," they say, "that prejudice toward Negroes is inversely associated with current occupational status for us to contemplate seriously the possibility that the zero order associations revealed by this data are substantively correct." The "independent evidence" they then cite consists of three community studies and one very erratic sample of veterans. All of those studies, incidentally involve very small percentage differences.[28]

Some intellectuals, those of more literary persuasions, are compulsively hostile to systematic data presentations, preferring instead their own "free" and uninhibited associations based on or stimulated by the *New York Times* accounts of the day's events. A few thousand construction workers, following a scenario very similar to that of the motion picture *Z*, attack peace demonstrators on Wall Street, and for these intellectuals the few thousand become the "typical" blue-collar workers. The demonstrations against open-housing marchers in working-class districts of Chicago and Milwaukee are presented as further proof of the sentiments of the entire population in that area. As mentioned above, that conclusion loses sight of a small survey of the area's population which showed 70 percent of them in favor of open housing. The literary-political intellectuals, in short, read their own special preconceptions into the day's news. In this respect they exhibit all the perceptual biases and distortions which have been so amply documented in experimental social psychological studies. A review of "the nation's *malaise*" by any of these writers will dwell on an assortment of awesome backlash campaigns. Such an account in 1972 would have Mayors Stenvig and Yorty (of Minneapolis and Los Angeles) figuring very prominently. When one asked about Peter Flaherty and Sam Massell (the mayors of Pittsburg and Atlanta), both of whom beat back the established powers in their respective cities, fighting all the standard weapons in the backlash arsenal, the characteristic response was to ask who they were. In such a case, the literary intellectual has either submerged the evidence or worse, failed to even see it. In the polite and antiseptic language of the social sciences, this would be called "selective perception."

If one compulsively rejects systematic evidence, if one has a trained (as with the Pavlov experiments) aesthetic disgust when faced with "data," with numbers, percentages, or correlation coefficients, then clearly that kind of contact with reality is never going to affect one's understanding of things. In great measure, the understandings that do come to dominate have roughly the same basis as the understandings of neighborhood or backyard gossips. That is, they pass on understandings within their circle; they support and mutually reinforce each other so that, in time, their special understandings appear to be "hard" and inescapable.

The selective perception, the continuous misreading of the evidence gives rise to the alarm felt by liberal policy-makers and that, in turn, provides the basis for "go slow" polices and for "benign neglect." The evidence reviewed here indicates that the policy-maker who is genuinely concerned with equality and human decency has considerably more support for his initiatives than he ever dreamed.

NOTES

1. The point has been made by Professor Zbigniew Brzezinski. As he put it: "A great deal of what we, the liberal establishment, but also the upper middle-class—which we are and which we hate to admit—really advocate, is social revolution at the expense of the lower white middle-class."

"This is not due to the racial prejudice of the lower middle-class alone. If they all had incomes of $25,000 a year they would be as liberal as we are. The fact is they live in marginal environments and the fact is that I—and I'll speak for myself here, feeling strongly about this issue—I do not really have to make many sacrifices on behalf of social revolution." From the New York Times, December 8, 1968, p. 76.

The leading work on the subject, of course, is Seymour Martin Lipset's *Political Man,* (Garden City: Doubleday, 1960), esp. chap. 4.

2. This point was made, just one instance among many, by John W. Gardner. He said: "The collision between dissenters and lower middle class opponents is exceedingly dangerous. As long as the dissenters are confronting the top layers of the power structure, they are dealing with people who are reasonably secure, often willing to compromise, able to yield ground without anxiety. But when the dissenters collide with the lower middle class, they confront an insecure opponent, quick to anger and not prepared to yield an inch." From Science 164: 3878 (25 April 1969) 379.

3. The account of the Milwaukee events is based on the reports of the Milwaukee Journal from 28 August to 21 September 1967. The study mentioned in the text is reported in their issue of 31 August 1967.

The actions of the Hard Hats have been treated as a spontaneous "uprising" on the part of New York City construction workers (for example, by

Victor Riesel, "The . . . confrontations were spontaneous," Madison, Wisconsin State-Journal, 21 May 1970). The original New York Times stories (9 May 1970) indicate much advance planning and advance warning. More important, there is evidence that the event was directed by men who were not wearing hard hats or blue collars. One observer said: "I turned around and [saw] men in business suits with color patches in their lapels—the color was the same on both men, and they were shouting orders to the workers." Similar reports appeared in the Wall Street Journal, 11 May 1970. The most detailed account of this stimulated "reaction" is that of Fred Cook, "Hard-Hats: The Rampaging Patriots," The Nation 15 (June 1970) 712-719. There was no mistaking the zeal of the construction workers involved. The other important lesson, however, is that it took some organizational effort from outside the blue-collar ranks to generate the action.

4. The precedure followed here is the same as that outlined in chapter 2. That is to say, we have taken only married respondents in family units where the head of the household is economically active. Males are classed as manuals or nonmanuals; wives are classified according to the husbands' occupations. See chapter 2 for further discussion.

5. See Richard Hamilton, *Class and Politics in the United States* (New York: John Wiley, 1972), chap. 11. Two comparisons are made in this source, one of manuals and nonmanual whites (in the South and elsewhere) and, with the same regional division, one of lower middle and upper middle nonmanual whites.

6. See my "Black Demands, White Reactions, and Liberal Alarms," pp. 130-153 in Sar Levitan, ed., *Blue-Collar Workers: A Symposium on Middle America* (New York: McGraw-Hill, 1971). Both manuals and nonmanuals were divided into "upper" and "lower" segments in this analysis so as to show the tendency of the "poor whites" and also of the "lower middle class." A similar break was made in the 1964 Survey Research Center study so as to allow a statement about the trends. The same South versus non-South break was maintained in this analysis.

7. The 1963 survey is their study no. 330. Some of the results from this study have been reported in the Hyman-Sheatsley review (see note 24). The study was also used by Donald J. Treiman. See his "Status Discrepancy and Prejudice," American Journal of Sociology 71 (May 1966) 651-664. I wish to express my appreciation to him for making the cards for this study available for my analysis.

8. Some sense of the complexities involved may be gained by consideration of the cross-tabulation of the two questions. The "percent tolerant" in the original table included a small group who were favorably disposed to the idea of a Negro's living in the same block and the much larger group who said it would make no difference. The data:

NORC, DECEMBER 1963
(Married, Economically active non-South Whites)

	Attitude toward Negro Family in Same Block		
	Unfavorable	Favorable	No Difference
Whites have a right to keep Negroes out:			
Agree	83%	63%	37%
Disagree	17	37	63
N =	(186)	(30)	(424)

There are other interpretations, aside from those discussed in the text, which are possible. The first question asks about "a Negro" in the block. Possibly the level of approval would decline if it were a question of "some" or "many" Negroes. There is always the possibility that the tolerant response is not sincere, that those who say that it would make "no difference" and who also say whites have a right to keep Negroes out really stand for the latter.

The table indicates nothing more than the attitudes. It is possible that larger minorities from among intolerant blue-collar workers would be willing to "take to the streets" than from among equivalent white-collar groups. That cannot be assessed with the data at hand. The evidence here indicates that there is considerable unrecognized support for equalitarian proposals, support which conceivably could be mobilized behind reasonable governmental initiatives.

9. But the backlash reaction, one will recollect, was anticipated already in the 1964 election. The reaction should certainly have appeared in the 1968 data. In October of 1968, Adam Walinsky, one-time legislative assistant to Robert F. Kennedy, was telling the organizing convention of the New Democratic Coalition that: "There are now only two identifiable ethnic groups—blacks and those who hate them." The speech appears in the Washington Post, 20 October 1968.

Findings similar to those presented here were reported by Walter De Vries, a consultant for Republican Congressional and Senatorial campaigns. In a 1968 letter to John Mitchell, then Richard Nixon's campaign manager, he wrote: "Parenthetically, the issue structure on racial problems still shows that most Americans still favor socio-economic aid, educational programs, the expansion of rights, and the elimination of discrimination; only a small minority go to the real hard-line approach." Despite the presence of the evidence, the campaign leaders chose to make a somewhat different emphasis in the campaign; and, it will be noted, the Democrats never seriously questioned the backlash assumption, thus allowing it to set the tone for the campaign. For the De Vries quotation, see Lewis Chester, Godfrey Hodgson, and Bruce Page, *An American Melodrama: The Presidential Campaign of 1968* (New York: Viking, 1969) p. 630.

10. The Survey Research Center studies have indicated one area of "backlash," this being with respect to federal government interventions to achieve school integration. The backlash is not within the working class; it is upper middle class and suburban. For a detailed analysis, see Rudy Fenwick, "White America Looks at School Desegregation: 1964-1968" (M.A. thesis, McGill University, 1974).

11. Theodore H. White, *The Making of the President: 1968* (New York: Atheneum, 1969), p. 369.

12. See Hamilton, *Class and Politics . . .* , op. cit., chap. 5. In the South there was some shifting in the opposite direction. This involved approximately 5 percent of the Southern white manual workers and still left the Democratic voting at approximately 80 percent. There is a question as to whether or not this is "backlash"—that is, a *reaction* to recent advances of the blacks—or whether it is continuity with the tradition, bigots at this point merely finding a new political instrument for achieving their aims.

For reasons discussed in chapter 3, the nonmanuals have been divided on the basis of income rather than by census categories. The cutting line is $10,000 (total family income) in 1964 and $12,000 in 1968 (as in Table 4.4).

13. For a more extended discussion, see Hamilton, *Class and Politics . . .* , op. cit., chap. 5.

14. Theodore H. White, *op. cit.*, pp. 368-369.

15. Commenting on the 1964 primary elections, Theodore White, the knight-errant of psephology, wrote: ". . . Wallace astounded political observers not so much by the percentage of votes he could draw for simple bigotry . . . as by the groups from whom he drew his votes. For he demonstrated pragmatically and for the first time the fear that white working-class Americans have of Negroes. In Wisconsin he scored heavily in the predominantly Italian, Polish and Serb working-class neighborhoods of Milwaukee's south side." From White, op. cit., p. 234. In point of fact, the heaviest Wallace support in that primary came from the most affluent of the middle class suburbs, and the level of Wallace voting there was almost twice that which he received on the south side. Crossover voting was allowed in the state. There was no significant contest in the Republican primary. It appears that much of the Wallace vote came from upper middle class Republicans who were out to embarrass the Democratic "favorite son," a governor who

had brought in the sales tax. The best account of the primary election is that of Michael Rogin, "Wallace and the Middle Class: The White Backlash in Wisconsin," Public Opinion Quarterly 30 (Spring 1966) 98-108.

16. The only other national study that has made the same division by class and region came up with a similar result. This study found that 9 percent of the non-South manuals voted for Wallace as opposed to 5 percent of the equivalent nonmanuals. The class difference here was a smallish 4 percentage points as opposed to the 1 percent difference found in the Survey Research Center study. See Seymour Martin Lipset and Earl Raab, "The Wallace White-lash," Trans-Action 7 (December 1969) 23-35. It seems likely that much of this "edge" of working-class voting for Wallace was linked to the southern origins of a large part of the non-South working class. Their report also shows that no Jews supported Wallace. If one controlled for both religion and Southern origins, it seems likely that there would be very little remaining difference. See Hamilton, *Class and Politics . . . ,* op cit., p. 504, for more detailed discussion.

The Gallup Poll results, unfortunately, are not presented separately by occupation and region. The overall presentations by occupation do not justify the extraordinary focus on the manual ranks. The Wallace percentages in April of 1968, for example, ran as follows: business and professional, 6; white collar, 8; and manual, 12. In July the equivalent percentages were 13, 20, and 16. The *Gallup Opinion Index* of December 1968 gives the final figures as 10, 12, and 15.

Theodore White, it will be remembered, said the Wallace votes were "overwhelmingly" those of white workingmen. The Survey Research Center study shows 63 percent of the non-South Wallace vote to have come from the nonmanuals. In the South, exactly half of his vote came from the nonmanuals.

17. There is a possibility that some of this support for Nixon's candidacy was not a principled rejection of the Wallace offering but rather was a *tactical* choice. See Hamilton, *Class and Politics . . . ,* op. cit., p. 505.

18. The small towns are those of fewer than 2,500 inhabitants. The middle-sized communities are those of 2,500 to 49,999 persons. The large cities are those of 50,000 or more. Included in the latter category are suburbs of the largest metropolitan communities. This pattern of the greater intolerance in the smaller communities is found only in the South.

19. It should be noted that we are dealing with a small number of cases. There were 34 "indigenous" small-town manuals and 27 nonmanuals.

20. I wish to express my appreciation for the services of the Roper Public Opinion Research Center of Williamstown, Massachusetts. I would especially

like to thank the Center's director, Professor Philip Hastings, for his assistance. Neither he nor the Center, of course, is in any way responsible for the interpretations given here.

The tables contain only white nonfarm respondents. The manual category contains the following occupational categories: skilled workers, operatives, nonfarm laborers, and service workers. The nonmanual category contains: professionals, business and executive employees, clerical and sales employees.

21. A useful account of Abraham Lincoln's campaign efforts is to be found in Richard Hofstadter, "Abraham Lincoln and the Self-Made Myth," chap. 5 of *The American Political Tradition* (New York: Knopf, 1957). More detail may be found in the following works: Leon F. Litwack, *North of Slavery: The Negro in the Free States; 1790-1860* (Chicago: University of Chicago Press, 1961); Lorman Ratner, *Powder Keg: Northern Opposition to the Antislavery Movement* (New York: Basic Books, 1968); Eugene Berwanger, *The Frontier Against Slavery: Western Anti-Negro Prejudice and the Slavery Extension Controversy* (Urbana: University of Illinois Press, 1969); and V. Jacques Voegeli, *Free But Not Equal: The Midwest and the Negro During the Civil War* (Chicago: University of Chicago Press, 1967); and Eric Foner, *Free Soil, Free Labor, Free Men: The Ideology of the Republican Party Before The Civil War* (New York: Oxford University Press, 1970).

The parties differed in their main tendencies. The Democrats were generally opposed to abolition. The Republicans tended to favor it. Their accompanying line of justification was not, however, an equalitarian or humanitarian appeal. The stress, rather, was that blacks were "unfitted" for anything but southern climes and also that colonization was a strong likelihood.

22. Chicago Tribune, 5 June 1938, p. 5.

23. Of some interest in this connection is an early work, that of Melvin Tumin, "Exposure to Mass Media and Readiness for Desegregation," Public Opinion Quarterly 21 (Summer 1957) 237-251.

24. The first of these studies is the work of Herbert Hyman and Paul B. Sheatsley, "Attitudes Toward Desegregation," Scientific American, 211 (July 1964) 16-23. The second work is that of Mildred A. Schwartz, *Trends in White Attitudes Toward Negroes* (Chicago: National Opinion Research Center, Report No. 119, 1967). The recent study, a continuation of the Hyman-Sheatsley work, is by Andrew Greeley and Paul B. Sheatsley, "Attitudes Toward Racial Integration," Scientific American 225 (December 1971) 13-19.

Another development which contributes to this trend is the increase in black-white contacts, especially of contacts which are relatively equalitarian in character, in neighborhoods, in schools, in workplaces. In general, the greater the percentage of blacks in such settings, the more favorable the attitude. See Hamilton, *Class and Politics . . . ,* op. cit., chap. 11.

25. The two questions read as follows (SRC 1968):

Q. 32. "How about white people in this area? How many would you say are in favor of strict segregation of the races—all of them, most of them, about half, less than half of them, or more of them?"

Q. 33. "What about you? Are you in favor of desegregation, strict segregation, or something in between?"

26. It seems likely that these exaggerated perceptions would also have some effect on the responses to survey questions. Conformists, those who give "conventional" answers, would be led, by virtue of the misperception, to give intolerant responses.

27. The Joseph Kraft quotations and the point about the rigged polls appears in Lewis Chester et al., op. cit., pp. 706-707. The reversal of the Flint Local's recommendation is mentioned in White, op. cit., p. 366.

28. The previous evidence is reviewed in Hamilton, *Class and Politics . . . ,* op. cit., chap. 11, pp. 454-460. Stember's work was published by the Institute of Human Relations Press, 1961.

CHAPTER 5

THE SUPPORT FOR "HARD LINE" FOREIGN POLICY

(with James Wright)

Some of the themes considered in the preceding chapter reappear in a transmogrified form in discussions of foreign policy preferences. The image of working-class life as a "state of war," as one of hostility and pugnacity toward "outsiders," reappears as a composite of jingoistic sentiment, chauvinistic attitudes, unreflective patriotism, and, most important, support for the toughest, the most bellicose of initiatives in foreign affairs.

Here too one finds the parallel lesson, the lesson of the reasonable and responsible elites, those who are conciliatory in their outlooks and who are willing to make the compromises necessary to avoid conflict. Once again, paralleling the lessons of the presumed working-class racism, is a lesson in the need for containment. It is necessary to support the responsible elites and upper middle classes in their efforts because otherwise the "thrust from below" would be irresistible.

These formulations invert the expectations which dominated in most circles prior to the 1950s. At least until 1914 the general expectation, shared by intellectuals and the population at large, was that tough and aggressive orientations in foreign affairs were most characteristic of elites, of the upper and the upper middle classes (the staunch Edwardians, the Kipling readers). These orientations were also shared, to a lesser extent presumably, by some elements of the lower middle class who identified with their own powerful nation and/or saw some profit to be gained through imperialism. For the most part, the manual workers were seen as pacifist, largely because the Socialist parties of Europe, the United States, and elsewhere were officially committed to that position. In later times this view still gained support as for example in France during the Algerian War where the middle and upper classes were more strongly in favor of hardheaded conduct of the campaign.

A diametrically opposed expectation is widely disseminated in the United States. Here, largely under the influence of a famous article by Seymour Martin Lipset, the expectation is that the "tough" position is indicative of "authoritarianism." It is the orientation of the anti-intellectual, vigilante mentality, of those who are tired of, or suspicious of, "talk." Presumably, the wish to "bomb an enemy back to the Stone Age" is one that would gain support from manual workers, from those with little education, from those with low status, and from the dispossessed and the alienated.[1]

The Survey Research Center election studies contain questions that allow some exploration of this matter. In 1952 a question was asked about the preferred policy in the Korean War, and in 1964 and 1968 similar questions were asked about the preferences with respect to the Viet Nam War. It is useful to consider these questions in serial order.

The 1952 question reads as follows: (Q. 27) "Which of the following things do you think it would be best for us to do *now* in Korea?" The responses were "pull out of Korea entirely" (a position chosen by only 9 percent of the respondents); "keep on trying to get a peaceful settlement" (that is, negotiate, chosen by 45 percent); and "take a stronger stand and bomb Manchuria and China" (38 percent). The remaining 8 percent were mostly "don't knows" and "no answers," together with a very small group wanting either a pullout *or* a bombing of China. The concern here will be with the 38 percent who favored more aggressive conduct of the war.

A summary examination of the basic cross-tabulations shows the exact opposite of the "working-class authoritarianism" assumption to be true. The "pro-bombing" sentiment is present to a greater than average degree among the following groups: males, whites, those in high status occupations, those with higher education, high income groups, Protestants, those outside the South, younger people, Republicans, the politically concerned, and those with high media attention, in particular those who followed the election in magazines or newspapers (Table 5.1). The only instance of what might be an authoritarian-vigilante mentality is in the case of the small number of "protective service" workers (police) where the pro-bombing percentage is well above that of all other occupations. A group that, in view of the received theoretical assumptions, might be expected to show the syndrome, the unemployed, have a pro-bombing level which is only half the sample average.

In this first view of the subject, the highest "bombing preference" appears among those who either obtain a "lot" of political information from magazines or who find magazines their most important source of news. Another important pro-bombing context is among the white Protestants, especially among those with middling or higher incomes (above $3,000 yearly) where the level reaches 49 percent. Because the conjunction of these two factors, better-off white Protestantism and media attention, are so peculiarly connected with the "bombing preference," it is useful to make a more detailed investigation here.[2]

The distinctiveness of this portion of the white Protestant population is not the product of a different income level, of different occupations or educational level. Their distinctiveness remained even when detailed controls were made for all of those factors. The basic lines of explanation to be suggested follow along two lines: that they are subject to some special mass media impacts, and that they have somewhat different initial predispositions with respect to national involvements.

The evidence shows quite clearly that, among both poor and better-off white Protestants, increased attention paid to magazines and newspapers is correlated with increased support for the policy of bombing (Table 5.2). The evidence also shows that the media attention is not sufficient to account for the attitude because, even where the reported levels of attention were the same, the

TABLE 5.1
ATTITUDE TOWARD KOREAN WAR POLICY BY BACKGROUND CHARACTERISTICS (Survey Research Center, 1952)

Background Characteristics		Percent Preferring			
	Pull-out	Negotia-tion	Bombing China	Other, Don't Know, No Answer	N
Total	9	45	38	7	(1613)
Race					
White	9	44	40	7	(1452)
Negro	15	55	20	11	(157)
Sex					
Male	7	43	44	6	(737)
Female	11	47	33	9	(876)
Occupation of Head					
Professional	9	47	37	7	(107)
Self-employed, managers	3	40	50	7	(224)
Clerical, sales	8	45	39	7	(154)
Skilled, semi-skilled	6	46	40	6	(459)
Unskilled, service	11	50	29	9	(174)
Protective service	4	27	65	4	(26)
Unemployed	4	56	16	24	(25)
Farmers	13	46	33	8	(178)
Education					
None	—	60	28	12	(25)
Some grade school	11	48	28	13	(335)
Completed grade school	13	51	29	7	(300)
Some high school	7	46	40	6	(248)
Completed high school	8	41	45	6	(245)
Some high school plus noncollege	9	40	47	4	(77)
High school plus non-college	4	51	40	4	(142)
Some college	7	32	57	4	(133)
Completed college	12	40	39	9	(105)
Income					
Under $1,000	10	53	22	15	(135)
$1,000-1,999	12	48	26	14	(177)
$2,000-2,999	11	49	30	9	(255)
$3,000-3,999	10	45	40	5	(364)
$4,000-4,999	6	49	42	3	(233)
$5,000-7,499	6	40	47	6	(273)
$7,500-9,999	9	42	46	4	(81)
$10,000 and over	11	26	52	10	(61)
Religion					
Protestants					
White	9	41	42	8	(1013)
Negro	15	54	19	12	(142)
Catholics	8	50	38	4	(335)
Jews	2	64	28	6	(50)
Other	7	50	21	21	(14)
None	18	61	15	6	(34)

TABLE 5.1 (Continued)

Background Characteristics	Pull-out	Negotia-tion	Bombing China	Other, Don't Know, No Answer	N
Region					
Northeast	8	49	36	7	(389)
Midwest	9	45	41	5	(580)
South	8	48	32	11	(440)
Far West	14	35	43	8	(204)
Age					
18-24	8	47	41	4	(101)
25-29	9	45	41	4	(182)
30-34	5	50	38	6	(202)
35-39	5	44	43	8	(189)
40-44	9	48	36	6	(191)
45-49	11	44	36	8	(148)
50-54	12	43	36	9	(136)
55-59	9	44	36	10	(128)
60-64	12	39	41	8	(105)
65 and over	11	47	31	11	(209)
Political Concern					
Care very much	8	44	43	5	(451)
Care pretty much	7	46	40	6	(616)
Don't care very much	13	47	32	8	(333)
Don't care at all	13	47	27	13	(159)
Party Identification					
Democrat	7	52	36	6	(751)
Independent	10	41	41	8	(356)
Republican	12	38	42	7	(439)
Media Attention					
Read about campaign in magazines					
Quite a lot	8	34	52	6	(227)
Not very much	8	45	39	8	(421)
No	10	48	34	8	(954)
Read about campaign in newspapers					
Quite a lot	7	39	47	6	(630)
Not very much	9	49	36	6	(644)
No	13	52	23	11	(332)
Most Important Soucrc					
Magazines	5	35	56	4	(80)
Newspapers	10	42	41	7	(353)
Television	7	49	38	6	(504)
Radio	12	44	36	8	(445)
None	13	54	15	18	(101)

TABLE 5.2
PERCENT FAVORING BOMBING BY MEDIA ATTENTION AND
INCOME: WHITE PROTESTANTS AND CATHOLICS
(Survey Research Center, 1952)

| | Percent Pro-Bombing | | | |
| | White Protestants | | White Catholics | |
Income:	Under $3,000	$3,000 and Over	Under $3,000	$3,000 and Over
Attention to Magazines				
Quite a lot	38	63	*	47
N=	(37)	(125)	(6)	(34)
Not very much	31	45	*	42
N=	(77)	(218)	(13)	(66)
None	28	45	30	37
N=	(239)	(287)	(56)	(155)
Attention to Newspapers				
Quite a lot	39	54	37	47
N=	(101)	(328)	(19)	(101)
Not very much	29	45	32	37
N=	(150)	(242)	(40)	(110)
None	22	34	25	30
N=	(103)	(61)	(16)	(46)

* Number of cases too small.

better-off Protestants were still more favorably disposed to the bombing.

The other explanation, at this point, can be only a suggestion since there is no evidence in the study allowing an assessment of the depth of national identification, of chauvinism, or what we might call the Stephen Decatur sentiments (". . . my country, right or wrong . . ."). It does seem likely, however, that the better-off white Protestants would be those who would have such attitudes and identifications. They would be the American equivalents of the Edwardians and the Kipling enthusiasts mentioned earlier. Some support for this view appears in the analysis of the minority groups in the society to be considered below.

The initial presentation also shows pro-bombing sentiments to be more frequent among younger people. Most of this variation by age is contributed by the better-off white Protestants. In part that appears once again to be a function of media influence, particularly newspapers and magazines. Even here, however, the better-off white Protestants with high school or college education who use magazines as sources of political information prove to be more favorably disposed toward bombing than the equivalent groups among the other religious bodies. Pro-bombing sentiment is not to be explained away, in other words, as merely an "intelligent person's reaction" to the then current state of affairs.

The best guesses are that the younger, better-off and educated white Protestants read different magazines and/or that they have different predispositions. Unfortunately, as already noted, the 1952 study does not allow us to test these guesses. The different predispositions, if they exist, might be the result of different training and experience in white Protestant circles. The older generation, moreover, may have experienced more pacifist, anti-war content in their education; the younger ones, by comparison, would have received a sustained lesson on the "need for war" (in the face of Nazism or Communism, the common thesis being that pacifism would "not work").[3]

Many people in the younger cohorts had direct experience with World War II, and that too may have affected their outlooks. The possibility that those experiences had some impact gains support since, in the detailed age breakdowns, males in the age groups most likely to have been in the war were most strongly pro-bombing. Among the women, the age group most likely to contain wives of World War II veterans was the most pro-bombing.[4] Once again, even this special impact among the veterans appears only among the better-off white Protestants. It does not appear among the Catholics. It does not appear, moreover, among the poor white Protestants. This again suggests a special predisposition among these better-off Protestants.

The second largest group in the society is the Catholic minority. In this group too one finds the pattern we have taken to be indicative of a media effect. The level of support for bombing, however, is somewhat lower, even at the same level of media attention. This would suggest either that they follow different media (with different political content) or that they have different orientations toward the same events (or possibly that both factors are operating).

The predisposition possibility is indicated by an important cleavage within the Catholic population. There is a decisive break along ethnic lines with those of three generations ancestry in the country and those of more recent English and Irish ancestry being above average in "pro-bombing" sentiment. All others are markedly below the Catholic average.[5] This suggests that it is the assimilated Catholics who hold the "white Protestant" position; the newer immigrants among them reject that position. The older Catholic groups, in other words, seem to have assimilated the dispositions of the better-off white Protestants and accepted their sense of the rightness or legitimacy of any such military initiatives.

The major point to be noted about the other groups in the society, the Negroes, Jews, and the small group of "others," is that they provide only very limited support for the bombing of China as an instrument of policy in the Korean War (Table 5.3). Moreover, among these groups, magazine reading had either no impact or, in two instances, was negatively related to pro-bombing sentiment. The best explanation that can be suggested is that they read different journals. Jews perhaps were reading the *Nation* and *New*

TABLE 5.3
PERCENT FAVORING BOMBING BY MEDIA ATTENTION: MINORITIES

	Percent Pro-Bombing		
	Negroes	Jews	All Others*
Attention to Magazines			
A lot or some	17	30	—
N=	(23)	(20)	(13)
None	21	27	23
N=	(131)	(30)	(34)
Attention to Newspapers			
A lot	27	33	21
N=	(30)	(21)	(14)
Some	27	30	12
N=	(55)	(20)	(16)
None	11	—	18
N=	(69)	(9)	(17)

* Number of cases too small.

Republic instead of *Time* and *Life.* Among Negroes this result may stem from a sweeping general alienation from the polity and a distrust of such massive uses of power.

In answer to the basic question, who supports the "hard line," the answer from the 1952 evidence is as follows: The strongest support is found among the better-off white Protestants and among assimilated Catholics. It is stronger in both groups among those who make use of magazines and newspapers as their sources of political information. In general, the support for that position, then, appears among the more dominant or "established" group in the society. And, by contrast, that position is avoided by all the other groups. The latter, the poorer white Protestants, the Negroes, Jews, the new ethnic Catholics, all tended to favor either the pullout or the other temperate option, to try for a peaceful settlement.

It is clear from this account that support for the tough option does not come from the dispossessed or the alienated. The location of the hard line sentiment does not accord with the expectations of standard, mass society imagery. A more direct investigation, using the 1952 study's political efficacy questions showed the same pattern indicated above. Those who felt able to influence politics were most strongly pro-bombing. Those who felt least able to influence events were most favorable to negotiation or pulling out. Of possible relevance to some conventional pluralist notions is the finding that pro-bombing sentiment also increased with the number of formal organizational memberships. It was the members of business, professional, civic, Parent-Teachers, and veterans' organizations who were most likely to support the hard line position.[6]

The long and the short of the matter is that the distribution of attitudes from this 1952 study is more in line with the "premodern" notion of the distribution of chauvinistic, jingoistic sentiments. More recent notions of upper or upper middle class moderation and working-class immoderation are not supported. In fact, they are decisively rejected.

The distinctiveness of the better-off white Protestants might reflect little more than the general "self-righteousness" likely to be found among elites and their associates in any society. This would involve a conception that the society and world are well-ordered as they are and that they have a special mission to maintain that "order." It is possible that, in this instance, one is dealing with a Calvinist concern with "moralizing the world," a concern that, for the sake of its high purpose, justifies some unusual, extraordinary interventions. Something of this orientation can be seen in the outlook of John Foster Dulles. As one biographer notes:

> Everybody who did ecclesiastical and political business with Dulles found his self-righteousness striking. . . . This self-esteem, this attitude of exclusive knowledge of eternal things coupled with a sense of moral superiority, is attested to by scores of witnesses . . . it is the temper of exclusive salvation. It easily leads to bullying others, even foreign statesmen, if they are deemed too slow, too unzealous, too wrong-headed—in other words, damned! This is what close and quite sober observers during the Suez crisis from the refusal of the Aswan loan to the end of 1956 have said: "A Calvinist atmosphere had come to prevail in the State Department, with the advent of Dulles," and again, "Dulles had the illusion of moral superiority over everybody else, with a pipeline to God." And once again, "He talked as though he had received a special message from on high—from the Almighty."[7]

The opposite case, that of the poor, of those on the margins of the society, the minority groups, and the late arriving immigrant populations, involves a propensity for more peaceful options, to be precise, a disposition to either withdraw or to negotiate. Persons on the "periphery" (to use Galtung's term) tend to have more fear of war. Relative to others in the society, they tend to be in a state of continuous anxiety about this possibility. The choice of pullout or negotiation may reflect the conditions of poverty and of marginal working-class existence. These groups, moreover, do not have the resources for taking "strong stands." The precondition for satisfactory living in such contexts is the avoidance of costly and unpredictable conflicts and, alternatively, the working out and maintaining of mutually beneficial supportive arrangements. This is to suggest that the response indicated here is a manifestation of a working-class subculture wherein the avoidance of conflict and the development of reciprocities (negotiations) are key necessities of existence. This order of values would be especially marked with respect to a distant conflict in which it would be most difficult for those "on the periphery" to appreciate the expenditure of funds and manpower. They might also feel that it would be their "manpower" that was going to be expended.[8]

The question arises as to whether that distribution of attitudes is stable. It is possible that "the masses" are volatile in their outlooks, perhaps coming down first on one side and then on another, depending on the winds of the moment. A question on Viet Nam policy contained in the Survey Research Center's 1964 election study, one that closely parallels the 1952 question, allows some assessment of this possibility. It reads: "Have you been paying any attention to what is going on in Viet Nam?" Those who answered "yes" were then asked: "Which of the following do you think we should do now in Viet Nam?" The responses were "pull out of Viet-Nam entirely," "keep our soldiers in Viet-Nam but try to end the fighting," and, "take a stronger stand even if it means invading North Viet-Nam." The results, twelve years later, in a different conflict and in a different country, are strikingly similar to those given in response to the Korea question (Table 5.4).

As of 1964, one third of the adult population indicated that they either had no interest in the matter or did not know what to do. When we took those who chose one of the three options and repercentaged, the result paralleled very closely the 1952 findings. For example, 26 percent of the most poorly educated favored either a pullout or an end to the fighting as compared to 12 percent who favored the stronger stand. The relationship is reversed among the college educated, where the equivalent figures were 35 and 48. When repercentaged the respective percentages favoring the stronger stand were 31 and 58.

The results here, in short, reveal the same pattern as in 1952. The preference for the "strong stand" is strongest among the higher occupational levels, among those with the most formal education, and in the highest income levels. The same age pattern appears with the youngest being most likely to favor the tough stand. And, there is the same relationship with media attention, the newspaper and magazine readers again tending to favor the

TABLE 5.4
ATTITUDES TOWARD THE VIET NAM WAR BY BACKGROUND CHARACTERISTICS: 1964-1968

	Total Sample										Those with Opinion			
	1964					1968					1964		1968	
	PO*	EF	SS	DK	(N)	PO	EF	SS	DK	(N)	SS	(N)	SS	(N)
Total	8	22	29	41	1,571	19	37	34	10	1,557	49	1,051	37	1,396
Race														
White	8	25	34	34	1,291	19	35	36	11	1,485	51	852	40	1,239
Non-white	11	22	11	55	148	27	46	18	9	168	25	67	20	153
Sex														
Male	8	22	41	29	642	16	33	41	10	686	58	520	45	697
Female	9	26	23	47	808	22	39	28	11	871	40	469	31	779
Occupation														
Professional	6	33	37	24	144	18	38	32	11	229	48	110	36	204
Managers	7	21	43	30	209	16	38	35	11	250	60	149	40	223
Clerical, sales	7	28	36	29	149	20	38	35	7	167	51	106	37	155
Skilled, semiskilled	8	26	31	35	423	16	36	39	9	463	48	273	43	420
Unskilled, service	9	23	23	45	145	20	36	31	13	107	41	89	36	93
Farmers	5	29	34	40	74	25	33	32	10	88	57	44	35	79
Unemployed	13	28	16	44	32	26	34	29	11	35	28	18	32	31
Education														
Less than 8 years	8	18	12	61	177	28	33	23	16	180	31	67	28	151
8 years	10	23	16	52	177	21	30	32	17	178	32	87	39	148
Less than 12 years	9	22	25	44	282	19	37	33	12	275	43	176	37	243
12 years	7	26	35	33	310	18	41	35	7	319	51	212	37	297
12 years, noncollege	10	26	41	22	148	14	39	39	8	175	54	114	42	161
Some college	7	25	47	20	175	20	31	41	8	223	59	138	44	205
College	8	27	48	21	163	18	44	31	8	202	58	135	33	187

TABLE 5.4 (Continued)

	PO*	EF	SS	DK	(N)	PO	EF	SS	DK	(N)	SS	(N)	SS	(N)
Income														
Under $2,000	11	15	11	63	159	32	22	26	21	136	28	60	32	108
$2,000-3,000	9	25	23	43	112	25	38	24	12	99	41	64	28	87
$3,000-4,000	13	24	27	36	129	20	43	23	14	114	42	83	27	98
$4,000-5,000	10	29	22	39	126	25	39	31	5	87	34	78	33	83
$5,000-6,000	9	25	32	34	161	16	31	40	13	115	49	106	46	100
$6,000-7,000	4	26	35	35	201	19	32	42	7	268	54	130	45	259
$8,000-10,000	6	28	37	28	220	15	38	39	8	196	52	156	42	180
$10,000 and over	9	25	43	33	285	16	42	34	8	481	56	220	38	421
Religion														
Protestant														
White	8	24	34	35	883	16	36	37	11	957	51	584	40	852
Black	12	22	11	56	139	27	46	17	10	141	24	63	19	127
Catholic	8	26	34	32	326	21	39	32	8	337	50	222	35	309
Jew	16	34	18	32	38	36	36	19	10	53	26	26	21	38
Other	15	21	21	42	52	29	26	38	7	58	37	30	41	54
Region														
East	9	22	26	43	351	24	40	28	8	370	48	204	30	339
Midwest	7	23	28	41	490	20	37	34	10	460	48	292	36	426
South	8	23	26	43	441	18	34	36	11	481	49	280	41	424
West	6	22	36	36	247	16	35	37	11	246	56	157	42	217
Age														
18-24	4	29	37	31	105	17	33	43	7	114	53	73	46	106
25-29	7	22	41	30	159	15	37	41	7	165	59	111	44	162
30-34	8	33	37	22	148	21	38	31	9	136	47	116	35	124
35-39	8	20	37	36	148	17	45	30	9	159	57	97	32	145
40-44	8	27	36	30	172	16	42	34	8	166	51	122	37	152
45-49	7	27	26	40	136	18	38	36	8	168	43	82	40	154

TABLE 5.4 (Continued)

	PO*	EF	SS	DK	(N)	PO	EF	SS	DK	(N)	SS	(N)	SS	(N)
Age (Continued)														
50-54	10	28	24	38	156	21	35	35	10	145	38	97	39	131
55-59	9	15	30	46	114	16	35	40	9	119	56	61	44	108
60-64	11	23	26	39	99	32	30	27	10	106	44	61	31	95
65 plus	13	20	20	47	210	23	33	25	19	269	38	111	30	219
Party Identification														
Strong Democrat	8	25	27	40	398	23	41	29	8	311	45	237	31	287
Weak Democrat	9	25	29	38	364	20	36	33	11	396	46	220	37	351
Independent Democrat	9	30	29	28	126	18	41	33	8	153	43	87	36	141
Independent	8	29	21	43	105	19	31	38	11	164	37	60	44	145
Independent Republican	9	19	47	26	81	14	30	48	7	135	63	60	52	125
Weak Republican	8	27	32	33	195	17	39	31	12	224	47	131	36	196
Strong Republican	11	16	49	24	157	23	36	33	8	149	65	119	36	137
Newspaper Attention														
Regularly	9	28	40	24	575	17	38	37	8	492	52	423	40	452
Often	9	25	38	27	204	18	34	40	8	166	53	147	44	153
Time/Time	9	24	27	41	263	19	39	34	8	247	45	158	37	227
Once in a while	7	21	20	52	85	28	26	33	13	92	42	41	38	80
Never	7	20	17	57	310	22	37	24	16	325	39	137	28	273
Magazine Attention														
Good Many	11	28	42	18	142	22	48	28	3	120	52	116	28	116
Several	9	27	41	23	234	11	40	39	10	156	53	180	43	140
1 or 2	11	26	37	36	185	20	36	38	8	199	50	136	40	184
None	8	22	26	45	877	20	35	33	12	862	46	491	47	759
Most Important Medium														
Newspapers	10	26	37	28	349	18	37	36	9	253	51	255	40	231
Radio	2	25	29	44	55	28	39	23	5	39	51	31	30	37
TV	9	24	28	40	836	18	38	35	9	700	46	510	38	639
Magazines	11	25	47	18	101	22	40	29	8	68	57	84	32	62

* PO = pull out; EF = end fighting; SS = stronger stand; DK = don't know; no answer.

tough policy. This study also indicates that the amount of atten-tion paid each of these media is correlated with increased support for the tough stand.

The same question was repeated in the 1968 study. The leading previous presentation of the findings reports as follows:

> . . . changes in public thinking about strategic alternatives in Viet-nam . . . over this period were rather limited. Where Vietnam was con-cerned, opinion was somewhat more crystallized in 1968 than in 1964 but there had been no sweeping shift of sentiment from hawk to dove.

That conclusion is based on the entire distribution of attitudes including those who "don't know" and those who had "no inter-est." Because the latter responses had declined from 33 to 10 percent in the four year time span, the results are not entirely comparable. Another calculation, taking those with opinions only, that is, taking the more active or informed public, yields a some-what different picture with support for the strong stand declining by some 12 percentage points and support for a pullout increasing by 9 and for an end to the fighting increasing by 14 percentage points.[9]

The location of this change is of considerable interest. In general, the groups that were the most "hawkish" in 1964 were the most likely to have changed by 1968. Taking those with opinions (as shown in Table 5.4) we find that 60 percent of the managers favored the tough stand in 1964, whereas this had fallen to 40 percent in 1968. The very hawkish college educated group, at 58 percent in 1964, had been dramatically transformed by 1968 with only 33 percent taking that same position. And similarly the very high income group of 1964 also was transformed, their 56 percent falling to 38. This means that the sizable relationship with these socioeconomic status variables indicated in 1964, be-cause of the change among the high status groups, had been reduced or eliminated. In 1968, in other words, the pattern of upper middle class "toughness" had disappeared. That did not leave a pattern of working-class "authoritarianism." For all prac-tical purposes, rather, it simply indicated little or no difference by occupation, education, or income level.

Still another of the 1952 and 1964 patterns disappears in 1968.

The relationship with newspaper and magazine attention is changed. It is strikingly reduced in the case of newspaper reading and is reversed in the case of magazine reading. The magazine readers who were very hawkish in 1964 were very dovish in 1968, the percentages for the stronger stand having fallen from 52 to 28.

There is not much mystery about these findings. The print media are most assiduously followed by the highly educated, well-off segments of the population. There was a significant shift in the orientation toward the war on the part of these media between 1964 and 1968, particularly on the part of the magazines. It would appear, in short, that this significant change in public attitude was a result of the change in media content.

The evidence as to the character of the audiences of these mass circulation magazines is clear. Studies done by the magazines themselves have shown the essentially upper middle class character of the audience.[10] The Survey Research Center studies also indicate much the same pattern. For instance, about 34 percent of all magazine reading is done by college graduates, a group which makes up only 14 percent of the adult population. Put somewhat differently, about half of the college educated in 1968 read magazines "regularly" or "often" for political information as compared to about one-fifth of the high school graduates and only about one-tenth of those with less than a high school education.

The change in the content of these magazines has been documented elsewhere.[11] The 1964 position of most of the major mass circulation magazines was that anything short of victory in Viet Nam was unthinkable. By 1968, with two exceptions, they were calling for settlements, de-escalation, and a bombing halt. Most now felt the war was a mistake. As one put it, the war had become "messy and formless." While there was no open advocacy of a settlement, the point was made differently, for example, with detailed attention to the increasing numbers of war dead. The two exceptions among the seven major national magazines were *Reader's Digest* and *U.S. News and World Report*.

It is much more difficult to asses the position of the 1,760 or so daily newspapers. It is clear that most of the major "prestige" newspapers had come out against the war in one way or another by 1968. This included the *New York Times,* the *Washington Post,*

the *Christian Science Monitor,* the *Atlanta Constitution,* and the
St. Louis Post-Dispatch. Even the *Los Angeles Times,* which had
been hawkish on the war from the beginning, had recently turned
"dove." These papers must have had some considerable influence
on a large range of the "next best" newspapers, both through their
own supplying of news stories and editorial material to other
papers and through imitative copying by other papers.[12]

To show the media impact it is useful to divide the population
by religion and socioeconomic class. For a number of reasons, we
have focused initially on non-South whites.[13] They have been
separated into manual and nonmanual subgroups with the latter
further subdivided into upper middle and lower-middle classes on
the basis of an arbitrary income line.[14] The comparison of the
1964 and the 1968 results, first of all, shows the "big change" (40
percentage points) to have occurred within the white Protestant
upper middle class. There was a very strong concentration of
"hawkish" sentiment within this group in 1964. In fact, almost
four out of five persons in this category favored an invasion of
North Viet Nam at that time. As of 1968, only two out of five
favored that option (Table 5.5).

TABLE 5.5
SUPPORT FOR THE STRONGER STAND BY CLASS AND RELIGION:
1964-1968; White, Non-South Respondents, as a Percentage of Those
with Opinions

	Percent Favoring Stronger Stand					
	Upper Middle Class	N	Lower Middle Class	N	Working Class	N
Protestants						
1964	78	(49)	53	(86)	49	(177)
1968	38	(95)	35	(120)	46	(229)
% difference	−40		−22		−3	
Catholics						
1964	55	(38)	58	(38)	49	(84)
1968	39	(65)	35	(51)	32	(101)
% difference	−16		−23		−17	

NOTE: There were too few Jews in the sample to allow a division by class level. The results for all Jews were: 1964: 26 percent (26); and 1968, 21 percent (38).

The changes for all other groups were much more restricted, ranging from 23 percentage points among lower middle class Catholics to only 3 percentage points among the Protestant workers. It will be noted that the class difference is eliminated by this shift among upper middle class Protestants. In fact, a reversal appears at that time with the latter group slightly less hawkish than the equivalent workers.

A still more detailed examination, this time linking the change explicitly to media attention, indicates that the transformation in the upper middle class white Protestant ranks was in great measure a change among those paying much attention to the print media (Table 5.6). Those paying much attention to the newspapers shifted some 42 percentage points. Those who were not regular newspaper readers shifted a mere 11 points. The latter groups, it will be noted, were not exceptionally hawkish to begin with in 1964 as contrasted with their newspaper reading peers. A similar

TABLE 5.6

SUPPORT FOR THE STRONGER STAND AMONG UPPER MIDDLE CLASS WHITE PROTESTANTS BY MEDIA ATTENTION: 1964-1968; Non-South Only, as a Percentage of Those with Opinions

	Percentage Favoring Stronger Stand			
	Reads Newspapers*			
	Regularly, Often	N	Less Frequently	N
1964	82	(34)	44	(21)
1968	40	(57)	33	(27
% difference	−42		−11	

	Magazine Articles Read*			
	Good Many, Several	N	One, Two, or None	N
1964	81	(21)	73	(22)
1968	32	(31)	42	(52)
% difference	−49		−31	

* The questions focused on attention paid to these media in the course of the campaign. They therefore exclude reading which is largely for entertainment. The questions read: "How much did you read newspaper articles about the election—regularly, often, from time to time, or just once in a great while." And, "How about magazines—did you read about the campaign in any magazines? [If yes] How many magazine articles about the campaign would you say you read—a good many, several, or just one or two?"

finding appears with respect to magazine reading. In this case the change was one of 49 percentage points among the heavy readers.

The causal argument is considerably tightened by consideration of an "experimental control," namely, the orientations of the *Reader's Digest* and *U.S. News and World Report* audience. Although the size of the sample prohibits the introduction of all the desirable controls (such as class and religion), the readers of these consistently "hawkish" magazines showed only a relatively restrained drop in support for the stronger stand, from 64 percent (N=50) in 1964 to 49 percent (N=39) in 1968. That still left these readers being some 15 percentage points more favorable to escalation than magazine readers as a whole.[15]

The lesson, it would seem, is that the "well informed" upper middle class white Protestants were "brought around" to a more "moderate" position on the war as a result of the changed content of the media they happened to follow. This evidence suggests support for the mass society theory to the extent that the media appear to have played a considerable role in stimulating this conversion. An error in the conventional formulations involves the emphasis on *the* masses as the key victims in the process. The present evidence would suggest, rather, that the manipulated persons happen to be from among the upper middle class masses. The working class and lower middle class, by comparison, were relatively immune to both original and subsequent influences.

The explanation for this paradoxical finding is relatively simple. One of the self-indulgent fancies of upper middle class intellectuals is that "other people" read those "mass" magazines: it *must be* the less-well-educated who follow *Life* and *Look.* But the available evidence once again does not support them in this congenial reading of the facts. The percentage of *Life* magazine readers increased with every level of educational "accomplishment" up to and including the holders of Ph.D.'s. Readership hits its peak in that rather exalted category with approximately half reporting that they were regular readers.[16]

Where the mass society theory, at least in its liberal or left variants, assumes that elites make use of the "mass" media to reach out and influence the vulnerable and easily swayed masses, this evidence suggests something quite different. The "transmission belts" in question reach out to the upper middle classes. On most occasions that is all that is required to control (or alternatively, to provide "order" in) the society. With the manual workers and the lower middle classes ordinarily passive and inactive, the key to "stability," to what is called *the* social order, is an accepting and approving upper middle class. When they give their consent and support, the entire mechanism will function more or less adequately. As the more visible local figures who "set tone" and provide authoritative declarations which both justify current practice and disapprove untoward initiatives by insurgent individuals or groups, as the dominating forces in the local media and in the local voluntary associational networks, they, in many if not most cases, unwittingly pass on the "lines" they have received through the so-called "mass" media.[17]

The mass society theorizing, curiously enough, probably aids in the maintenance of this process in that it allows upper middle class persons to avoid the realization that it is they themselves who have been influenced or manipulated by the media. Misdirecting attention, saying that it is other people who are vulnerable (or gullible), lowers the defenses of the upper middle class and allows a certain degree of self-satisfaction in that an "informed" upper middle class man, for example, can think the views he has are his own, something he has carefully thought out and developed by himself.

Another important feature of the situation involves the incapacity of academic and journalistic intellectuals who, one might think, could point out the mechanism involved and expose the dynamics of the process. But the fact that these astute commentators "misplaced the masses" indicates their unawareness of the actual circumstances of their own peers within the upper middle class, let alone their lack of awareness of the much more distant blue-collar "masses." In short, it points to the isolation of those intellectuals inside their own special enclaves within the upper middle class. Associating with their own kind, reading each others works, and following their own journals ("transmission belts"), they had effectively cut themselves off from any serious contact with the outside world. In addition, the distinctive anti-empirical bias which is present in at least some of these circles has also helped them remain unaware of the world they purport to know so intimately.

The discussion thus far is still basically within the framework of the mass society viewpoint. That viewpoint, in its most alarming presentations, assumes an extreme vulnerability on the part of the masses. The manipulators manipulate, and it is assumed that, with their "clever" techniques, they are also successful; the manipulators do accomplish their aims. Although in some ways intellectually satisfying to its exponents (they, after all, have a "clear understanding" of the mechanisms involved and hence, being somewhat above it all, are not moved by those influences), the view does overlook some elements which, on the surface at least, would seem to be both real and important.

It should make a difference, for example, what subject matter was being propagated. If it was some distant matter, such as the behavior of destroyers in the Gulf of Tonkin, just for example, it seems likely that the influence of media and their controllers would be very great. The average person would be totally dependent on those sources and would have no other information within his experience with which to check or assess the claims offered. Much the same can be said for other "distant" subjects, such as the activities of foreign and domestic communists, subtle degrees of softness on Communism on the part of distant political figures, definitions of national interests in faraway countries, and so forth.

On the other hand, there are many events which are much closer and much more pressing to the average household. When it is a question of the state of the domestic economy, the average person or family has many very direct indicators which are quite independent of any claims put forth in the mass media. While it may be convenient for a politican to claim that his audience "never had it so good," the average person can assess that claim with the simple facts of paychecks, grocery prices, rents or home payments, medical costs, and the like. And with that "independent judgment" one may provide some check on the manipulative or distractive intention of that politician. It seems likely that the immediate economic situation would have a saliency which would tend to outweigh almost all other concerns.

Another kind of event, wars, also provide at least some basis for realistic assessment. One might not understand the ins and outs of their origins and there would ordinarily be much effort expended to ensure support and to quiet dissent, but there are, nevertheless, "feedbacks" which, over time, would be likely to erode even the most well-planned propaganda campaign. Aside from the economic effects, there would be a return of dead and wounded which, in the ordinary run of things, would check the artifically contrived zeal.

It would be a mistake to assume that military experience (or, for a family, having a relative in the military) would have a simple unambiguous relationship to attitudes. The literature is replete with opposing claims, some saying that combat experience creates opposition to war, others saying that it inures one, that it creates more and more ruthless outlooks. It would seem that the key to the outcome depends not merely on being "in the military." One would have to specify in more detail the character of the military experience (e.g., short-term versus long-term combat experience, leadership versus follower role, winner versus loser, sense of the rightness or wrongness of the outcome, tough versus gentle prior attitudes, and so forth).

It was noted above that the blue-collar ranks change only very little in their attitudes. While to all appearances the entire society was in uproar, while dissent was spreading to all communities and all sectors of the society, this context, curiously enough, provided a significant pocket of stability. Although there was some decline in the support for the stronger stand, the change was relatively small. One explanation might be that they were relatively untouched by the new directions provided in the print media. This one could refer to as the inertial explanation.

Some combinations of military involvement with certain background experiences did seem to generate hawkish outlooks. There was very little difference in the hawkishness of non-Southern white manual and nonmanual families who did not have any family members in the armed forces. But among those who were so involved there was some difference, 50 percent of the manual respondents favoring the stronger stand as against 35 percent of the nonmanuals. One can make a further specification and ask whether the family member in question was in Viet Nam or not. For both manuals and nonmanuals the tendency was for those with family members in Viet Nam to be somewhat more in favor of the strong stand.

One may look at the pattern from another perspective, this time focusing on the education of the respondents who had relatives in the military. Those with a college education tended to avoid the hawk response. Among those with less than a high school education, by comparison, having a family member in the military was associated with relatively strong hawk sentiment. It is impossible to say with any certainty just what dynamics are operating. One reading is that those who have college education and who are likely to have received the new media message find the solution to their personal dilemma within the terms of the framework offered them. Their "solution" to the problem of the endangered relatives is to pull out or to end the fighting. For those who have not been supplied with that option, their solution is to go in and "get it over with" using all means available. If this assumption were true, it would mean that the responses were "situational," that is, dependent on the frameworks present and available for interpreting a difficult and threatening personal problem. This would be opposed to the Lipset reading which sees the attitudes rooted in "character," as the product of punitive childhood training, deprivations, and so forth.[18] If this reading is correct, it would mean that the lessons of the protesters had not reached these populations, at least not in any intelligible form.

All of the above analysis has been focused on the non-Southern population. In the South, a different constellation of factors was operating, not the least of which was a Southern presidential candidate with a very distinctive message. It is useful, for this analysis, to consider the messages in some detail and to consider also some aspects of the "conservative" variant of the mass society theory.

The "messages" offered by the three leading candidates in the course of the campaign differed significantly. Candidate Hubert Humphrey began the campaign as the "continuity candidate," following through the Johnson policies with no evident change. The immensely hostile receptions given him in the early days of the campaign (to be sure, by small "minorities" of active protesters) led him to initiate some significant changes in his position. He came out for a bombing halt and, in the final days of the campaign, President Johnson was able to arrange one. Nixon had some ideas for ending the war which could not be disclosed to the public. And George Wallace was highly vocal in his advocacy of the stronger stand in the conduct of the war. To emphasize the point, he had selected Air Force General Curtis LeMay as his running mate.

In the conservative variant of the mass society theory, the established elites are portrayed as "responsible" and the destabilizing threat is posed by what are referred to as "demagogues." In the ordinary case they are not members of the established elites. Rather they are portrayed as upstarts, the location of their activities is generally "the streets" (or in the classical formulation, the Roman Forum). Other than these crude benchmarks, the specifications of what a demagogue is, or the exact character of his activity, remain only vaguely defined. It will be noted that the framework is a convenient one for denouncing enemies (real or perceived) of established powers. In the present case, it was George Wallace who was being cast in the role of the threatening "demagogue." In point of fact, however, one would be hard put to it to distinguish the performance of the contenders since there appear to be important "demagogic" elements in all three efforts.

In any event, Wallace's candidacy and his position on the war constituted another factor, another influence in the period. Given the concentration of his forces in the South, it is reasonable to expect that a different pattern would be found there, different from the one we have already discussed for the non-Southern states. It is also reasonable to expect that the Wallace influence would be found only with the white population.

This was in fact the case. Among those white Southerners with an opinion, the support for the stronger stand increased from 47 percent (N=202) in 1964 to 50 percent (N=321) in 1968. This slight increase occurred at a time when the "toughness" of the non-South white population declined by 14 percentage points. The support for the strong stand was especially heavy among the Wallace followers, a fact which carries the suggestion, at least, that he had done much to make and sustain the outlook.[19] This increase in hawkishness, moreover, occurs in a context where Wallace was especially strong, in the middle-sized cities of the South. There the sentiment for an invasion of North Viet Nam had increased by 7 percentage points over the four year period. In the larger cities, as well as in the small towns and rural areas, such sentiment had diminished. It seems likely that organized Wallace support was strongest in the middle-sized cities and that informal pressures in his favor would also be strong in that context. Wallace did have the support of some newspapers, and it seems likely that they too would be located in cities of this size rather than in metropolitan areas.

The major lessons of this analysis would appear to be the following: The image of the blue-collar workers as "tough" and combative, as disposed to support the most bellicose of foreign policy initiatives, appears to be one of doubtful validity. The generalizations based on the performance of a few thousand Hard Hats in the Wall Street area is challenged by the systematic evidence drawn from both the 1952 and 1964 studies which show the blue-collar workers as favorably disposed toward both a pull-out and toward a conciliatory policy of, at minimum, ending the active fighting.

The parallel lesson is one of the "hardheadedness" of some very well-established groups, in particular, of the well-educated, upper middle class white Protestants. It seems unlikely, however, that this indicates an "upper middle class authoritarianism." The evidence from the 1968 study, showing sweeping changes in attitude on the part of just this group, suggests rather that the attitude is closely dependent on the messages passed to them through the mass media. Borrowing from the "mass society" line of theorizing, it would make sense to refer to these groups as the "upper middle class masses," those who are vulnerable to and easily moved by the "persuasive communications" of elites as transmitted through the media.

This adds up to saying that the mass society theorizing needs both specification and supplementation. It is necessary to specify the "affected" populations rather than focusing on some large and undifferentiated "mass." And, as has been suggested, it is necessary to specify the possibilities of influence according to the kind of message involved; in the face of some messages, those involving distant events, most people are highly vulnerable. In other instances people have some independent evidence within their own experience which allows a check on the attempts of the would-be manipulator.

This means that the special alarmist lessons offered by those intellectuals pushing the mass society themes, whether in its left, liberal, or conservative variants, need to be tempered by some consideration of the factors that provide constraints on the outside manipulative effort and that, in a sense, provide a more or less consistent focus on those problems central to the question of human improvement and liberation.

This "corrective" attempt should not be misconstrued as adding up to some cheery lesson in pluralist democracy. To say that large segments of the population are not subject to manipulation as described in the mass society formulations does not mean that there is *no* manipulation. That has been explicitly disclaimed. And it does not mean that their existential problems are solved. The directions of policy in many cases, as in the decade of direct United States involvement in the Viet Nam War, proceed with only limited change. As of 1968 a majority favored either a pullout or an end to the fighting, yet four years later the fighting still continued.

In essence, the above comments say one ought to avoid both the silly claims about widespread power and influence (effective "veto powers") argued by some pluralists and the spectral claims about sweeping manipulative powers offered by alarmed liberals and leftists, claims drawn from their hoary mass society repertory. The problem of gaining effective public control over policy, of "taming power" as one of the pluralist potentates has stated it, is still to be solved. It is a complicated and difficult task. It is not, however, as if those concerned with that task were up against some overwhelming "magical" media powers. It is also not the case that they are up against overwhelming opposition from the blue-collar ranks.

It is useful, once again, to give some consideration to the sources of the standard misrepresentations. Some of the problems have been touched on in previous chapters. One of these, a key problem, is the anti-empirical bias of many intellectuals, both those of literary-political persuasions and those in journalistic lines of endeavor. Another consideration, this operating within the more restricted bounds of those favorably disposed toward empirical inquiry, involves what one might term the politics of publication.

It is ordinarily assumed that publication in academic scientific sources is a neutral enterprise. Books or articles are presented for review and, if the argument is sound and the evidence adequate, the work will be published for a larger audience. But that viewpoint fails to recognize that here too "human passions" are involved. In all fields one finds dominant orientations or mainstream tendencies, positions that are accepted by the majority of the practitioners. Some of those practitioners will be the researchers or scholars who have made the mainstream position. Others will be merely the camp followers, those who learned the position in their graduate school training, who have a psychological investment in its manifest and evident verities, and who therefore would be unlikely to challenge that position, who in fact would find themselves threatened by a challenge. The assessments of new challenging work would tend to be made by persons with "direct investments" in the "established" or conventional wisdom of the age. The innovative viewpoint (or finding) must, in order to reach that larger audience, be passed on and approved by "gatekeepers" with "loyalties" to the conventions.

Some of the findings in this chapter were originally submitted to journals in 1965. One editor found the contribution to be "competently prepared, well-written, clearly analyzed and carefully developed . . ." but "more specialized than we would like for the general audience" of that journal. One commentator found the work "low in theoretical relevance."

One tactic of the interested gatekeeper is to recommend reformulation or reworking, one that would push the analysis in the direction of the received or conventional wisdom. One commentator, for example, recommended that the "data be reanalyzed to conform with [my] approach." Another recommended the use of the "much more sophisticated model" put forth by another author even though the findings were diametrically opposed to the assumptions of that model. This author also recommended against publications on the grounds that he would have judged "*ab initio*, that white, male, WASPS would come out high." Another tactic consists of a demand to change the formulation. One commentator wrote the editor saying: ". . . it requires one small but important type of editing before it is suitable . . . it must be rendered value-free." Specifically, this commentator: thought it "mandatory" that "the author . . . delete the . . . paragraph . . . in which he refers to 'upper middle class authoritarianism.' " "I have a similar feeling," he continued, "about [the] use of the term 'upper middle class masses.' "[20]

The findings relating media attention and support for the strong stand in 1964 and 1968 were submitted to a prominent quarterly devoted to the study of public opinion. In this case the editor explained that their "basic problem" was that they were currently receiving "many more good articles" than they could publish. Also by way of explanation he noted, "We have published so much material on attitudes toward the war in Vietnam." The journal in question, in the years from 1964 to 1968, had published one article on attitudes toward the war and that one was based on a rather limited sample of 152 college professors in the Boston area. In subsequent years through to early 1971, they did publish some additional contributions to the subject. There were none in 1969, but in 1970 they published an essay on "The Protestant Clergy and the War in Vietnam" (which turned out to be based on a sample of California clergymen). They also published a review of polls on wars, whether they were viewed as a mistake or not. They published one study of attitudes based on a national sample and one analysis of the treatment of violence, protest, and the war in the United States and Canadian television news. That amounts to a grand total of four articles on the subject plus the review of poll data over the entire seven year period. This was amid a thicket of approximately 70 articles or notes on public opinion methodology ("The Sample Cluster: A Neglected Data Source") and such substantive contributions as "Somali Proverbs and Poems as Acculturation Indices" and "Some Effects of Radio Moscow's North American Broadcasts." It would seem, in other words, that there is more than just "technical" judgment in operation here. In part, at least, the distortion of both intellectual and public awareness of opinion is a function of the special concerns of the gatekeepers.

NOTES

1. See Seymour Martin Lipset, *Political Man* (Garden City, N.Y.: Doubleday, 1960), Chap. 4. In the first pages of this chapter he presents a long quotation from a "Short Talk With a Fascist Beast" which he says "portrays graphically the ideological syndrome" (i.e., working-class authoritarianism). One entire paragraph (of three) is given to this casual laborer's enthusiasm for the Soviet Union's 1956 action in Hungary, an action which he compared to the weakness of British policy in Cyprus. On the following page Lipset makes a contrast between what once appeared to be true (the parties of the middle and upper classes supporting "jingoistic foreign policies") and what presumably is now true (working-class groups in some nations being "the most nationalistic sector of the population"). At a later point, in a key formulation, we find this statement: ". . . when liberalism is defined in noneconomic terms—as support of civil liberties, internationalism, etc. [the] more well-to-do are more liberal, the poorer are more intolerant." At a still later point Lipset summarizes Eysenck's research on the "tough-" and "tender-minded," the latter being described as "tolerant of deviation, unprejudiced, and internationalist." He then proceeds to indicate the relationship with class. I dwell on this matter at some length because Lipset, in a response to an earlier publication of some of the findings in this chapter, asserted he "never related the effect of education or class to foreign policy concerns." See the exchange in the Revue francaise de Sociologie 11 (janvier-mars 1970) 100-104. For further discussion, see note 18.

An article making much the same point is that of Johan Galtung, "Foreign Policy Opinion as a Function of Social Position," Journal of Peace Research 3-4 (1964) 2-6-231. He makes a distinction between persons at the "center" (essentially higher status, more informed) and those at the "periphery" (those with the opposite characteristics) and ends with the following comment: ". . . let us summarize conditions that would probably contribute to a stable, peace-oriented and effective public opinion in the field of foreign policy: 1. Elimination of the periphery from influence on foreign policy, for instance through a party-structure that does not adequately reflect periphery foreign policy orientations . . ."

On the Algerian War attitudes, see the various issues of Sondages: Revue française d'Opinion publique, 1956, no. 3, pp. 23-29; 1957, no. 2, pp. 37-50; 1958, no. 3, pp. 39-46; and 1958, no. 4, especially pp. 24, 52, 54. The meager results from the United States are summarized by Milton J. Rosenberg, "Images in Relation to the Policy Process: American Public Opinion on Cold-War Issues," pp. 277-334 in Herbert C. Kelman, *International Behavior:*

A Social-Psychological Analysis (New York: Holt, Rinehart and Winston, 1965). See also James N. Rosenau, ed., *Domestic Sources of Foreign Policy* (New York: Free Press, 1967); Gabriel Almond, *The American People and Foreign Policy* (New York: Praeger, 1950); William A. Scott and Stephen B. Withey, *The United States and the United Nations* (New York: Manhattan, 1958); Joel T. Campbell and Leila S. Cain, "Public Opinion and the Outbreak of War," Journal of Conflict Resolution, 9 (September 1965) 319-329.

Some works more specifically focused on the Viet Nam War are: Sidney Verba, Richard A. Brody, Edwin P. Parker, Norman H. Nie, Nelson W. Polsby, Paul Ekman, and Gordon S. Black, "Public Opinion and the War in Vietnam," American Political Science Review 56 (June 1967) 317-333; Philip E. Converse, Warren E. Miller, Herrold G. Rusk, and Arthur C. Wolfe, "Continuity and Change in American Politics: Parties and Issues in the 1968 Election," American Political Science Review 63 (December 1969) 1083-1105; Richard F. Hamilton, "Le Fondement populaire des Solutions Militaires 'Dures' " Revue française de Sociologie 10 (1969) 37-58; and John E. Mueller, "Trends in Popular Support for the Wars in Korea and Vietnam," American Political Science Review 65 (June 1971) 358-375; and, also by Mueller, *War, Presidents, and Public Opinion* (New York: John Wiley, 1973). An article covering much the same ground as that of the present chapter but which is based on independent evidence, referenda results, is that of Harlan Hahn, "Correlates of Public Sentiments about War: Local Referenda on the Vietnam Issue," American Political Science Review 64 (December 1970) 1186-1199. His findings parallel closely those presented here. A related historical study of some interest is that of Richard Price, *An Imperial War and the British Working Class: Working-Class Attitudes and Reactions to the Boer War, 1800-1902* (London: Routledge and Kegan Paul, 1972).

2. Combining these two characteristics with some others shown in Table 5.1 yields some extremely high levels of pro-bombing sentiment. Among better-off white Protestants who are young, who identify as Independents or as Republicans, and who pay a lot of attention to magazines, for example, 79 percent (N = 33) favor bombing.

3. Of special importance in this connection is the article by Snell Putney and Russell Middleton, "Some Factors Associated with Student Acceptance or Rejection of War," American Sociological Review 27 (October, 1962) 655-667. The findings of this article point in the same direction as those in the present account. They report that "at least among college students, it is the most sophisticated who find nuclear war most credible and acceptable" (p. 666). They also link this result with media attention, reporting some experimental studies which made use of different content and which resulted in a marked shift in a more pacifist direction.

A useful account of the changing content of college texts in the Cold War era is provided by William L. Newman, "Historians in an Age of Acquiescence," Dissent 4 (1957) 64-69. The changing content of courses is indicated by the words of a professor commenting on the "trend toward conformity." Said he, "Five years ago they picked John Maynard on Russia, now they pick Rostow." See Paul F. Lazarsfeld and Wagner Thielans, Jr., *The Academic Mind: Social Scientists in a time of Crisis* (Glencoe: The Free Press, 1959), p. 199. This comment refers Walt Whitman Rostow's *The Dynamics of Soviet Society.* One source describes this as "a CIA-financed book." See David Wise and Thomas B. Ross, *The Invisible Government* (New York: Bantam Books, 1965) p. 260.

In another development the New York Public Library dropped its sponsorship of a program entitled the "Faces of War" (which consisted of readings on the subject from the works of Euripides, Shakespeare, Cervantes, Twain) because it was a "sensitive area" and, said one trustee, an argument for peace was "not in the public interest." This episode is reported in Marjorie Fiske, *Book Selection and Censorship* (Berkeley: University of California, 1959), p. 59n.

4. A more explicit test may be made based on the one-third of the sample that was asked about the veteran status of the respondent or of the head of the house. The basic result is as follows (all respondents):

	Men		Women	
	Veteran	Not a Veteran	Head a Veteran	Head Not a Veteran
Percent pro-bombing	51	35	39	27
N =	(89)	(139)	(87)	(204)

Although the number of cases is very small, when we examine the religious subgroups by age, the results based on this third of the sample generally support the claims made in the text.

5. Forty-nine percent (N=76) of the Catholics with grandfathers who were born in the United States favored the bombing. Among those of more recent English or Irish descent, 44 percent (N=57) were pro-bombing. The maximum level for any other Catholic subgroup was 35 percent.

6. It might be argued that the results shown here reflect a special "organizational" contribution. In both 1952 and 1964 some leading Republicans advocated the tougher line; conceivably they brought their upper middle class followers around to acceptance of that position. It is possible that Democrats (who are disproportionately in manual or lower middle class

occupations) adopted the moderate position either as a defensive reaction or, especially in 1964, they were led to the position by their presidential candidate's apparent stand. An examination of the pattern with party identification controlled (based on the 1952 study) showed clearly that the policy preferences were more closely linked with rank than with party. In both camps it was the low-educated who favored negotiation and the highly educated who favored the attack on China. The 1964 results showed this same pattern.

7. Herman Finer, *Dulles Over Suez: The Theory and Practice of His Diplomacy* (Chicago: Quandrangle Books, 1964), p. 78. The same self-righteousness, again coupled with a very pronounced willingness to use war as an instrument of policy, is to be found in the work of elites of earlier generations as, for example, in the cases of Theodore Roosevelt and William Randolph Hearst.

8. Some evidence on the fear of war may be found in Richard Hamilton, *Class and Politics in the United States* (New York: John Wiley and Sons, 1972), p. 124. Some suggestive work on the working-class subculture indicating the stress on and the need for reciprocity are the following: William J. Newman, "The Culture of the 'Proles' " Dissent 5 (1958) 154-161; Richard Hoggart, *The Uses of Literacy* (London: Chatto and Windus, 1957); Michael Young and Peter Willmot, *Family and Kinship in East London* (London: Routledge and Kegen Paul, 1957); Andrée Michel, "Relations parentales et relations de voisinage chez les ménages ouvriers de la Seine," Cahiers Internationaux de Sociologie 17 (July-December, 1954) 140-153; Donald E. Muir and Eugene A. Weinstein, "The Social Debt: An Investigation of Lower-Class and Middle-Class Norms of Social Obligation," American Sociological Review 27 (August, 1962) 532-539.

9. The original formulation is that of Converse et al., op. cit., p. 1086. For a discussion of the percentaging and the implications of each alternative, see James D. Wright, "Support for Escalation in Viet-Nam, 1964-1968: A Trend Study" (M.S. thesis, Department of Sociology, University of Wisconsin, 1970), pp. 11-14. One of the alternatives presented in the question, "Keep our soldiers in Vietnam but try to end the fighting," is mistakenly labeled "status quo" by these authors.

10. See, for example, the publications of Newsweek magazine, *The Characteristics of the Reading Audience of Newsweek, Time, and U.S. News and World Report*, 1959; *Reading Audience Characteristics: Age, Income and Occupation of Readers of the Three Newsweeklies*, 1960; and *The Audience of Five Magazines*, 1962.

11. James Wright, op. cit., pp. 25-32. This review of the magazines ap-

pears in "Life, Time and the Fortunes of War," Transaction 9 (January 1972) 42-52.

12. There does not appear to be any systematic study of the change in press opinion on the war. Of some interest is the work of James Aronson, *The Press and the Cold War* (Indianapolis: Bobbs-Merrill, 1970). Another account, this one stressing newspaper positions in the early years of direct United States involvement, is that of Susan Welch, "Viet-Nam: How the Press Went Along," Nation 213 (11 October 1971) 327-330.

13. The Negro population was consistently opposed to the "tough" options of 1952, 1964, and 1968, hence there was little change to report among members of this group. There were some special factors among the Southern white populations, and it proves useful to consider them separately at a later point.

14. Given the inflation in the period from 1964 to 1968, there is some question as to whether using the same $10,000 income line for both years is legitimate or whether a somewhat higher line, perhaps $12,000, ought to be used for 1968. An examination of attitudes toward the war using finer income distinctions, however, revealed that the added confusion of the different cutting points would be unnecessary. In 1968, 35 percent of those with incomes from $10,000 to $12,000 (N=105) supported an escalation, and this compares with an identical 35 percent support figure among those whose incomes exceeded $12,000 (N=210).

15. It is possible that the direction of causation is the reverse of that being argued in the text. The populations in question may, for quite extraneous reasons, have come around to a dovish position and then, as a consequence, have switched to dovish magazines. An attempt was made to test this possibility, but there was little evidence to suggest support for this alternative. See Wright, op. cit., pp. 36-38. The overall level and pattern of magazine reading was very similar in both years. Some of the shifts were just the opposite of what would be expected in this alternative reading, the hawkish *U.S. News* gaining readership and dovish *Life* losing.

A test of this opposite hypothesis—the magazines *reflecting* outlooks rather than creating them—should be relatively easy. What is needed are decision-making studies, investigations of the decisions within the magazines to change their policy on Viet Nam. It seems likely that only a relatively small number of persons would have been involved in any given magazine. One could simply ask them why they had changed, what were the factors involved.

It is of interest to note that while *Reader's Digest* claims the largest circulation of any United States magazine (reaching some 17 million readers), only about 5 percent of the 1968 nonmanual respondents gave the magazine first mention as one they would turn to for political information. This compares, for instance, with a 19 percent mention for *Newsweek*, a magazine of much lower circulation. This is to say that circulation is by no means a measure of influence.

16. See *Newsweek*'s publication, *The Audiences of Five Magazines*.

17. It will be noted that there is a fair amount of change even among some of those who are not diligent readers of the print media. It seems likely that those who are active readers of magazines and newspapers are at the same time the informal opinion leaders within their various settings and that they in turn pass the information and political preferences transmitted by the media on to their less active and less "well-informed" relatives, friends, and associates. For a discussion on this indirect media effect, called the "two-step flow" of communication, see Elihu Katz and Paul F. Lazarsfeld, *Personal Influence: The Part Played by People in the Flow of Mass Communications* (Glencoe: The Free Press, 1955).

18. This is speaking of the formulation in Lipset's *Political Man*. In later work he has shifted his emphasis: at one point he says that "unions, parties, regional cultures, religions, will be *most determinative* of specific political actions." He has yet to present evidence which controls for all of these *most determinative* factors so as to allow his readers to assess just how much, if any, working-class authoritarianism remains after controlling. The little new evidence he presented in *Political Man* involved only simple two-variable tables (occupation and measures of tolerance). He also showed the same with an education control. For a much more detailed exploration of that evidence plus a consideration of the sources he cites as supporting his position, see Hamilton *Class and Politics*, op. cit., chap. 11, as well as chap. 4 above. His new formulation appears in the preface (p. xvii) to his and Earl Raab's *The Politics of Unreason: Right-Wing Extremism in America, 1790-1970* (New York: Harper, 1970). Despite this new concern with "particular institutional structures," the substance of the book is remarkable for its avoidance of these matters.

19. Thirty-three percent (N=84) of the Southern white Humphrey supporters favored the "stronger stand" as opposed to 43 percent (N=134) of the equivalent Nixon supporters and 57 percent (N=75) of the Wallace followers. Some Nixon voters (see chapter 6) were actually Wallace supporters who, for tactical reasons (to avoid a Humphrey victory), had made a late shift.

20. This version, without the "mandatory changes" did appear as "A Research Note on the Mass Support for 'Tough' Military Initiatives," in the American Sociological Review 33 (June 1968) 439-445. I wish to express my appreciation to the then editor, Norman Ryder, for his support.

The account here should not be construed as suggesting a "conspiratorial" plot. The problem is much less sinister and hence much more difficult to counter. It is a matter of a majority of the practitioners in a profession *individually* protecting their "investments" in the mainstream position. It is a struggle at long odds to find, say, two anonymous commentators who would approve a "deviant" work for publication or, as in this case, to find an editor who will overrule censorial intentions.

CHAPTER 6

THE MYTH OF THE ELECTORAL TECHNOCRATS

The previous chapters have dealt with what might be described as myths about the general public or segments of that population. In this chapter we will examine some claims about the people who "deal with" the general public, in particular with those who stage electoral events.

A major source of concern for many liberal as well as radical commentators in recent years has been the appearance of a new species of political engineer, one with a very high level of knowledge and technical sophistication who, with complete amoral cynicism, goes about the task of delivering votes to any client willing to pay. Because the clients who are willing and able to pay are characteristically on the other side (it is the rich and conservative enemy), the activities of these agents on the scene are said to provide a new, dangerous, and very disturbing element. The combination of their sophisticated technique and their moral indifference would allow a manipulation of the average voter such that the interests of the general population would be continuously thwarted and the democracy itself undermined.

Probably the most important recent work containing these themes is that of Joe McGinniss, *The Selling of the President: 1968.*[1] The basic point is made on the dust jacket which contains the Nixon visage on a cigarette package. And on the inside cover the publishers quote Hubert Humphrey as saying, "The biggest mistake of my political life was not to learn how to use television." The book generated the appropriate sympathetic vibrations in liberal circles. The editor of one "fighting" Democratic newspaper, for example, referred to it as a "sensational" book which provides "a chilling insight" into the practices of "high-pressure public relations experts" with their "cynical . . . bizarre techniques."

For all of the talk and all the concern, one fact has been persistently overlooked: it was a very poor sales effort. The product, Richard Nixon, had gained a 49.5 percent share of the 1960 political market on the basis of a badly organized campaign. In 1968, however, the new sales organization managed to capture only 43.3 percent of the market. The "high-pressure" sales effort, in short, was followed by a *loss* of 6.2 percent of the market.[2]

The real lessons of the book are quite different from those that have been suggested. A reconstruction of the McGinniss work, together with a consideration of other sources and evidence, makes possible a more realistic assessment of the role of the political salesmen.

The political merchandisers, to be sure, are cynical. They are highly contemptuous of the capacities of the general population. Nixon speech writer Raymond K. Price, for example, feels that the "natural human use of reason is to support prejudice, not to arrive at opinions." Voters, he says, "are basically lazy, basically uninterested in making an *effort* to understand what we're talking about." His main point is that "emotions are more easily roused, closer to the surface, more malleable."

Harry Treleaven, a man with years of experience at J. Walter Thompson, felt that "most national issues today are so complicated, so difficult to understand, and have opinions on that they either intimidate or, more often, bore the average voter." Few politicians, he claimed, "recognize this fact."

Another of the coterie's theorists stated, with evident pride, that in their 60-second spot announcements, "Nixon has not only developed the use of the platitude, he's raised it to an art form. It's mashed potatoes. It appeals to the lowest common denominator of American taste. It's a farce, a delicious farce; self-deception carried to the nth degree."[3]

The assumptions about the cynicism of the would-be manipulators, in short, are quite accurate. In the alarmist readings, however, there is a correlated assumption, that the cynics are also highly intelligent, that they really know their stuff, in this case, the effects of their "bizarre techniques" on the electorate. With rare exceptions, the alternative hypothesis, that they might not be all that sagacious, is completely ignored. There is one fragment of evidence in the McGinniss book which is of relevance here. Harry Treleaven at one point wanted a commercial on black capitalism. A white photographer was sent off to Harlem to take pictures of happy working blacks. When the photographer explained his purpose, he was told to move on, and to do it quickly. Treleaven, on hearing the news, said, "Gee, isn't that strange. I can't understand an attitude like that."[4]

There is, by the end of the book, a recognition that the sales effort had not been all that successful. Nixon was president: by virtue of a third party candidacy, he had managed to squeak through despite his loss, from 1960, of more than 6 percent of the vote. There was a recognition by all the participants that, despite their very knowledgeable use of the media and their "understanding" of the voter's mind, Nixon was slipping in the polls. And that was happening despite very sloppy, unprofessional media use by Hubert Humphrey's people. McGinniss says the campaign "collapsed beneath the weight of Nixon's grayness." Treleaven concluded that it was the "total split between the advertising and political people" that was the problem. "It left us much less effective than we could have been."[5]

It is to be expected that the critic-commentator who is "exposing" the operation of the technocrats, most especially one who is presenting an alarmist exposé in the best liberal tradition, should introduce the subject in its proper context. The proper context in this case means the framework provided by other intellectual commentators. McGinniss does not fail us in this regard. He leads in with Daniel Boorstin; but the decisive claims, the cornerstone of the edifice, are by the house critic, Marshall McLuhan. "In all countries," McLuhan tells us (via McGinniss), "the party system has folded like the organizational chart. Policies and issues are useless for election purposes, since they are too specialized and hot. The shaping of a candidate's integral image has taken the place of discussing conflicting points of view."[6]

Poor McLuhan! What world has he been living in all these years? Somewhere in the past there was discussion of conflicting points of view? Is that what log cabin and whiskey campaigns were all about? Is that what is meant by "Tippecanoe and Tyler too"? What did Thurlow Weed, who managed the Whig campaign of 1848, mean when he "ascribed the successful election of General Taylor to his complete silence on any and all public questions"?[7] The poor chap's mind is befogged with children's histories of Lincoln-Douglas debates. And aside from that exercise in historical romance, what was there? Did Winfield Scott discuss the issues with Franklin Pierce? Where are the Cass-Polk debates to be found? What was it that Millard Fillmore and James Buchanan said when discussing conflicting points of view? And Blaine? Or Cleveland? Or Benjamin Harrison? Or Calvin Coolidge?

McLuhan's fantasies are one thing. McGinniss's use of McLuhan as appropriate stage setting in a liberal melodrama is another. But in still another context, in the real world, the one dominated by the hard and cynical practitioners, by the knowledgeable politicians themselves, and by their technocratic aides, from them we can and do expect something quite different.

From another source, however, we learn the following:

> In studying the 1960 contest [Nixon's campaign experts] had concluded that the key to a victorious campaign was the skillful use of television. . . . they also decided that TV was not the appropriate medium for discussing issues.
>
> Within the Nixon staff, memoranda were circulated quoting typical passages from Marshall McLuhan which included statements such as "policies and issues are useless for election purposes since they are too specialized and hot to TV."[8]

It is to be expected that liberal commentators (who are, after all, secret schoolmen at heart, descendants of scholastics) would find Truth in the words of sacred and holy texts; but that hardheaded, realistic politicians should be doing exactly the same thing, that, for many reasons, should give the concerned citizen pause.

It is easy to understand why both Nixon and the team should be so attracted to this position. For him, and for the Republicans in general, "the issues" have always presented an almost insurmountable problem. Because they had no wish to outbid the Democrats in domestic welfare offerings, they were left in an extremely vulnerable position with respect to those matters of greatest concern to the general population. This fact has been clearly recognized by the Republican leadership for many years. In 1960, discussing the choice of a vice-presidential candidate, Nixon said, "If you ever let them [the Democrats] campaign only on domestic issues, they'll beat us—our only hope is to keep it on foreign policy." At the same meeting of Rupublican chieftains, Thomas E. Dewey expressed the "sense of the meeting" as follows: ". . . he [Henry Cabot Lodge] would put the emphasis on foreign policy, where it should be."⁹

The dynamics of the Nixon campaign, the pressures for issue-avoidance, are considered in greater depth in another study of the man. The organization did have the usual speech writers, idea men, and the like. And it was expected that there would be the usual spontaneous confrontations, meetings with the press, and so forth where ideas and issues would play some role; but it was also clear, from long experience, that Nixon did not "go over well" in the spontaneous encounter. The unexpected question and the ill-considered answer with the television cameras catching all could easily lead to the irrevocable disaster. And it was to guard against this difficulty that Nixon's law partner, Len Garment, in the fall of 1967 recruited Harry Treleaven from J. Walter Thompson where he had been selling Pan Am, Ford, and RCA. And there was also Frank Shakespeare, who has been described as "a refugee from high-level internecine combat at CBS." The three of them, together with some later additions, developed this "second track" approach to the public, the controlled, insulated presentation with a heavy use of television.

The men from the first track, the "issue" men, patiently waited for their time to come. After the primaries it was thought that they would then go to work developing their specialty. But it never happened. One of them, Richard J. Whalen, author of *The Founding Father,* a biography of Joseph P. Kennedy, finally left in disgust. His parting comment was: "What really does the man stand for?"

John Mitchell, also from the law firm and the boss of the

campaign, was another aide "not big on issues." Together with Maurice Stans, the campaign finance chairman, they divided the campaign budget so as to play up the second track approach, that is, it went heavily to support the television shows.[10]

Both by reason of their unpresentable politics and their, to say the least, problematic candidate, the entire team was strongly predisposed to accept the use of television as the medium and the view that issues were to be avoided.

Both the claims of the cynics and the judgment of McLuhan, the all-knowing sage, constitute hypotheses. The validity of those claims, if one were going to be "realistic," would have to be tested. The impressive thing about the Nixon experts, the sellers of the president, is that they did *not* test those basic assumptions.

There is, at present, one published account which gives an indication of the response to the offerings of the electoral technocrats. This account, by Samuel Lubell, is unsystematic and impressionistic, but it constitutes the best information currently available.

The assessment of the Nixon campaign, first of all, must be seen in the context of the assessment of Hubert Humphrey. The voters, Lubell says, saw Humphrey as meaning "four more years of Johnson."[11] And against that eventuality, they were looking for a more attractive alternative. But the problem was that there was none available. Lubell concludes that, despite all the "technical efficiency" of the Nixon campaign, it "had little effect on the voters." People turned from the Democrats to Nixon, Lubell says, but few did so with any sense of enthusiasm. Instead, they "saw Nixon as little more than a convenient collection basket, the only one available, into which they were depositing their numerous discontents with the Johnson Administration." There was a widespread sense, one accompanied by bitter resentments, that the party system "didn't give the people a chance to name the candidates." Lubell reports that many people were put off by both major party candidates. One is quoted as saying, "I'm sitting on a fence and I don't know which way to fall." And Lubell adds that rarely have "so many voters felt so lonely with their fears and hopes, trying to guess what the candidates meant." Another voter says, "Nixon's so ambiguous. He answers questions, but when he's finished you don't know what he meant." One voter expressed resentment about the Nixon-Mitchell-Shakespeare-Treleaven et al. operation saying, "Nixon is so cocksure, he seems to think he doesn't have to tell us what he's going to do."[12]

Lubell's interviews give a picture of a different kind of Wallace voter, that is, different from the pure liberal stereotype. One man indicated that "right now Wallace would get my vote." But he went on to indicate that he had doubts about what Wallace could do if elected and then added, "I'd go for Nixon, if he made clear where he stood." Some sense of frustration involved is indicated in another voter's comment. She had originally intended to vote for Wallace but then "found out a lot about him . . ." and became afraid he might win. Her earlier support for Wallace was intended as a lesson for the other candidates, "so the politicians will wake up and realize that people won't go along with what we have now." After rejecting Wallace she was still faced with the original problem, lack of a clear positive choice. "I don't know what Nixon will do about our racial troubles. You don't hear much about what he thinks. I'm not happy about voting for the quiet one." Many others, Lubell reports, were using Wallace as a means of "talking back to the politicians."[13]

It would be a mistake to read a racist or repressive lesson into this "talking back." Lubell says, "A majority of voters felt quite strongly about the need for action to end racial violence, but, . . . they did not want Negro repression." And again, the point overlooked by the media technocrats, he adds that no candidate "really spelled out such a position." Elsewhere he states with respect to the "law and order" theme that most of those advocating stiffer law enforcement did not want to stop Negro advances. Again it will be noted that the liberals have read in a meaning which for them is self-defeating.[14]

The contrast between Wallace and Nixon, that is between Wallace and the Nixon image, was very striking during the campaign and was clearly recognized, and appreciated, by many voters. Speaking of Wallace, one man put it simply: "He speaks flat out like us."[15] The blandness of Nixon's formulations and the mealy-mouthedness of Humphrey's, by comparison, were simply insulting.

It is of some interest to see these comments in conjunction with the judgments of the technocrats about the voters, the claims about the voters as "basically lazy," as uninterested, or as unwilling to make an effort, and their claims about the issues as too complicated, as intimidating, or boring. The Lubell portrait of the average voter shows him or her to be a lot more capable than Raymond Price and Harry Treleaven ever dreamed. Given the difficult position of the average voter, having been denied any candidate who might have represented them and spoken for their interests, they had a solution and that was to avoid the candidates who did not speak "flat out", who for their own inscrutable reasons found it necessary to hedge on all issues.

It seems likely that the Treleaven strategy triggered off the Nixon backlash, that is, the reaction against his candidacy. As Lubell puts it:

> . . . Nixon's silence was politically dangerous in view of the gains that Humphrey was making beginning in early September. These gains did not reflect any major change in how Humphrey was regarded personally, but he did have two assets. Many anti-war Democrats were searching eagerly for some sign that would justify their voting Democratic. Even more important, the economic appeal of the Democratic Party was steadily reasserting its strength week by week. More and more voters, when asked whom they were going to vote for, were replying, "I'm a Democrat" or "I'm for labor."[16]

The electoral technocrats' definition of the average voter as lazy and ignorant and their consequent choice of the issue-avoiding strategy left the voters with no very attractive options. One possibility was to "come back" to the party they had always supported, to the party that, despite the recent betrayal on the war, had done more for them than the Republicans. For those voters who were using the Wallace candidacy as a means of punishing or disciplining the major parties, the Republican issue-avoidant strategy provided no alternative.

The "bizarre techniques," in summary, appear to have repelled the voters rather than to have attracted them. Instead of "selling" the candidate, the "experts" very nearly succeeded in defeating him.

This lesson seems to have been largely overlooked by the

technocrats. Treleaven, as we have seen, blamed the "split between the advertising and political people." There was also the problem, in his view, of Spiro Agnew. "More than any other single thing," he said, "I think that damaged the image we were trying to build."[17]

The Republicans did make extensive use of election polls, the largest effort ever in fact, but these seem to have been used to measure candidate popularity rather than substantive concerns. That is to say, they brought in information about the division of sentiment and about the changes in sentiment, but they do not appear to have been used to find out why that change was occurring. Although they had created "an enormous amount of information-gathering machinery," one of the persons involved expressed doubts that "it led to any serious policy movement in the campaign."[18]

The McGinniss book is impressive for its suggestions of competence and sophistication in the management of Nixon's campaign on the national level (where it turned out to be a near disaster) while, at the same time, it overlooks the one area where the Republicans appear to have had a clear success, namely in the South.

While the trend elsewhere was against Nixon, within the South, specifically within the Southern middle class ranks, there was a very large and sizable shift from Wallace to Nixon. The apparent key to this movement was a series of radio and TV spots broadcast in "some southern cities" which contained a very simple message. It went: "A vote for Wallace is a vote for Humphrey." The Wallace support there seems to have been based on conviction (rather than tactics, as a means to punish other parties). Lubell quotes one voter as saying "I really wanted Wallace but I got too scared 'cause I didn't want Humphrey to get in." Another said, "I think like George Wallace but I'm afraid Humphrey will win, and he would be worse than Johnson."[19] Five states of the old Confederacy and three border states eventually came to provide electoral votes for Nixon. If the Wallace-to-Nixon movement had not occurred, some of those states would probably have given their electoral votes to Wallace and in some Humphrey would have squeezed through. Shifts of three or four of the eight would have been sufficient to throw the election into the House of Representatives.[20]

One curious feature of these liberal histories, with all their concern and alarm, is that they are unfinished. They characteristically do not tell the "end of the story." A favorite subject of liberal concern in the 1950s, for example, was a California firm called Whitaker and Baxter. They were one of the earliest of the professional political merchandising establishments. Unlike some later firms, they did not work for just any client. They would not sell Democrats, and they apparently did not like liberal Republicans. They worked for Earl Warren in his first run for the governorship in 1942, but that was the last time. The interesting thing about Whitaker and Baxter is that they, as one writer put it, "stood almost alone." When Clem Whitaker died in 1961, the firm, it is said, "lost its genius." Although still active, they have had no recent spectacular successes and are no longer on the agenda of special liberal concerns. All of this is reported in a less well-known work of liberal alarmism, this being James Perry's *The New Politics: The Expanding Technology of Political Manipulation.*[21] Perry finds it "somewhat puzzling" that "no other comparable management firms were organized during Whitaker & Baxter's heyday."

In the liberal dramaturgy one reports the *apparent* successes but not the failures. If the latter are reported, the finding is played down or set aside as "somewhat puzzling." The typical concerned liberal then "hears" a never-ending series of tales about the wiles of the political manipulators. He is given the image of an unbroken development, of a multiplication of the number of practitioners, and a continuous improvement of technique. In point of fact, however, the history is one of appearance and disappearance, of many failures, and, remarkably enough, of a lack of cumulation of technique.

Perry tells of the emergence of a Democratic firm, operated by two "old Kennedy hands," which did much the same kind of thing as Whitaker and Baxter—and then records its demise after "a staggering record for losses." Milton Shapp, with the aid of the new manipulators, defeated the Democratic machine candidate in the 1966 primary in Pennsylvania. After chalking one up for the manipulators, Perry then says, "We shall (with a touch of guilt) lightly pass over the general election." Shapp lost. "For a number of reasons," Perry says, "the general election was not relevant to the purposes of this book." One of the reasons given was a "national surge" favoring the Republicans. But that presumably is what the "expanding technology of political manipulation" is all about. The technology presumably *determines* mass political behavior; it is supposed to dominate the unexplained "surge."

Perry touches on the Rockefeller campaign of 1966. Rockefeller had the most expensive nonpresidential campaign in history with the political technicians hard at work for him. The campaign of his opponent, Frank O'Connor, was in great disarray. Rockefeller and the technicians also developed some low level slander against O'Connor. In a TV commercial, Rockefeller informed his audience that "If you want to keep the crime rates high, O'Connor is your man." The net result of all this political manipulation was that he made the poorest showing of his career.[22]

Perry discusses a computer simulation effort done for Kennedy in 1960. This very complex and costly venture yielded the prediction that John. F. Kennedy, on balance, "could gain" as a result of the religious question. The best available study of the election indicates that he, in fact, suffered a net loss due to the religious question.[23]

Perry then considers John V. Lindsay's campaigns as managed by Robert Price. Price, however, is not of the new school: he "never takes professional polls" and thinks radio and television advertisements are "usually just a waste of good money." Price has never lost an election. He also managed Rockefeller's Oregon primary campaign in 1964. It was, one will recollect, the only campaign that year in which Rockefeller was successful.[24]

Another difficulty with this kind of alarmist history is its persistent use of *post hoc, ergo propter hoc* arguments. The candidate hires the firm of political manipulators; they do their stuff; and he wins the election. The connection, presumably, is obvious. This involves the taking of an immensely complex set of events, an election campaign, and singling out one of the many factors involved and declaring it to be *the* cause. Did Rockefeller's technicians "win" him the 1966 gubernatorial contest? Or did the disorganization in the O'Connor camp lose it?

Some firms are in a position to select their clients. There is considerable incentive for them to do so, most especially to select likely winners and to avoid the obvious losers. Their future business depends on their record of campaigns won. In some ways it is relatively easy to develop an impressive record. If, for example, the firm handles only Republican candidates in a generally Republican state and even there makes some selection, it would not be difficult to create an impressive record of wins. Even a near-certain winner, it should be noted, will have reason to employ such a firm. They are geared up, after all, to handle the welter of detail work that would overwhelm the candidate and his own personal staff. And the question in such a case would be: Is the record a result of their "sophisticated technology" or of their selection of clients?

There are two systematic biases present in such histories. First, the accounts record the successes of these firms but do not record their failures, or, as in Perry's discussion, they are recorded but then denigrated so that their possible importance is not recognized. And second, there is a persistent tendency to attribute the result to the efforts of the firm. The correlate here is the failure to consider the possible impacts of the many other factors present in any election. The review of the cases indicates a rather spotty record for the new manipulators. Perry nevertheless concludes by saying: "We need not, then, labor the point: The new techniques as practiced by these professional managers win elections." They might. Or they might not. It would take much more detailed study than has been done thus far to carry that point.

The same conclusions may be reached by considering the subsequent history of Treleaven and Company. Two years after having "sold" the presidency, Treleaven was indeed thriving. In the 1970 elections he was managing six candidates, five Senatorial aspirants and one gubernatorial hopeful. Five of the six lost. Here again we may see the truncated character of liberal history. We have the book-length alarmist overture which introduces the theme, which shows the clever, calculating, and sophisticated manipulators at their work. But the next episode of the story, their rather abysmal failure two years later, receives almost no mention.[25] Months after their 1970 failure, the alarmist text is still selling well, still misrepresenting the realities for thousands of readers.

It would be easy and inviting to conclude that Treleaven had been successful in that one case. His candidate William Brock had come through in Tennessee against the veteran Southern liberal, Albert Gore. But closer examination yields a much different picture. Gore was in trouble before Treleaven appeared on the scene. He had just barely managed to survive in 1964, in a year when everything was going for Democrats. And he had won the Democratic primary in 1970 with only 51 percent of the vote, against a newcomer to politics. The early polls showed Brock to have a commanding lead over Gore. Thus, like Nixon, he was winning before the selling job began.

The Brock-Treleaven campaign was in many ways a redoing of the Nixon campaign. Brock could not openly front on any domestic liberalism issues. The staple of his campaign was the sustained use of lies and half-lies about Gore's record. Without making clear what he, Brock, stood for, the point was made that Gore was not representing the people of Tennessee.

Harry Treleaven, it will be remembered, when last seen in the McGinniss work, was complaining about Spiro Agnew who, in his view, more than any other had "damaged the image." No lesson appears to have been learned from this, because in 1970 there was Spiro Agnew in Tennessee generously providing his support. The Republican polls showed an immediate 7 percentage point drop in Brock's popularity following the visit.[26] The smear campaign also seems to have worked against the client so that Brock, who began with a sizable edge in popular support, almost lost it. As in 1968, had the campaign gone on for another two weeks, it seems likely that Treleaven would have "unsold" this client too. The message seems to have finally come through to Treleaven. After the election he said: "I've got to go back and figure out what really does elect candidates." Not very much insight, however, had been gained. A similar Treleaven smear attack on Senator Quentin Burdick of North Dakota was a failure. "It didn't work the way we planned in North Dakota," he said. But then he added, apparently unaware of or unwilling to recognize his "unselling" job, "The same approach did work in Tennessee."[27]

Once again, there is the *post hoc, propter hoc* problem. Did Treleaven win it? Or did Gore lose it? Gore did not maintain any on-going local organization in the state. He was very short on money. In fact, he was outspent by a ratio of 3 to 1. He also "did not believe in organized campaigning." When on the road, for example, he had no advance men with the predictable result that some audiences were minuscule.

The Gore case gives some sense of the forces working *against* the manipulators. With extremely meager organizational resources, with little money, with opposition within his own party, and in the face of a lying campaign effort, he still had managed to come from behind and get 47 percent of the vote. Had he maintained even a minimal organization during his term of office and had he developed even a passable organization in the course of the campaign, it seems likely that he could have picked up the additional 3 percent that would have given him a win.[28]

There are a number of summary conclusions to be noted. The appearance of the political technocrats, as has been noted repeatedly, is not a new thing. Every election brings a new range of "original" quotations to the effect that the technicians were selling the candidate as if he were a soap product. But, going back at least as far as 1896, we find a similar observation made by Theodore Roosevelt about Mark Hanna's "selling" of McKinley: "He has advertised McKinley ... as if he were a patent medicine!"[29] And, to be sure, one can always find ancient Greek antecedents in the sophists, those experts at making the worse cause appear the better. Aristophanes portrays a team of them baiting their breath with garlic before going out to woo the masses.

The one "hard" point that the alarmist commentators have is the one about the cynicism of the manipulators. That claim, as the McGinnis quotations make perfectly clear, is beyond dispute. The next step of the argument, however, is a questionable one. Cynicism associated with intelligence, with capability and means is one thing. Cynicism associated with blindness, with obtuseness is quite another. As has been indicated, the assumption of clear intelligence and of capability in the 1968 case (and in some of the others) is open to considerable doubt.

It does not follow from this that *all* technicians are obtuse or blind. One expert wrote campaign manager John Mitchell a letter on September 26, 1968, in which he outlined the current state of the campaign and the likely development through October to election day. He noted that Nixon had not gone much over 40 percent and that among the rest of the voters there was a high degree of volatility indicated. There was, therefore, a strong possibility that they would revert to their traditional party behavior. He noted also, quite accurately, the "issue structure on racial problems" which "shows that most Americans still favor socioeconomic aid, educational programs, the expansion of rights, and the elimination of discrimination; only a small minority go the real hard-line approach."

He noted further that one of the strongest of their appeals to frustrated and alienated Democrats was the idea that Nixon offered "at least" the opportunity for change. His suggestion was that if a return to the Democrats began, they should stress that Humphrey did not "even offer the *opportunity* to do things differently." He indicated that it was necessary to "hit this theme harder, and add the programmatic specifics to back it up." The first item on his list of programmatic specifics was to "reduce our commitment in Vietnam." Mitchell did not even answer the letter.[30]

The lesson is that there are a wide range of capacities to be found among the "experts" who offer their services. There is no inherent necessity that the parties and candidates who hire the experts will be able to distinguish the capable from the incapable.

Is there a "developing technology"? The evidence does not unambiguously show this to be so. There is much discontinuity, in short, many starts and many stops. To an extent this stems from the ad hoc character of American political organization. The parties have only skeletal operations between elections. When the campaign season arrives they extemporize. Many snap judgments have to be made. These include the questions of who shall be the campaign manager, which technicians to hire, which advertising agency, which strategies to use, which media to emphasize, and so on. The choice of electoral technocrats in this process is likely to be hit-or-miss, based on casual recommendation rather than on careful examination of performance.[31]

The electoral technology business is a highly speculative business with fluctuating and very uncertain profits. Essentially one is in business only at election time. Between seasons one must lay off staff and lose much of the talent and knowledge developed while on the job. Given the concern with stable and more remunerative employment, there are regular losses, especially of the more talented personnel, to other related lines of endeavor (such as the selling of soap). The business is subject to all the hit-or-miss determinants affecting the granting of contracts. One might, on the basis of a few successes, be set up for a large volume of business in a subsequent election. A few losses, however, can wipe out all previous gains. The nervous and not-too-sophisticated candidate may then chose the next, the latest, the newest entrepreneur on the scene, the one who has just been sold to him in the most recent work of liberal alarmism.

Because of the turnover in the operations, the "development" of the technology is not always continuous. Some knowledge gets lost when an organization folds. Much of the knowledge gained in a campaign is guarded with the greatest of care and made available only to a handful of loyal party operatives. Many of them are not likely to be completely aware of the implications of that knowledge. This secretiveness also limits the development of an electoral technology. It is rare, moreover, that anything more than a rule-of-thumb evaluation of methods and techniques is undertaken. When the election is over, the candidates, both the winners and the losers, turn to other matters. It is extremely difficult, for that reason, to know whether it was the "sophisticated techniques" that generated the win or whether it was some of the "other factors" present in the campaign. Without that detailed evaluation it is difficult to cumulate or develop techniques.

The final point implicit in the alarmist accounts is the assumption of manipulator's omnicompetence. They, the manipulators, do their thing, and the rest of the population helplessly responds. In some ways this portrayal, which we might refer to as liberal bathos, is as naive as the assumptions held by the technocrats themselves. It agrees, in essence, with their assumption that "the people" are lazy and ignorant, that they are not interested in issues. The limited evidence reviewed here, however, suggests a markedly different relationship between the manipulator and his supposed victim. Rather than helplessness and passivity, the Lubell interviews show anger, frustration, and resentment at being treated in that manner.

In response, many voters chose a punitive tactic, voting for Wallace to give the Democrats and Republicans a lesson. Others, in reaction to Nixon's nebulous offering, eventually returned to their traditional loyalty. The range and attractiveness of the options, to be sure, were very limited. At minimum, however, this alternative reading of the evidence indicates that there was some awareness of the demagogery. And some defenses were available to the general public restricting the impact of the would-be manipulator.

While on the subject of "defenses," it is worthwhile to add one further observation. Various Democrats played a major role in giving Nixon the substantial lead he had as of September 1968. It was, after all, a Democratic administration that had cheated on its 1964 promises. After offering "responsibility" in foreign affairs and the Great Society at home, it forthwith provided irresponsibility in the Viet Nam effort and gradually was forced to withdraw the Great Society offerings. Initially, Hubert Humphrey chose to offer more of the same (out of "loyalty" to the president we are told). A combination of factors, dissatisfaction over the nomination, the police riot in Chicago, and the refusal to offer anything different on Viet Nam led to organized heckling at the start of the Humphrey campaign. All the major sources agree that the heckling led to a reconsideration of the strategy and to the eventual very hesitant declaration of support for a bombing halt. And that, in turn, set the stage for the last minute de facto halt in the bombing a few days before the election. Here again it would appear that "the public" is not as helpless as liberal ideologues would have one believe. This is not to say that it is an equal battle or to argue for any of the wide-eyed pluralist claims. It clearly does not add up, at present, to an account of "flourishing democracy."

NOTES

1. Joe McGinniss, *The Selling of the President: 1968* (New York: Trident Press, 1969). The book has had an extraordinary sale within the United States and in other English-speaking countries. As of August 1971 it had also

been translated and published in the following languages: Spanish, Norwegian, French, Portugese, German, Swedish, Italian, Flemish, and Dutch.

2. Based on the figures provided by the Republican National Committee in their *The 1968 Elections: A Summary Report with Supporting Tables* (Washington, D.C.: 1969), p. 25.

3. McGinniss, op. cit., pp. 37-38, 44, 115.

4. Ibid., p. 96.

5. Ibid., p. 161.

6. Ibid., p. 28.

7. The quotation is from Matthew Josephson, *The Politicos: 1865-1896* (New York: Harcourt, Brace and World, n.d.; originally published in 1938), p. 74.

8. Samuel Lubell, *The Hidden Crisis in American Politics* (New York: W. W. Norton, 1971), p. 55.

9. The first quotation is from Theodore H. White, *The Making of the President: 1960* (New York: Antheneum, 1961), pp. 206-207. The Dewey quotation comes from William J. Miller, *Henry Cabot Lodge* (New York: James H. Heineman, 1967), p. 320.

10. Jules Witcover, *The Resurrection of Richard Nixon* (New York: G. P. Putnam's Sons, 1970), pp. 364-366. Chapters 15 through 17 contain a very useful account of the development of and operation of the two-track approach.

11. Lubell, op. cit., p. 51.

12. Ibid., pp. 53, 54, 58, 59, 61.

13. Ibid., pp. 61, 77.

14. Ibid., pp. 71, 76, 77.

15. Ibid., p. 75.

16. Ibid., p. 62.

17. McGinniss, op. cit., p. 161. The lesson was also missed by David S. Broder, the well-known political correspondent of the Washington Post. He writes: "As Joe McGinniss demonstrated in *The Selling of the President*, it is ridiculously easy to gull us with a modern media campaign—and indeed to maneuver us into playing our predetermined role in carrying out the candidate's media strategy." This appears in the Foreword to Walter De Vries and Lance Tarrance, Jr., *The Ticket Splitter* (Grand Rapids, Mich.: William B. Eerdmans, 1972), p. 12.

18. See Lewis Chester, Godfrey Hodgson, and Bruce Page, *An American Melodrama: The Presidential Campaign of 1968* (New York: Viking, 1969), p. 618. Pages 630-631 are also of considerable interest in this connection.

Theodore White reports the awareness in the Nixon camp of the unfavorable trend. A three day strategy meeting was called in mid-October to discuss the matter. There does seem to have been a recognition that the slippage was linked to obscurity on the issues. Ten radio broadcasts were planned. These, says White, would be "serious, scholarly, thoughtful discourses on welfare, youth, education, arms, peace and those other holy subjects of American politics." Also, two "instant books" resulted from the meeting, *Nixon on the Issues* (published in six days) and *Nixon Speaks Out*. It seems unlikely that these late contributions to the campaign reached a very large audience. As for Nixon himself, White reports that back on the campaign trail there was "little fresh that one could report." See Theodore H. White, *The Making of the President: 1968* (New York: Atheneum, 1969), pp. 370-373. See also Witcover's account of *Nixon on the Issues,* p. 383. Another source says, "He dealt with troublesome issues in statements and position papers that few read, but that he could cite when he was accused of ducking comment on the nation's major problems." Of *Nixon on The Issues,* this same source says, "The volume usually ended up on a shelf." See Ralph de Toledano, *One Man Alone: Richard Nixon* (New York: Funk and Wagnalls, 1969) p. 354.

19. Lubell, op. cit., pp. 63, 80.

20. Lubell seems to be the only commentator who has picked up this special Southern tactic. Witcover makes no mention of it. Chester, Hodgson, and Page make mention of the usefulness of such a strategy for Nixon's purposes and indicate that the Nixon people saw the need, but they then go on to say that it was never carried off (p. 627). McGinniss has some discussion of Nixon's Southern operation which was under the direction of Fred La Rue. He does not, however, mention the specific effort discussed by Lubell. He also states that Treleaven had "nothing to do with" the Southern media campaign. "He did not even see it," because Treleaven "was considered Madison Avenue, and it was felt that Madison Avenue did not understand The South" (pp. 122-123).

21. James Perry, *The New Politics: The Expanding Technology of Political Manipulation* (New York: Clarkson N. Potter, 1968), p. 15. The thrust of Perry's work is contained in the following quotation: "These new managers . . . can play upon the voters like virtuosos. They can push a pedal here, strike a chord there, and presumably, they can get precisely the response they seek" (p. 213). A recent contribution to the genre is that of David Lee Rosenbloom, *The Election Men: Professional Campaign Managers and American Democracy* (New York: Quadrangle, 1973). The advertisement reports that "a calculating cynicism unprecedented in American politics has finally demolished the 'American Dream.'. . . Here, at last, is the book that dares to describe . . ." etc.

Other works that one might consult are those of: Dan Nimmo, *The Political Persuaders: The Technique of Modern Election Campaigns* (Englewood Cliffs, N.J.: Prentice-Hall, 1970); Karl A. Lamb and Paul A. Smith,

Campaign Decision-Making (Belmont, Calif.: Wadsworth, 1968); Harold Mendelsohn and Irving Crespi, *Polls, Television, and the New Politics* (San Francisco: Chandler, 1970); Herbert M. Baus and William B. Ross, *Politics Battle Plan* (New York: Macmillan, 1960); David A. Leuthold, *Electioneering in a Democracy* (New York: John Wiley 1968); Cornelius P. Cotter, ed., *Practical Politics in the United States* (Boston: Allyn and Bacon, 1969). And last but not least, we have Rodney G. Minott, *The Sinking of the Lollipop* (San Francisco: Diable Press, 1968).

22. Perry, op. cit., pp. 33, 42-43, 128-132. Rockefeller received 54.9 percent of the vote in his first election to the governorship in 1958. In 1962, he received 54.6 percent. In 1966, in the campaign discussed above, he received only 45.0 percent of the total. There were defections to Liberal and Conservative party candidates in this election.

23. Perry, op. cit., pp. 165 ff. For the "best available study" see Angus Campbell, Philip E. Converse, Warren E. Miller, and Donald E. Stokes, *Elections and the Political Order* (New York: John Wiley and Sons, 1966), chap. 5. Perry quotes Theodore Sorensen to the effect that the whole effort was not very valuable ("... no more valuable than the 'issue polls'... restated the obvious... reflected the bias of the original pollsters... incapable of direct application"). Perry, nevertheless, refuses to take the comment at face value. "Except as a historical footnote," he says, "Sorensen's criticism is academic. A simulator was built and it did supply information that was read by the ten or fifteen men who actually ran a presidential campaign. More importantly, the simulator seemed to be at least partly effective."

24. Perry, op. cit., chap. 7. Not one to give up easily, Perry claims that Lindsay would have had a "smashing victory" if Price had been using the new techniques.

25. See the account by Christopher Lydon, "TV Political Advertising Loses 'Magic'," New York Times, 5 November 1970. Other than the Treleaven losses, the firm of Bailey, Deardourff and Bowen "did not have a single winner in its several statewide races although it had massive spending advantages." Deardourff, incidentally, figures prominently in Perry's account. Charles Guggenheim had five losers and four winners. Two of those winners, Edward Kennedy and Philip Hart, had a lot of other things going for them aside from the efforts of the political technocrats. See also the article by Warren Weaver, Jr., "Media Investment a Loser in Florida," New York Times, 18 March 1972.

26. Richard Harris, "Annals of Politics: How the People Feel," The New Yorker 47 (10 July 1971) 34-54. Also of some interest is David Halberstam's "The End of a Populist," Harper's 242 (January 1971) 35-46.

27. See the Lydon article.

28. For a more extended discussion of Tennessee politics covering the period of Kefauver and Bass, see Richard Hamilton, *Class and Politics in the United States* (New York: John Wiley, 1972), pp. 423-427.

29. Thomas Beer, *Hanna* (New York: Knopf, 1929), p. 165.

30. Chester et al., op. cit., pp. 630-631. This description of the public orientations toward the civil rights area, it will be noted, is consonant with the evidence presented in chapter 4 of this work. It will also be noted that, even though this evidence was "available," the 1968 campaign and later ones were planned on entirely different principles, those of the Southern Strategy. These principles were largely the work of the Nixon's specialist on "ethnic affairs," Kevin Phillips. Phillips's work is based largely on analysis of aggregate voting data. His interpretations involve the *imputation* of the motives underlying these votes. He was also the chief aide to John Mitchell and, so it seems, his voice was heard and that of Walter De Vries, author of the insightful letter to Mitchell, was not.

31. Although Humphrey had every reason to know he would be nominated, it was not until August 30, the Friday before Labor Day, that he approved his campaign plan. The latter could not have been approved much earlier because it was only being written on Tuesday of that week. Humphrey had also neglected to find himself a campaign manager. That, too, was arranged on August 30. Two weeks later, on September 13, they changed their advertising agency. The state organizations were in disarray. The one in California, for example, was described as "a ghost army." The California chairman was in Europe, not expected back "for weeks." For the details of Hubert Humphrey as the Disorganization Man, see Chester et al., op. cit., pp. 632, 639, 644, and White, op. cit., pp. 337-339.

CHAPTER 7

SMALL BUSINESS ORGANIZATIONS: MALFUNCTIONING PLURALISM

In classical pluralist accounts, a healthy democratic society is portrayed as a three-tiered structure. At the bottom one finds the general population, diverse and heterogeneous, subject to many whims and fancies, given to many different and changing interests. At the top there is a government managing the enterprise. And intervening between the People and the Government one finds a congeries of voluntary associations influencing and checking the latter so as, in some limited way, to represent the former.

These associations and their activities are seen as central to the entire democratic enterprise. Without them, the individuals in the general population would be isolated, weak, and helpless. As individuals they would not be able to influence governmental policy for their benefit and they would not be able to defend themselves against policies detrimental to their interests. In short, the notion of a direct democracy, of individuals themselves nego- tiating or influencing, proves to be unrealistic. Under such an arrangement, the individuals in "the mass" would be completely subject to the dictates of that government or to the dictates of the elites or ruling classes that controlled the government. In such a condition, so it is argued, they would be susceptible to the blandishments of the interested demagogue. And that course, in the usual reading of the pluralist scripture, would make matters even worse.

In somewhat greater detail, the classical pluralist account goes as follows. Individuals who share common interests or concerns will get together (or "aggregate") so as to form associations to represent them in political struggles. These organizations, unlike individuals, are large enough and of sufficient strength to effect policy decisions within the government. They can thereby achieve some benefits for their members; they can also serve defensive purposes by fending off the initiatives of other associations which threaten member interests.

It is further assumed that the interests are not clustered nor are they permanent. The ordinary individual would join a number of special purpose organizations and, to some extent at least, his or her interest in one would conflict with the interest of another. Recognizing this fact, the member and the organization leaders would not press matters with single-minded insistence but would look for some way to achieve a satisfactory compromise. Some bargaining would occur; the skills of compromise would be further developed; and, with time, a nonconflictful political process would result.

It is important to note the direction of influence in this process. The action originates at the grass roots. The associations are formed by people at the grass roots and in response to their needs or concerns. The key assumption is that these associations are internally democratic, that they do in fact respond to the members' interests. The arrangement would be functioning improperly, in an undemocratic way, if the direction of influence were otherwise, that is, if the associations were directing the members rather than being directed by them.

So much for the model. It is useful to make inquiry as to whether things do in fact work that way.

An across-the-board assessment of organizational performance is clearly impossible. In one sector, however, with respect to small businessmen, a study exists that does allow some detailed insight into these matters. This study proves especially useful because it allows us to contrast the performance of the small businessmen's associations with the actual orientations of their clientele as outlined in chapter 2. The work in question is that of Harmon Zeigler, specifically his book *The Politics of Small Business.*[1] Much of the data in the following pages comes from that source although the framework of the analysis is somewhat different.

In much of pluralist speculation there is an assumption of "automaticity" about the process of forming associations. Where there is a problem or a threat, some "countervailing power" will be created. The use of that simple declarative avoids consideration of the dynamics involved in the process.

One might easily assume that the history of small business has been one of continuous problems. For small businessmen, the need for some organizational weaponry has been a constant over the entire history of the nation. But, curiously enough, the major national organizations representing their interests (or at least saying they represent small business interests) did not appear until the late 1930s. And even then, their creation was dependent on a rather important outside stimulus.

The occasion was a conference on small business called by no less a figure than the President of the United States. Faced with heightened opposition from big business interests, Roosevelt hoped to create "the impression that . . . small businessmen were grateful for the help they had received from the New Deal agencies." About 500 persons were invited to this affair, most of them being businessmen "who had written to the President about small business problems." Little was accomplished. Zeigler describes it as "a ludicrous affair." One result was "a general condemnation of the President and all he stood for." They gave no indication "that small businessmen felt that they were any different from big businessmen."

It was from this beginning that the national interprofessional small businessmen's organizations developed. As *Business Week* described it, "Organizers figured that here was a new and profitable field. . . . Promoters swarmed to the promised harvest." Some fifty organizations had appeared within the year after the conference. There was a scramble for members and a flurry of competitive claims about which one of them really spoke for small business. As would be expected, as among the small businesses being spoken for, there was a high mortality rate.[2]

It is useful to review this development in the light of the standard pluralist assumptions. Key to the process of "aggregation" was the action of the President of the United States.[3] Although the problems facing small businessmen were of long standing, it was not until 1938 that general associations acting in their name became a fact. This might be set in contrast to an equivalent organization of big business, the National Association of Manufacturers, which began in 1895.

The assumption of internal democracy is also one that is open to some question. Possibly the leading association of this kind is the National Federation of Independent Business (NFIB). The federation is a private property. It is, in fact, "a private corporation owned by C. Wilson Harder [its founder] who is the principal share holder. The members do not have any opportunity to offer any alternative to Harder as president. No elections are ever held." There is, Zeigler tells us, "no attempt to stimulate any sort of interaction among [its 150,000 members]." Membership in this organization, in short, involves no more than the payment of dues in exchange for various printed materials. The ideas of involvement, participation, interaction, office holding, and bargaining—all key notions in the pluralist repertory—are distinctive only for their absence from this association.

Another such organization has roughly similar arrangements. This is the National Small Business Men's Association founded by DeWitt Emery. The NSBMA, Zeigler reports,

> ... provides for a president who is elected by the Board of Trustees. The latter is supposed to be elected at annual meetings. However, there is no record of any polling of the annual meetings on the choice of trustees. The powers of the president are virtually unlimited; according to the constitution, he is a member of all committees, has "general supervision" of association affairs and "such powers and duties as the Board of Trustees shall from time to time prescribe."

Emery moved out of the presidency from time to time. At one point he left to form a public relations firm in Chicago. His first client was the NSBMA.[4]

In still another organization, the American Association of Small Business, we learn that "... the president appoints an elections committee of seven which appoints a national board of directors of 91 people who in turn appoint the president."[5]

Another feature of these organizations that does not accord with the image of grass roots spontaneity involves a peculiarity of the staffing. Under the president of the NFIB one finds 3 field directors, 26 division managers, and 200 district managers. The latter, in fact, are salesmen who receive a commission of 50 percent of the first year's dues. The NSBMA also has 35 professional salesmen, not themselves members, who operate on a strict commission basis. Another of these organizations, the Conference of American Small Business Organizations (CASBO), also has a staff that operates on a 50 percent commission basis.[6]

These organizations, in summary, turn out to be essentially private businesses. The leaders, rather than being the elected representatives of a highly motivated group of supporters, turn out to be the merchandisers of services that would find no clientele at all were it not for their use of a sales force.

Membership figures are hard to come by and even when available are open to some question. The NFIB claims to be the largest small business organization in the nation. In July 1959 it claimed 130,000 members. By mid-August of that year it claimed 142,000, and at the end of August it claimed 150,000. Zeigler reports an estimate giving the yearly turnover as 90 percent. The NSBMA claims 20,000 members. Other organizations claim even fewer.

One peculiarity of the membership deserves special attention. It might be thought that a small business association, unavoidably, would have to define the word "small." But curiously enough, this is an endeavor all of them have rejected. The NFIB stated that they saw "no real need for any technical breakdown on the overall basis."

The constitution of the NSBMA allows all businesses to join. As they put it, "We know a small business when we see one." Their constitution allows for membership by a division of a corporation. Their recruiters show no interest in the "independence" of a prospective client. Firms with over 200 employees are given ten memberships at ten dollars per member. Zeigler cites an estimate that the "average" NSBMA member has 500 or more employees.

CASBO has a somewhat different character in that it is a bridge organization; as the name makes clear, it is a conference of organizations. Representatives from these organizations attend the annual meetings. The conference has developed the notion of "underlying membership" which allows it to speak for all the individuals in the member organizations. CASBO also has individual members. One of these was a director with a firm having 1,600 employees. "Many members," Zeigler tells us, "have 1,000 or more employees."[7]

All of this suggests that the entrepreneurial interests of the association's owners are somewhat more important than their concern with representing the members. Those interests can best be served by avoiding the definition of "small" and thus allowing the support of anyone willing to make a contribution. Thus, the first convention of the NSBMA was subsidized largely by Atlantic Refining, Borg-Warner, Curtis Candy, Greyhound Bus Lines, H. J. Heinz, Kohler, Lambert Pharmacal, McKesson Robbins, National Steel, Quaker Oats, Remington Rand, Sun Oil, and Westinghouse. Later meetings had the same kind of corporate sponsorship. In 1947, the association's head, DeWitt Emery, set up a Small Business Economic Foundation which was to be financed by contributions. The contributions came from Standard Oil of New Jersey, United States Steel, Standard Oil of Indiana, Socony-Vacuum, and the Texas Company. Among the smaller companies who contributed were Chrysler, Republic Steel, Firestone, and Inland Steel. There were many others. In addition to the grants and the membership contributions, financial support comes in the form of institutional advertising in the occasional publications.[8]

The analysis thus far has been concerned largely with what have been called "inputs." One must raise the corresponding question about the "outputs." It is possible that the pluralist governmental process has been short circuited as far as the internal democracy is concerned. It could, nevertheless, be true that the organizations perform "responsibly" and represent the interests of the membership although there would be no good reason for them to do so, the membership not having direct means to "punish" unresponsive leaders.

There appear to be two major varieties of public outputs: some literature is produced and some kinds of lobbying activities are undertaken.

There is little that need be said about their literature. It is sweeping, general, and filled with clichés; the content is heavily focused on the threat of big government and trade unions. The NSBMA, speaking of the Federal Trade Commission regulation of dealer-manufacturer relationships, called it "intolerable federal regulation" and indicated its "opposition to federal regulation in any form." The government is portrayed as a collection of single-minded "bureaucrats" who have nothing else to do with their time than to plot "socialism." The same organization saw labor unions as "monopolistic combinations" and demanded that they be placed under the antitrust law. They would, however, regret seeing labor "placed under the thumb and at the mercy of the bureaucrats." They portray their task as one of liberating the working man from the snares of the unions. "Can we, the small business-men of the country," they ask, "free the hands of the loyal, patriotic factory workers? Can we?—You bet we can. And what's more the workers themselves . . . will flock to our support."

Zeigler points out the use of the absolute dichotomy; it is either laissez-faire capitalism or socialism. The platforms, he notes,

> are of sufficient generality to encompass a highly emotional type of appeal while avoiding the intricacies of specific legislation. The develop-ment of technical proposals which have the possibility of receiving serious Congressional attention is not the purpose of their platforms.[9]

Another way of putting it would be to say that exerting influence on the government for the benefit of their clientele was not a major concern.

The one exception to this pattern is the National Federation of Independent Business. Their literature is more focused on the problems of small business and more concerned with big business as the source of the difficulty. Their major solution is the use of antitrust laws against big business. Beyond that difference in focus, however, there is little to distinguish them; their argument also tends to be sweeping, general, and leaning toward the cliché. For example,

> "Yes, another smashing blow against 'Mom and Pop' and other neigh-borhood enterprises . . . who is [sic] considered too small to be impor-tant. Well, brother, we told you all about this 25 years ago and we're still tellin' and yellin' . . . mostly for enough help to put a damper on these monopolies before they plunge this country into an economic dark age."[10]

There still remains the question of their legislative lobbying activity, conceivably, the principal justification for their existence.

Here too the behavior of some of the organizations is, to say the least, somewhat curious. One might think that it would be useful to have a standing committee of the House of Representatives devoted to the subject of small business. The members of such a committee would have a continuing obligation to study small business problems and, possibly, to introduce supportive legislation. The NSBMA, however, opposed the formation of the Small Business Committee. At a later point, this committee introduced legislation to get a larger share of defense contracts for small business. CASBO opposed this legislation.

One might also think it a useful thing that there be a Small Business Administration within the Department of Commerce, that in other words there be an administrative agency present to follow small business developments, to generate data on the developments, and also possibly to initiate and/or support legislation. Both CASBO and NSBMA opposed the creation of the Small Business Administration. They argued that the Department of Commerce represented all business. The American Bankers Association made extensive use of NSBMA and CASBO resolutions against the Small Business Administration as "proof" that small business did not want this.

The NSBMA argued that "small business is not a class—it is a fluid part of the American economic system." They objected to "political token relief of any kind, even for small business." DeWitt Emery said: "We seek no special consideration. . . . Small business does not need or want any special privileges or consideration." CASBO has much the same outlook.[11]

We have a rather unexpected curiosity here, a lobbying organization whose main concern is that the agencies of government *not* give their clientele special consideration. If one were to make the conventional democratizing assumptions and were to take the evidence at face value, one would have to note the remarkable self-abnegation on the part of small businessmen. Not only are they not interested in special purpose legislation to improve their situation, they have gone out of their way to form an "organizational weapon" to make sure they do not get special consideration. Alternatively, and probably more realistically, one should *not* take the appearances at face value.

As noted earlier, the NFIB is different. It does not, however, provide much of an alternative to the concerned small businessman. Zeigler writes that the NFIB "showed . . . little knowledge of the intricacies of the legislation [setting up the Small Business Administration] by first demanding that credit sources for small business must be expanded and then by supporting legislation which would restrict these sources." They were also concerned that the Small Business Administration "be free of control by the Department of Commerce, yet remained unaware that the House bill which it supported was written by Commerce to do just that." Another organization that supported the creation of the new agency was the American Association of Small Business. Zeigler describes their understanding of the issues as "equally vague."

At one point the small business committees of the House and Senate attempted to generate external support from the small business organizations. Zeigler says that the NFIB "was not regarded . . . as being of value for the pursuit of specific legislation." Summing it up, a member of the Senate Small Business Committee stated that "the real possibilities for small business lie in the trade associations not specifically small business groups. We get 100 boosts from trade associations for every one from small business groups."[12]

If one were not aware of these matters, if one did take the organization's claims at face value, and if one did assume a general business conservatism, it would be easy to assume that the NFIB was both representative and somehow effective. Acceptance of that position would come even easier if one were convinced of the adequacy of the pluralist world view. A political scientist, for example, has described the NFIB as ". . . one of the most vigorous spokesmen for the interest of small businessmen."[13]

The NFIB, the largest of the organizations under discussion and the one with the most distinctive political line, is different in another respect. It does have a link to the membership in the form of a regular survey called the *Mandate.* Members have an opportunity to respond to a set of questions affecting their interests and these results, presumably, then provide the basis for legislative lobbying. Zeigler estimates that the response rate is something less than one in five. It is possible, of course, that the low rate of response is a function of an inflated estimate of the number of members in the association.

The quality and uses of the survey are open to doubts on other grounds. Zeigler points out that the members have no control over what questions are to be asked. Complex questions have to be reduced to a "few explanatory sentences." Some of the descriptions of the options would tend to force results consonant with the views of the association's leaders. On one occasion, also, the legislative representative gave testimony in support of a bill before the *Mandate* results had come in, this on the assumption that "the Federation will in all probability be committed" to the measure.

The results of their poll are sent off to the members of the House and Senate as well as to the Small Business Administration. The recipients send letters of acknowledgment and these are duly printed in subsequent issues of the *Mandate* thereby providing unambiguous evidence of the close linkage between the federation and the lawmakers. Senator Warren Magnuson wrote to say that he would consult their poll "as the various issues listed come before the Senate for action." Senator Wallace Bennett said: "This information is helpful to me and I appreciate your courtesy in providing it." And Senator Roman L. Hruska wrote: "Certainly do appreciate having this information in my file for ready reference."

On occasion there has been serious conflict in the opinions of small businessmen as reported by the various organizations representing them. The NFIB, for example, claimed that 90 percent of small businessmen were opposed to the basing point system of pricing while the NSBMA claimed overwhelming support for that arrangement.[14]

The public utterances of these small business organizations may best be described as "conservative." There is nowhere any suggestion of the liberalism indicated in the surveys reviewed in chapter 2. It seems unlikely that the organizations could systematically miss the liberal majority in the small business ranks; it seems unlikely, in short, that selection could explain the outlooks of the organizations. On the whole it seems best to discard the persistent democratic assumption and simply to assume that these associations are not representing the "underlying" clientele at all. Although this might be disturbing to some, it is useful, nevertheless, to recognize the reality of the matter. If one thinks of Robert Michels and the Iron Law of Oligarchy, the recognition may come somewhat easier; at least, one may recognize that there is some theoretical justification for acceptance. Unlike the Michels' discussion where, in some measure at least, the development was unplanned, these organizations were never intended to be democratic. Unlike German Social Democracy, there were no formal provisions made to assure at least the appearance of member control. So, rather than focusing on mechanisms of inadvertence, in this case one would be better advised to focus on the original plan or calculation.

The discussion thus far has been concerned largely with the negative task of showing how these organizations do not perform according to the model provided by the theory of classical pluralism. The business organizations in question were not spontaneous emanations from the grass roots. That was not true of their origins nor is it true of their persistence since their continued existence depends on a large staff of commissioned salesmen. There is very little evidence to show that the top levels of the organizations represent, follow, or are in any way sensitive to the wishes and desires of the membership. And finally, the actual behavior of these organizations can scarcely be said to be consonant with the interests of the underlying membership. As Zeigler puts it, "We have a situation wherein the small business groups do not support, in fact oppose, special legislation for small business; do not concern themselves with the presentation of issues of interest primarily to small business; and yet claim credit for achieving the special recognition the small business has received."[15]

If small business organizations do not perform at all in the way the pluralists anticipate what alternative account proves more appropriate to describe their actual operations?

The three-tiered formation with influence passing from the bottom upward, as in the classical pluralist framework, is clearly inappropriate as applied to these associations. A more adequate image would drastically restrict the role of the lowest level, of the clientele. They are involved through the efforts of the sales force and they make a financial contribution but otherwise their influence is negligible. Other agencies present in this more realistic view

of the "political process" are major corporations, their own lobbying or trade associations, and the federal government. The small
business organizations might be called "outliers." They are
not directly controlled by the major corporations; they lie just
outside their direct lines of control. The major activity of these
outlying associations, some of them, is the working out of linkages
or alliances with the major corporations or with their directly
controlled agencies. Rather than thinking in terms of representative agencies, it is more appropriate to think of these organizations
as themselves being small businesses. Their owners, one might say,
are in the voluntary association business. In effect, they are
merchandizers of services, the services in this case being political
support, endorsements, and lobbying.

One of the difficulties with legislative lobbying is that some
efforts are highly predictable and hence unimpressive as far as
their impact on "the political process." It is to be expected that
trade unions will testify on labor legislation, bankers on banking
legislation, manufacturers on laws affecting manufacturing, and so
on. A key feature of the lobbying effort is either to create a larger
coalition or, at least, to create the appearance of such an alliance.
To do this, one can arrange tradeoffs with other lobbying agencies: you favor my bill and I'll favor yours. The lobbyist may be
aided by the presence of organizations actively seeking out clients
for willing to pay for these testimonial services.

In 1950, Zeigler reports, major steel companies were attempting
to legalize the basing point system of prices. Under this arrangement with the "base point" being Pittsburgh, all steel sales were
treated as if they in fact originated in that city. It allowed the steel
companies to add on enormous sums of fictitious transport
charges. Steel made and sold in Birmingham, Alabama, would be
treated as if it were made and shipped from Pittsburgh with the
steel companies pocketing the nonexistent costs of transporting
the goods between the two cities. Testifying in favor of this
legislation was DeWitt Emery of the National Small Business Men's
Association. He maintained that the legislation was imperative for
small business survival. United States Steel and Republic Steel,
leaders in the struggle for this legislation, were contributors to
Emery's Small Business Economic Foundation.[16]

Fred Virkus, Chairman of CASBO, sent out a letter to the presidents of large corporations in which he explained the advantage of using their services. It read, in part:

> We were called in on the provisions of the . . . Taft-Hartley Bill, and we believe we were effective in the passage. . . . These are merely illustrations of legislation affecting our overall economy in which we have taken an interest, and in which big business, as such, cannot come out into the open for obvious reasons. . . . Big business should be as keenly interested in consolidating the efforts of its smaller partner . . . as we are to bring this about, and we hope that we may have your cooperation.[17]

In this case the "cooperation" requested was the payment of printing costs for literature.

In another instance, the Association of American Railroads wished to have support for the Reed-Bulwinkle Act which removed railroads from some restrictions of the Sherman Act, notably with respect to rate making agreements. Virkus's assistance in this case was linked with another kind of support. His letter read as follows:

> Your suggestion that a large company might be willing to pay the membership dues of its customers is a good one, and we would prefer it that way rather than have a large concern contribute $1,000. Some of the larger companies make their officers and branch managers members.[18]

NSBMA and CASBO both opposed legislation that would provide government loans for small business. Such activity would provide competition for banks and, not unexpectedly, they were opposed to the legislation. The American Bankers Association, Zeigler reports, made extensive use of the NSBMA and CASBO resolutions as "proof" that small business itself did not want this government aid. Virkus also endorsed candidates for public office.

Linked to this salesmanlike effort is a wider ideological task. In the case of CASBO and NSBMA, a major aim is to submerge the distinction between big and small business. Again in opposition to a standard claim, the task of these organizations is to prevent the aggregation of an interest group; these are organizations that stand in the way of the realization of an interest. The NFIB case, once again, is somewhat different. While they do speak of a separate small business interest, their organization appears to be independent of the large corporations and its directions tend to be those of the owner-oligarchs.

It would be a mistake to see these organizations as simply "fronts" for big business, as if they were directly owned and operated by the major corporations. Rather they are the creations of the entrepreneurs who saw the opportunities in an exchange of services and made use of them. The organizations were not created by big business; it is not as if they were direct "transmission belts" owned and operated by the giant firms. For the latter there is some advantage to be gained by the fact of their independence. The outcome, again recognizing the difference in the case of NFIB, is much the same as if they were the direct agents of the giants. The organizations helpfully offer their services, and the giants are more than willing to be of assistance in exchange for these services.

The usual pluralist account, to recapitulate, sees associations as representing their normal clientele. In these instances, however, they prove to be neglectful of their own clientele and instead endorse the programs of other groups. Rather than accepting the outlines of received formulations it seems more appropriate to see these organizations as businesses, owned and operated by their founders or their successors. These businesses, like any other, provide income for their owners and make possible a way of life.

The organizations have an ideological impact in another way: they aid in the creation of, or rather, in the sustenance of, the belief that small businessmen are arch conservatives. When one's knowledge of small business outlooks comes largely through the pronouncements of such organizations, a distorted understanding of those outlooks is a highly probable result. Many observers engage in what might be called ad hoc democratizing, that is to say, they read in an assumption of democratic process when discussing organizational behavior (this occurs despite their knowledge of and occasional reference to the work of Robert Michels). If one makes such an assumption, it is that much easier to take organizational pronouncements as indicative of membership sentiments.

By so misprepresenting a segment of public opinion, these organizations (and the intellectual commentators who accept their pretensions) again contribute to the submergence of an interest. If it were recognized that the small businessmen share the same outlooks as blue-collar workers and the lower middle classes, it would be possible to make appeals to them and form coalitions with them. Instead, basing policy on misrepresentations, liberals and leftists denounce them, attempt to isolate them, and try to limit their influence.

It would be extremely difficult for a small businessman to organize an alternative, more representative association. He works long hours; he cannot get away from the shop at convenient meeting times; he does not have much money to support associational efforts. Many other groups "naturally" congregate in the course of their everyday activities. Workers come together in factories, employees come together in offices, but small businessmen work in relative isolation from their occupational peers. Territorially scattered and tied to the shop, it is difficult for them to even come together, let alone work together long enough to allow the development of a program and an effective plan of action. The relatively low educational levels found among small businessmen must also be a hindrance as opposed to the wide experience of the upper middle classes and the well-educated white-collar workers. With the possible exception of the farmers, who suffer many of the same difficulties as small businessmen, they are about the most difficult group to organize in the entire population.[19]

While pluralists make an assumption of the ease of organization or aggregation, conditions in the real world pose enormous difficulties. Another implicit assumption, at least in the more classical versions of pluralism, is the relative equality of organizational resources. But it is easy to see that the sheer facts of occuaptional life give rise to significant differences between groups, some having it easy, some not so easy.

One might raise the question as to why things operate this way. If the small businessmen are welfare state liberals as indicated in chapter 2 why do they continue to support organizations that are diametrically opposed to their viewpoints. One possibility is that we are talking about different groups. The refusal to define "small" means that many middle-sized businesses may be among the clientele of these organizations. The really small businesses, those without any employees, may not be present at all.

Another possibility is that the small businessmen do behave as expected; that is, they leave the organization. As was seen with respect to the largest of these, the National Federation of Independent Business, yearly turnover is approximately 90 percent. It is possible that many members are brought in through the efforts of the sales staff but then, in the course of their first year, find the "outputs" rather disappointing. And they simply do not renew their membership. In the meantime, the sales department recruits new members to replace the old ones who have defected. Given the rapid turnover in the field of small business, it is always possible for them to find new, not yet disenchanted, members.

It is not surprising, given these difficulties, that small business organizations tend to be the most oligarchic and least responsive of any trade or professional organizations in existence. Given the dispersion and given the difficulties of congregation, it is difficult to have any other result but self-appointed and self-perpetuating oligarchs "speaking for" a voiceless clientele.

Not all small business organizations follow this pattern. The most striking contrasting instance discussed by Zeigler is the Smaller Business Association of New England. Its proposals are concrete, detailed, and workable; its legislative liaison work appears to have been very effective. Key to its "difference" is the fact that it has fewer members than the other organizations discussed here. It is also a membership organization characterized by frequent interaction of the participants. It also appears to be, as is suggested already in the name, an organization of middle level independents rather than small ones. This means they would not have the same extreme difficulties faced by small businessmen. These members would be able to "get away from" the shop, would have financial resources, would have technical expertise, and so on. They would not be facing an all-powerful owner-oligarch with aims and interests different from those of the clientele.[20]

Still another variety of experience is to be seen in the experience of a trade association. In 1931, California passed the first of the so-called fair trade laws. It exempted a seller of a brand product from state antitrust laws where he had bound a retailer to sell at an established price. The law was ineffective because it did not bind nonsignators so in 1933 a "nonsigner's clause" was added which bound all sellers on the basis of the contract between the manufacturer and any single retailer. This law resulted from the efforts of the National Association of Retail Druggists.

This law was imitated in forty other states and was passed with "breakneck speed." The development has been described as follows:

> There is no record of hearings having been held in 40 states . . . the California law was supposed to contain a provision authorizing a producer to require "any dealer" to maintain a stipulated price. The text enacted, however, was garbled. Instead of "any dealer," it read "in delivery," so that the authorization made no sense. The care with which the laws were considered is indicated by the fact that this version was passed by the House and the Senate and signed by the governor, not only in California, but also in Arizona, Iowa, Louisiana, New Jersey, New York, Pennsylvania, and Tennessee. The N.A.R.D. held the hoop and cracked the whip. The legislators and the executives obediently jumped.

One might describe this as instant legislation.

The organization blacklisted products of manufacturers who refused to cooperate. When Pepsodent refused to sign contracts, it is reported, their product "went under the counter in practically every California drug store." A few months later, they agreed to cooperate and came back above counter.[21]

Some organizations, in short, do operate along the lines of pluralist theory. Some are internally democratic (although that in any case is going to be a matter of degree, of more or less). Some are effective in representing their members' interests. The major point is that there is a diversity of experience. Some associations follow that model and some do not. There is a need for a more empirical orientation with respect to the actual behavior of voluntary associations. It will not do to simply impose the ever-ready framework on all voluntary associational experience. One cannot, in short, simply point to the activities of voluntary associations and declare that their sheer existence is proof of a flourishing pluralism. And the parallel need, going along with the need for closer empirical work, is a need for sensitivity to and development of alternative theoretical models to describe what is in fact happening.

NOTES

1. Harmon Zeigler, *The Politics of Small Business* (Washington, D.C. Public Affairs Press, 1961).

2. Ibid., pp. 17-18.

3. Zeigler mentions other organizations, the Association of American Railroads, the National Association of Manufacturers, and the Chamber of Commerce, as having been "directly encouraged by the government in their organizational attempts" (p. 19). One of the organizations to be discussed, the National Small Business Men's Association, was organized just prior to the conference in 1937. Another organization, the Conference of American Small Business Organizations, was an offshoot of this one. The Senate Small Business Committee wished to see some coordination of these diverse small business groups and suggested to Fred Virkus, Chairman of the Illinois Division of NSBMA, that he form them into a single unit to work closely with the Committee. He left NSBMA and formed CASBO. Virkus and CASBO went on to oppose "most of the Committees' legislative proposals and eventually advocated the abolition of the Senate Committee" (Zeigler, pp. 89-90). The coordination effort failed. The attempt at co-optation also failed.

4. Ibid., p. 24. Emery died in 1955 and the organization floundered a while until a new executive director was named. Without consulting the members, the new director reversed many of Emery's policies.

5. Ibid., p. 26.

6. Ibid., pp. 32-33.

7. Ibid., pp. 22-24.

8. Ibid., p. 74.

9. Ibid., pp. 54, 57.

10. Ibid., p. 48. Some of their literature is rather fanciful. One publication explains "why it is vital that you cooperate in this Federation survey." It quotes a Rep. Ray. J. Madden of Indiana who said that "forty-one years ago Lenin stated the United States would crumble to Communism from within, except for ONE obstacle to U.S. Communism. This was the number of small businesses existing at that time. Small business with rights to fair play, Lenin saw as the strength of America." The Federation writer went on to explain that "through this survey Small Business teams up with Congress to

strengthen our Country against Communism." From a NFIB Mandate of the early sixties (no date).

11. Ibid., pp. 106, 42.

12. Ibid. The quotations in the above two paragraphs come from pages 106, 112, 101, and 113, respectively. See also page 132.

13. John H. Bunzel, *The American Small Businessman* (New York: Knopf, 1962), p. 68.

14. Zeigler, op. cit., pp. 28-32. The letters from the Senators are reproduced in "Action through Your Mandate Votes" (no date), a federation publication.

Possibly the all-time tendentiousness prize goes to a question in a study done for Quality Brands Associates of America. It reads: "If a manufacturer is forced to reduce his own prices . . . to avoid losing the business of discounters . . . and so decides to use . . . in making his trademarked products . . . fewer and less skilled employees . . . at cheaper pay rates . . . and decides to use lower and lower grades . . . of inferior material . . . do you believe that homemakers who buy that downgraded product get less . . . or more . . . in value . . . for what they pay?" Amazingly, 12,349 persons or 93.7 percent of those with opinions thought they would get less. From John W. Anderson, the president of Quality Brands Associates, "Outlaw Trade Tickery Now! Or See Producers and Consumers Made Hopeless Slaves of Mass Monopolists!" (Gary, Indiana: The Anderson Company, 1963).

15. Zeigler, op. cit., p. 43. Zeigler shows that small business actually lost through this "special recognition." The formation of the Small Business Administration was followed by a reduction in the volume and amount of government loans to small business and by a reduction in the small business share of defense contracts. See pages 120-130.

16. Ibid., p. 75.

17. Ibid., p. 76. After Virkus's death, CASBO was led by Fred Hartley, the co-author of the Taft-Hartley Law.

18. Loc. Cit.

19. For an account of the American Farm Bureau Federation and its activities, one that closely parallels this discussion of small business organizations, see Robert Sherrill, "Harvest of Scandal," The Nation 205 (November 13, 1967), pp. 496-500.

20. Zeigler, op. cit., pp. 56-57.

21. Clair Wilcox, *Public Policies Toward Business* (4th ed.; Homewood, Ill.: Richard D. Irwin, 1971), pp. 701-702.

CHAPTER 8

THEORIES AND REALITIES

The procedure adopted in this work was outlined some years ago by C. Wright Mills. Referring to the intellectual "craftsman," he said that such persons did not usually "make up one big design for one big empirical study." Rather their policy would be:

> ... to allow and to invite a continual shuttle between macroscopic conceptions and detailed expositions. He does this by designing his work as a series of smaller-scale empirical studies (which may of course include microscopic and statistical work), each of which seems to be pivotal to some part or another of the solution he is elaborating. That solution is confirmed, modified, or refuted, according to the results of these empirical studies.[1]

Having done the smaller-scale studies, we may now return to the macroscopic conceptions outlined briefly in the opening chapter. Those three orientations are: the revisionist or "centrist" theory, the mass society view, and pluralism. In this chapter we will, as economically as possible, review the results of this research. A second task will be to discuss once again the positive alternative outlined in chapter 1, the "social-bases" or "group-bases" position. The aim here is to indicate the ways in which this view provides a more adequate "fit" with current realities than do the rejected alternatives. And finally, another obvious task, one that has been touched on in passing in the previous chapters, is to provide some explanation for the peculiarities of the intellectual accomplishments criticized here. How have they managed to persist for so long in an age which, presumably at least, is surfeited with empirical studies?

The first of the theories outlined was the "centrist" position of the contemporary social sciences. This viewpoint derives from revisionist Marxism, in particular from the work of Eduard Bernstein. The key elements of the position are the claims that the lower middle classes—both the "independent" and salaried components—will be anxious about their social position and will be opposed to the concerns and interests of manual workers. They will, so it is said, cling desperately to their "middle class" position and, the ultimate "threatening" claim in the centrist repertory, they will be latently or manifestly reactionary, restorationist, and fascist in their politics.

There is a clear lesson of a need for restraint in this line of theorizing. It would be an obvious disaster were one to aggravate the condition of these lower middle classes or in any way contribute to the unleashing of their destructive potential. And so, the lesson, where one is indicated, is to remain quiet; it is a counsel of nonintervention.

But the alarm and the counsel of restraint depend on the original diagnosis, on the initial claims that these groups do feel threatened, that they fear "proletarianization," and that they see "restorationist" politics as the solution to their problem. Because these are the "building block" assumptions of the whole theory and the basis for the accompanying politics, if the diagnosis were wrong or inaccurate on these points, the entire structure would have to be reconsidered. It might be that none of its claims and prescriptions were valid, or alternatively, that only parts of the general structure were invalid and in need of reconstruction.

Evidence with respect to the situation and outlooks of independent businessmen was reviewed in chapter 2. For all practical purposes this is the first systematic review of the national evidence on this question. That review finds the major claims in the area to be unsupported. Some formulations have treated all (or almost all) independents as economically marginal, hence subject to the predicted strain and given to the predicted reactions. An examination of the first of these points showed the initial assumption to be questionable. The independents differed only slightly in their earnings pattern from salaried white-collar groups. The most that one could say for the marginality thesis is that a slightly larger percentage of independents fell into the low income categories than was true with the new middle class groups.

The Lipset variant portrays all independents, the small and the large, those of modest means and those of some affluence, as being rightist in their propensities. There are somewhat different bases for their choices of such politics, but, regardless of the origins, the end result is the same. An exploration of this possibility, contrasting all independents with the various salaried middle class groups, found this claim to be unsupported. The best overall judgment is that there were no clear differences between old and new middle classes, this in response to questions on party identifications, candidate choices, and political issues.

The principal tendency of the business conservatism claim was then tested, that being the focus on the small independents. Because it has been claimed that the more affluent independents and the well-off salaried employees (managers, professionals) are more moderate than the reactionary small businessmen, comparisons were made with those two groups. These claims were also found to be unsupported. In this case, there were substantial differences in opposition to the claims of the received hypothesis. Small businessmen were more likely to be Democratic in identification and in party choice than the other groups; they were more likely to take liberal positions on the economic liberalism issues. Rather than a monolithic identification with the middle class, a sizable majority of the marginal independents identified with the working class.

This all adds up to the conclusion that the small businessmen are not the threat to decent, humane, progressive values that nervous speculative theorists have claimed. Put positively, it means that they are very much like blue-collar workers in their orientations and outlooks, in their class identifications, in their support for economic liberalism measures, and in their support for the most liberal of the available political options. Rather than being a threat, they turn out to be supporters of many of the things championed by "centrist" liberals.

It was not possible to make any detailed inquiry into the

reasons for this dominant liberalism among the small businessmen. It does seem likely, however, that they have come out of working-class ranks and have working-class relatives and friends, as well as working-class customers. When conditions for blue-collar workers in the neighborhood are good—when there is full employment, overtime, and/or favorable strike settlements—conditions will also be good for the local proprietors. Given such circumstances, it would be unthinkable for a small owner to "put distance" between himself and others in his milieu, or for him to think of himself as set apart, as "middle class," and as needing to maintain some visible signs of his own distinction.

The "business conservatism" claim, in short, at least as far as this evidence goes, is a myth, one with very serious "restraining" implications. This demand for restraint, it would appear, has no realistic basis.

Centrist theorizing offers a parallel claim about lower middle class white-collar workers. They too, like the independents, are being squeezed. They suffer "proletarianization," loss of distinctiveness vis-a-vis the blue-collar ranks, and they too prove susceptible to fascist appeals. Again, as with the independents, one may raise the simple question as to whether or not the claim is accurate.

A review of relevant evidence showed the main lines of the argument to be unsupported. Significant percentages of those in the major white-collar categories chose the label "working class" when asked about their class identification. The claim that lower white-collar workers would avoid such an identification, that they would strongly resist any "proletarianization," simply does not hold true for this sizable minority. The line of theorizing which purports to describe *the* lower middle class, in other words, proves woefully inadequate as a beginning fundamental assumption.

The salaried "lower middle class," the category of white-collar employees with relatively low incomes, contains people with very different kinds of careers. Some of them are simply at the first point in what is basically an upper middle class career. They come from upper middle class families, they have learned the values of that rank, they received a "good" education, and they have begun careers in the corporate hierarchies. A key feature of such careers is that one begins at a lower level in the hierarchy and from there one moves upward following a planned succession of jobs. A "normal" or routine aspect of the upper middle class career is that it involves a period during which one is "temporarily" lower middle class. In the same occupational and income categories one will find persons who are, essentially, "permanents" in the lower middle class. There are also some "late additions" to the lower middle class. This refers to semiskilled blue-collar workers who, if lucky, obtain routine clerical jobs when they are no longer able to work at the machines. When one focuses on the marginal middle classes taking income as the defining characteristic, one will be mixing two sharply divergent kinds of experience. The characteristics of a well-educated group from upper middle class backgrounds are thereby "averaged" with a poorly educated group from working-class and farm backgrounds.

Given the differences in background and future careers, it is not all that surprising that the former tend to be Republican in party choice, conservative in values, and are middle class identifiers. And the latter groups prove to be Democratic, liberal on the issues, and to have working-class identifications. This is the "lower middle class" that is genuinely marginal, that is not "going places," and that will always be earning less than the skilled blue-collar workers. They do not show a fetishistic attachment to "middle class" attitudes and life-styles, and they do not show monolithic or even majoritarian rightist sentiments. And, the obverse of the coin, that part of the lower middle class which is conservative and which does identify with the middle class is not exactly "marginal." None of the major component segments of the lower middle class, in other words, are adequately described by the received theory.

Another difficulty with the received analysis is its indifference to other cross-cutting factors. An examination of attitudes contrasting those of the white Protestants with the other members of the middle class showed some very sizable differences. These are greater, on the whole, than the differences between the upper and lower middle class segments. The analysis that focuses exclusively on the class dimension is once again averaging very diverse experience, the Protestant segment being strongly Republican and the others very strongly Democratic.

These findings would come as a surprise were one armed solely with this received line of theorizing. From another perspective, the results provide no surprise at all. If one recognizes the differences in background and training and the differences in subsequent careers, the correspondence of the current outlooks and attitudes with those differing experiences is more or less to be expected. Like the independents discussed earlier, the low income white-collar worker who comes from a working-class background, who still lives in a working-class neighborhood, and has working-class relatives and friends is not likely to aspire to membership in some far distant community nor is he likely to reject the persons, values, or life-styles within his own community. Even if he were so motivated (which in itself would take a very unusual set of determinants), to do so would be to court personal disaster. On the whole, it seems highly unlikely that any significant number of such persons would be so motivated: few people voluntarily choose to reject family, friends, or neighbors and few choose personal isolation.

This adds up to saying that the image of a tense, angry, status-ridden lower middle class is a mistaken one. It also means that the notion of the "dangerous" or proto-fascistic character of this class is also open to some considerable doubt. The evidence reviewed here shows them as having no special propensity for two rightist candidates, Goldwater and Wallace. In terms of their values, the economically marginal members of the middle class prove to be economic liberals and in favor of general welfare state measures. They do not, in short, show rightist propensities.

The further implication is that the restraining character of this line of theorizing is mistaken. Rather than viewing this "class" as a dangerous, ominous, and threatening segment of the population, as a segment that is inimical to humane values, it is—if one subscribes to those values—useful to see them as a potential part of that coalition of forces. Rather than pointlessly and erroneously denouncing them as not-yet-fully-developed fascists, it might be worthwhile to listen to them and work with them. Rather than cordoning-off, isolating, and villifying a large segment of the population, it might be of some use to speak with them, to work out programs of joint interest and mutual benefit, in short, to form a coalition with them.

The other "threatening" segment within the United States, in the views of the "centrist" theorists, is the white working class. An examination of the attitudes of the white workers in regard to questions of tolerance and the rights of blacks revealed a complex pattern. In its main outline, however, the pattern did not support the commonplace claims about white workers. The responses to questions asking about the major controversies of the day, those that presumably at least were at the heart of the black-white struggle, jobs, housing, and equality in public facilities, showed that outside the South there were no significant differences. For three-quarters of the American population, those in the East, Midwest, Mountain, and Pacific states, the notion of middle class or upper middle class virtue on the one hand and working-class viciousness on the other was not supported.

Some limited class differences were revealed in the South, especially in response to questions about more personal contacts. That again does not mean a night-and-day contrast; the differences might be better summarized with "more or less" instead of the categoric assertion.

This review of the evidence showed also that the levels of intolerance were not constant. The best available studies of the subject indicate a steady improvement of the outlooks—in all major segments of the population, including the white working class. Despite the alarmist claims about a "backlash" and "growing" antagonisms, that is not indicated in the available data. There are instances in which the levels of tolerance or support for equalitarian moves have declined but the overall tendency has been positive. It would be a mistake to equate opposition to a given spokesman or to a given line of campaigning with opposition to the general principle involved. Some tactics repelled various segments of the population but without turning them around on the issue.[2] There is, in summary, no support for the notion of a substantial, clearcut, across-the-board retreat on civil rights.

The research presented here can only provide some very limited clues as to the sources of intolerance. Some of the current intolerance is clearly linked to the special regional inheritance. Some of it may be the residue of past religious teaching. Some of it may be a handed-down product of highly inflammatory newspaper content in times past. It would be a mistake to place a near-exclusive emphasis on training or conditions inherent to the class situation, that is, to the exclusion of such "outside" impacts. The trend in the attitudes might well be the result of changes in the lessons offered by organized religion and by the mass media. If the determining factors were "exogenous," that too would add up to an optimistic lesson, one involving liberation as opposed to the lesson of restraint.

A similar lesson is to be learned from the analysis of the attitudes toward "tough" versus more moderate policy options in the Korean and Viet Nam wars. The received image from the original discussion of working-class authoritarianism has been reinforced by the attacks of a few thousand blue-collar workers on peace demonstrators in the Wall Street area in May 1970. The present review of national evidence has shown that enthusiasm for the tough option was lowest among the blue-collar workers both in 1952 and in 1964. The "toughs" were white, Protestant, upper middle class, highly educated persons who were well-read, that is, who followed newspapers and magazines closely. The typical hawk in 1952 and 1964 had just the opposite traits of television's famed prototypical worker, Archie Bunker. At a later point, in 1968, there was very little difference between the white collars and the blue collars in the preferences: majorities of both favored the cease fire option or the pullout. This convergence in outlooks resulted from a decline in the bellicosity of the upper middle class. They, in short, "came around" to the moderate blue-collar position.

The findings in the foreign policy chapter also have some relevance for the mass society theory. A key assumption in this view is the belief that *the masses* are highly individualized, isolated, anxious, and lacking in political capacity. Without traditional communal supports, the individuals in this "mass" are highly vulnerable to the suasions of the interested demagogue or to the efforts of manipulative elites. The key vehicle for this manipulation is the mass media.

In this connection it is interesting to note that the print media, newspapers and magazines, were strongly supportive of the Viet Nam War effort in 1964 and that very strong support for that effort was found among the readers. By 1968 most of the major magazines and many of the leading newspapers had changed position on the war. The attentive audience had also changed position and, as was previously indicated, they were then little different from the remainder of the population in their expressed policy preferences. Both the 1964 position and the changed 1968 position would appear to be the results of media efforts.[3] The victims in both instances were not the isolated and helpless individuals lost in the mass but rather were the well-placed, the well-integrated, and, presumably, highly competent members of the upper middle class.[4]

This would indicate that the mass society theory does have some viability. The location of the thrust and the emphases, however, need reconsideration. Those most influenced by the media, a first difficulty, ironically prove to be the very groups that are most vocal in ascribing vulnerability to others in the society. A second difficulty is the failure to recognize the extent of interpersonal integration within almost all segments of society. This is to argue that the portrait of isolation, helplessness, and anxiety is a read-in. A third problem involves the assumption that the mass media are followed by "the masses." The basic generalization to be derived from media studies in the United States and elsewhere is that attention to print media varies direction with class level. The lower status, less-well-off groups, those with limited education, simply do not make contact with the major mass magazines. As for the newspapers, attention appears to be rather limited and rather selective, the focus being largely on local news and entertainment as opposed to the "persuasive communication" found on editorial pages and in the formulation of national and world news.

A fourth difficulty with this line of theorizing stems from the sweeping assumption of indeterminateness. Aside from the anxiety-producing isolation and the link to the manipulator, there are, presumably, no other significant forces in the life of the "mass man." There are no personal ties that count. There are no interests or concerns of sufficient importance to outweigh the blandishments of the manipulator. There is no defense sufficient to ward off the threat. In some formulations the mass man is portrayed as incapable of even recognizing a threat to his interests or autonomy.

It is in this connection that we may review the second of the chapters dealing with the manipulative attempt, this being the work of the electoral technocrats. Despite the claim that they are shrewd and capable manipulators, we have seen that the efforts of one such group were detrimental to the clients, in 1968 and in 1970. With the materials at hand it is not possible to say *how* it happened, that is, what was going on in the minds of the voters. Nevertheless, the results themselves do make it clear that people moved away from the candidates rather than toward them. This indicates a peculiarly inept "expert" performance.

It would be a mistake to conclude from this discussion that there is no media influence or no cause for concern. The evidence reported in chapter 5 suggested a considerable influence. The heart of the critique involves two questions: Where is the influence felt? and, How much influence? The conventional formulations being challenged here have asserted an impact where there is none or have asserted a "positive" result where the result was, in fact, "negative." As for the location of impact, the problem is with the steady focus on the movement of "the masses"; whereas, in the foreign policy questions reviewed here, it appears to have been the non-masses who were moved.

These chapters, to be sure, present only two case studies. There can be no assurance that these instances are typical of the entire universe of manipulative attempts. The next cases to be studied might provide complete support for the outlines of the theory. The lesson, however, is one of a need for a more detailed specification of this line of theorizing—to indicate where it is applicable in its pure form and where modification of the focus and the emphases are necessary. A continued recitation of the school verities will not suffice.

If the basic claims of the theory rest on an unsound base, then the consequent alarm is unwarranted as is also the recommendation of restraint. Perhaps the masses are more reliable than previously thought. And maybe the educated and responsible upper middle classes are not quite so reliable (or autonomous) as previously believed.

The third of the theories considered here, pluralism, holds that "power" has been widely distributed within the society. There is no one center of power since every group has some resources it may use in the competitive struggle. The key means in such contention is the organizational weapon, the voluntary organization. These voluntary organizations are portrayed as emanations from the grass roots, as growing out of the felt demands of the underlying populace. They not only emanate from the grass roots, they are also internally democratic: they represent their memberships.

The discussion of pluralism must be even more limited than that of the mass society theory: what we have here is again an instance or case. While case studies cannot provide the basis for a rejection of a position in its entirety, they can provide a challenge to key assumptions. If in some cases things do not work out as they are supposed to, one must then specify what differentiates those cases from the others where things do work as claimed. The case studies also invite a specification of frequencies—what proportion of the practice is in accord with the claims of the theory?

The business organizations discussed here have beginnings which do not accord with the outlines of the pluralist theory. They made their first appearance as by-products of a presidential public relations effort. They were set up by entrepreneurs and run essentially as private businesses. Little or no provision was made for grass roots influence. In fact, the zeal of the members was so limited that large sales organizations have been necessary to keep the operations going. An examination of some of their legislative lobbying efforts indicated a fair amount of opposition to small business interests rather than service for them.

The dynamics of the arrangement appear to be rather simple. The organizations appear to be in the business of selling or trading legislative services, recommendations, endorsements, testimony, and so forth. The small business link is necessary so as to allow them to say they are speaking "for" some clientele. But the heart of the operation involves "exchanges" with much more affluent clients, many of them usually referred to as big business.

The restraining impact of this theory derives from the related "democratizing" assumption, from the notion that such organizations do in fact "represent" grass roots opinion. Because the pronouncements of these business organizations are consonant with a well-established belief about the arch-conservatism of small businessmen, it is easy to take such claims at face value, as the coin of the realm. A direct inquiry into the subject through the use of surveys in which businessmen, big and small, were asked about the various issues of the day (in chapter 2) showed these claims to be the direct opposite of reality. To the extent that people are taken in by the belief that the organizations "speak for" the underlying clientele, their efforts to mobilize for liberal or left options would be undermined. If they were not immobilized by the apparent size of the conservative opposition, they would be led to avoid discussion with these populations in the belief that businessmen were completely out of reach for such purposes. In doing so one would leave them to any other political direction that chose to pay them some attention.

The three theories discussed contain differing portraits of the majority, of "the masses." The respective critiques offered here may be summarized as follows: The majority are not as closely subject to "class" determinants as has been suggested in Marxist or centrist theorizing. There is much greater latitude for variation within each of the settings discussed and, another way of saying the same thing, there is greater possibility for persistence of subgroup traditions than has been suggested. There is reason to believe that the focus on lower middle class economic stresses and the resultant anxieties is also mistaken.

As for the mass society theory, the emphasis on rootlessness and isolation is probably mistaken as is also the emphasis on the presumed consequence, that is, stress, anxiety, and panic. The condition and the consequence presumably set the stage for the "reaction"—a ready availability for the cynical demagogue, or, in the left critique, a ready availability for the overtures of cynical elites. The critique of this position has noted that most people are "integrated" in one way or another in some community setting, that is, among friends, relatives, neighbors, and co-workers. Most people do not live in a constant condition of anxiety and panic. And people have some resources allowing them to screen out and reject at least some of the manipulative attempts. And finally, some question has been raised as to the abilities of the would-be manipulators. In the cases discussed they do not show the capac-

ities they are said to possess. The relationship between manipulator and manipulated is not as direct, not as ineluctable as has
been claimed. There would appear to be a considerable degree of
autonomy among the masses as well as a fair amount of good
sense. In some instances, the "fool" of the piece appears to be the
would-be manipulator.

The critique of the pluralist theory made here is focused on the
claims made about the role of voluntary associations. In the cases
studied here, the associations were not instrumentalities of the
grass roots. They did not, in other words, provide a power base for
such businessmen. Put another way, "power" was not redistri-
buted as a result of their existence. At best one may say that the
location of power was *misrepresented* as a result of their existence.
It would clearly be a mistake to underestimate the importance of
such "distorted perceptions." It is central to the restraining impact
of this viewpoint.

It is useful to consider, at least in broad outline, a positive
alternative to these portraits of the majority.

At a first element, let us consider the possibility, at least as an
hypothesis, that most people's lives are conducted within the
context of viable, friendly personal relationships. That is to say,
most people are raised within the context of a family, and most
people, no matter how geographically or socially mobile, maintain
contacts with that family. In addition to the family, most people
form interpersonal relationships with friends, co-workers, members of their church, and so forth.

Most attitudes and outlooks are the products of such interpersonal influences. To answer the question of why individuals hold
the views they do, one must explore the original social training
they received and any subsequent reinforcing or transforming
influences. To answer the question of why a group of persons
jointly share a given position, one might have to do a historical
study, going back to the time the view was first adopted. It would
be a mistake to assume that the viewpoints contained within these
primary group contexts are "irrational," the products of supersti-
tion, prejudice, or idle gossip. Much of the content of a group
heritage makes sense to the individuals involved (as well as to
outsiders who are privy to the "group" understandings). That

heritage, in the ordinary case, provides a set of understandings that enable one to get along in the world. Where the ability to "get along" is impeded by some element of the "world view," that element would ordinarily be corrected, reinterpreted, or discarded. This is not to say that there is any great sophistication about the viewpoints being discussed; it is only to say that they constitute a set of working procedures which allow a "reasonable" kind of life.[5]

The group heritage provides a kind of framework for handling the routine events of human existence. There are, however, new events that impinge on the members of any group, events which have not been defined within that framework. The extent of individual or subgroup vulnerability depends in part on the "location" of these new events. Some of them take place at some distance: a foreign minister signs a treaty, a president attends a summit conference, or a senator makes a statement about a labor settlement. The knowledge of these events will ordinarily be known only through the mass media. It is in such situations that the public is most vulnerable: they have no way of checking their media sources. The clearest and least ambiguous instance of media—or news source—influence is where suppression or heavy censorship of information occurs. One cannot respond to the message that is never received. And, should the first step in a series of events be omitted from an account, it is impossible to have an adequate understanding of the second.

Even in such cases, the local primary groups are not entirely helpless. One's interpretations of those distant events will ordinarily be mediated by the preexisting understandings. A key role in grass roots interpretations of things is played by "political experts" within those groups. They may provide the "clear and unambiguous" fact with an interpretation or meaning which is consonant with (or provides no threat to) the subgroup traditions. Such an interpretation or reading of the evidence serves to protect personal and/or group interests. In the process, what appears to be a manipulative threat will be screened out and rejected. The event, offer, or claim that "looks suspicious" will be held at a distance, its impact thereby limited. Some of the defenses are rather commonplace as in the definition of someone as a "fast-talker." That definition, it will be noted, screens out the entire content of that person's message. In some contexts, particularly among the poor and in working-class communities, that definition makes a lot of sense because fast-talking outsiders have, with considerable frequency, done damage to individuals or the community.

Again a note of caution is in order. This is not to say that such defenses are in a high state of perfection. One protects with the means that are available. Possessing little possibility for getting adequate information about the distant event, one can take the easiest, the most economical option, rejection of the entire communication. Or, alternatively, one can accept the judgment of the friend, acquaintance, or political figure who in times past proved reliable and trustworthy. There is an obvious parallel defense, that is, rejection of the once trusted figure on the occasion of betrayal. It seems likely that many of the swings in American electoral history may be explained as the result of such rejections.

Some distant events provide "returns," that is, they yield information allowing a judgment independent of the media or news source contributions on the subject. Some "distant" economic policies might have local effects such as reduced business or enhanced inflation. Wars may involve hundreds of thousands of persons, each of whom is in a position to render an independent account of the otherwise very distant event. Again the primary group influences may prove decisive in determining which of the many possible alternative readings will be accepted. The same fact, continuing inflationary tendencies, for example, might be associated with condemnation of business profiteering or with condemnation of union wage demands–depending on who does the interpreting.

Probably the central features of most peoples' lives, at all times and in all places, are job and home. The immediate problems of "earning a living" would ordinarily outweigh the more distant concerns discussed above in their felt importance. Most lives are spent in the prosaic activities of working, eating, sleeping, and recreation. Much of that life is necessarily occupied with the once again very prosaic questions of money, of "making ends meet." This "fact of life" provides a very central life focus for most people. It is only the rich and the well-born or the well-rewarded intellectual (or the mentally distracted) who are in a position to organize their lives otherwise.

In an age of generally improving living standards, most people will experience real improvements in their living conditions.[6] The average person in the United States can back up that judgment with solid evidence drawn from his or her immediate experience. They live in better housing than they did when growing up. They eat much better than they did in the past. The schools in their communities provide a range of amenities that would have been beyond belief in the schools of thirty and forty years ago. And most people do not work as long or as hard as their parents did. All of these observations are based on direct personal experience. As such, they escape completely the determinations that are supposed to operate in the mass society.

The significance of this point is that, if opposite claims are made, they will be running against rather strongly held judgments. When some intellectuals talk about the alienation of contemporary society, about the stresses of bureaucratization, and about the repressiveness of modern living, such claims are likely to be greeted with incredulity. The argument of "false consciousness" (they do not *know* how bad they have it) is likely to set an even greater distance between the "advanced" intellectuals and the people whose condition they are so solicitously "describing."

It is possible that all groups are experiencing improvement but at different rates, thus giving rise to some *relative* losses of position. As applied to the lower middle class and the white working class, this alternative line of analysis does not appear to be realistic. If there are widespread feelings of relative loss, these feelings do not appear to weigh very heavily in their overall assessment of their condition. And they do not appear to have triggered reactions against groups, such as the blacks, who might be seen as "getting ahead." One alternative reading—one with some empirical support even—would recognize a rather unusual fund of decency and generosity within the general population. They do not wish hard times or misery on anyone. Instead, they support moves to improve the condition of those who, through no fault of their own, are disadvantaged. The central tendencies in alarmist liberalism, the focus on scarcity and on competition, have led observers to overlook these opposite behaviors.[7]

Again, a precaution is in order. The statement is that people on the whole have better housing than did their parents. Or that they are working shorter hours and, on the whole, doing less onerous work. (People used to dig with picks and shovels, whereas nowadays that is done with machines and a few machine operators.) Such statements are not meant to excuse or overlook real current problems. Some housing in the United States, hundreds of thousands of units, is disgraceful when seen in comparison to genuinely advanced countries such as those of Scandinavia. Given the national wealth and the available technology, all dilapidated and slum housing should have disappeared long ago. It goes without saying that the problems of poverty, of urban sprawl, of pollution and mass transit are also inexcusable given the availability of plans and technology that would make possible superior alternatives.

The basic feeling within the general population is one of having achieved a rather desirable condition. That does not imply or suggest some permanent or final state (in the sense suggested by the expression "having arrived"). It is just that the outlook for the future, the direction of one's effort, is likely to be toward building on the achievement rather than, as in apocalyptic leftism, destroying the entire operation and beginning again with new management and new principles. The average person, in searching for or evaluating the options, is likely to prefer those that do not threaten current achievement but will somehow add to it. As indicated, this does not necessarily involve a narrow self-seeking orientation: there is a considerable willingness indicated to see to it that all groups participate in the accomplishment.

One final observation ought to be added in this connection. The general population is highly pragmatic. The concern is to find means that have a high probability of leading to the achievement of one's goals. The drawing of surrealist connections, offering of symbolic gestures and the like, those efforts so much appreciated by the more ethereal intellectuals, earn little more than contempt or bemused curiosity from the general population. The intellectual who condemns the pragmatic or compromise approach in favor of the pure, untrammeled procedure (toward somewhat obscure goals) is likely to be one who, for good defensive reasons, would be held at a considerable distance.

For most members of the citizenry, the choice of a political party and of candidates is another matter rooted in primary group training and allegiances. Most people are trained in a tradition; most people identify with that tradition; their social contacts are such as to reinforce that loyalty; and most people vote accordingly. This procedure too may not be as irrational as it might first appear. The group loyalty may well have some basis in terms of group interests even though that might not be known in all detail to individuals in the group. Such loyalties do change from time to time when there is a serious disparity between the aspirations of group members and "their" party's performance. Again the group heritage does not provide a perfect arrangement or even a high degree of alignment between interests and party. It provides an economical, minimally adequate way of sorting out complex political issues and providing some limited direction to those affairs.

Not all voting, to be sure, is of this traditional variety. When it comes to political parties and candidates, the options available to the average man are very limited. The general public has the choice of voting for one or another of those persons who have been so kind as to offer themselves and their services. Given the costs involved, only the very affluent (or those supported by the very affluent) are in a position to present themselves.[8] The options available to the machinists, the punch press operators, the warehousemen, the sheet metal workers, to their wives and their families, are the choice of one or another of those candidates. The carpenters, the plumbers, electricians, clerks, and comptometer operators are not ordinarily in a position to offer candidates of their own. The initial choices of candidates, in other words, are made for them. The option remaining to them is to choose among those placed before them.

In some cases there might be a real choice, Candidates A and B representing different meaningful positions. In some cases there may be only the appearance of a choice, with the popular candidate offering different policies once he is elected. And in some cases there may not be any attractive candidates, that is to say, ones who offer policies favored by significant segments of the electorate.[9] In this case a vote cast out of a "citizen's sense of duty" may be a random decision, like flipping a coin. In some instances one is voting "traditionally" because there is no serious alternative option. And in some such instances one might find significant quantities of "negative voting," that is, a vote intended to punish an incumbent for either real or sensed betrayal. That may constitute a rational choice, particularly where a Tweedledum-Tweedledee option is presented. With rare exceptions such election results are written up as expressions of the "will of the electorate." The will of the voters, however, had little to do with the original sponsoring of candidates. All the primary allowed was a narrowing down of the field, a choice among the self-selected or sponsored candidates. Where a punishing vote was intended by the voters, rather than seeing such action as a communication, under the aegis of the mass society notions those results come to be counted as further evidence of the unreliability of the masses.

At this point one may well raise the following question: Why the persistent misperception on the part of the intellectuals?

Misperceptions may result from ambiguous cues or they may result from imperfect appreciations on the part of observers. It is also possible, clearly, that both factors may be operating in any given relationship. In the discussions contained in previous chapters, it is the "ambiguous cues" that have been emphasized. Here attention will be given to the condition of the observers.

Many of the problems of perception discussed in this work have their roots in the peculiarly isolated social circumstances of intellectuals and in the defects of the most frequently used procedures within those circles.

Intellectuals, with rare exceptions, live in somewhat isolated circumstances. The large proportion of them come from either upper or upper middle class backgrounds and live within that milieu during their entire lifetimes. Where one can claim to have a "broad background" or to have "traveled widely" or to have a "wide circle of acquaintance," that means little more than extensive contacts within these circles. Even this focus exaggerates the range of personal contact. The upper class in the United States may include some 200,000 nuclear families, and the upper middle class may contain 10 to 20 million families. The range of contact, typically, is restricted to the intellectual circles within those classes, to those in the academic enclaves, to circles of journalists and writers, to those in book publishing or in the foundations. When one talks of a "wide circle of acquaintance," that refers to contacts with such circles in other cities and in other countries. It would be a mistake to exaggerate here either. The contacts of intellectuals in "other cities" are also very restricted. That means New York City, Cambridge, New Haven, Princeton, Berkeley, San Francisco, and possibly a few other minor centers. Seldom does the intellectual based in one of these enclaves have even a remote passing acquaintance with life and conditions in Indianapolis or Houston or Iowa City or Seattle. A knowledge of conditions in Youngstown, in Mansfield, in Akron, or McKeesport is an even greater rarity. This is to say that, as far as personal contact and acquaintance goes, knowledge of the world outside these restricted intellectual circles is very limited.

Because personal knowledge of that "outside world" is non-existent or rare, it follows that these intellectuals must depend on some other means or source to provide themselves with "information" about those distant realities. In great measure the "intellectual authority" for the typical intellectual is another intellectual.

That might provide an adequate "standard" were the intellectuals widely dispersed throughout the society or were they in touch with some source of information providing them with systematic accounts of how things were outside of their immediate purview. But where that is not the case, the "authority" rests on a rather infirm base. In essence what one has is an extended interpersonal network with information being passed around within its confines. "Truth" comes to be that view or judgment which is repeatedly confirmed within the network of trusted associates. The truth in this case has an interpersonal basis (many friends and associates vouching for it) rather than an empirical one. In this respect, speaking that is of the form of the arrangement, the "truth" has exactly the same basis as the truths passed among neighborhood gossips. There are differences, to be sure, in the abilities of the participants, in the quantities of information generated, and in the extent and character of the respective "neighborhoods." One should not, however, be misled by inessentials.

Intellectuals are voracious in their reading. American intellectuals read the *New York Times* for their daily fare, and they read the "leading" intellectual journals for further detail and analysis. The writers for the leading journals, however, in the main happen to be "literary-political" in orientation, that is to say, their major work is in literary fields rather than in social sciences. In fact, as has been mentioned previously, there is within this network what amounts to a "school" position on the latter subject, this involving a compulsive hostility toward any kind of systematic social science research.

The field of attention for this group is limited in another way: their view of the world is rather strikingly New Yorko-centric. The *Times,* perhaps understandably, makes that focus. The overwhelming majority of the writers for the leading intellectual journals live in New York, or more specifically, in Manhattan. Many of those currently living elsewhere came from there originally. These journals are heavily focused on events in "the city," for the reason that they find other locations scarcely worth one's attention. One weekly news magazine, for example, turned down an article on the planned destruction of commuter transportation into the city of Chicago because of its "limited interest." The same tendencies operate in the field of book publishing. A work on the politics of the city of Houston was rejected initially because of its "limited interest." After all, it is only the sixth largest city in the country. For these intellectuals, then, who have themselves determined what shall and what shall not be of interest, "the world" comes to be New York City and its immediate environs. If they know more about Queens and Nassau counties than about Pittsburgh or Philadelphia (or Trenton or even Jersey City), there is no great loss involved because the latter places are of no great importance anyway. One of the most ingenuous arguments put forth in this connection is that the rest of the nation is a mirror image of "the city." Hence if one "understands" ethnic relations in Brooklyn, one understands ethnic relationships no matter where they appear. One might call this the provincialism of the cosmopolitans.

Such delimitations of their field of endeavor mean that their efforts are even more closely akin to those of the neighborhood gossips than would at first appear. Much of their reading material is produced by other persons within their network, many of them friends (or enemies) and neighbors. The refusal to make use of nonliterary sources means that they have cut themselves off from an independent source of evidence about the larger society. It means that they must rely on impressions and guesses, on the same kinds of judgments offered by their trusted fellow intellectuals.

It is not too surprising that one finds within these circles a development which might be called the "cult of sensitivity," a notion that they are graced with special powers of feeling and understanding, powers which surpass those of ordinary people or of their upstart competitors, the "crude" social researchers. One may denigrate the contemporary social sciences as much as one likes: there is much obscurantist language and procedure in the contemporary social sciences which hides rather than reveals. Pointing to someone else's fault, however, says nothing about one's own virtue. It would require very unusual powers (or "sensitivity") to divine the outlooks of blue-collar workers in Canton, Ohio, from the vantage point of one's exclusive neighborhood and life in Manhattan.

This adds up to saying that the literary-political intellectuals have cut themselves off from most of what goes on in their own country. And, compounding the difficulty, they have developed a style of "inquiry" which justifies (to them) the rejection of a major alternative procedure for finding out about this "larger society." It amounts to the creation of a self-encapsulated existence.

Intellectuals do operate differently from other people in one significant respect: they reach "across centuries" to discover their conceptions. The intellectuals themselves customarily count this as one of their most valued and cherished accomplishments. They "know" the past; they "preserve" the "cultural heritage." They rescue the apothegms of intellectuals of previous generations, such as, "Those who do not know the past are destined to repeat it."

There are a number of difficulties involved in this reaching across the centuries. The contemporary intellectuals reach across and make contact with the *intellectuals* of previous eras, this to find out how "life" was then. But if intellectuals of previous eras operated in the same way as the contemporaries, it would mean that they are again picking up information from within self-isolated groups. The knowledge that is thereby "rescued" may have been "problematic" in its own day. If that were true, one would have "rescued" or "preserved" a peculiarly useless bit of information to use as a guide to the present. Unless an independent assessment of the adequacy of the original claims were made, one would be taking the matter on faith.

Such intellectuals prove to be rather disadvantaged. Ordinary people, those not burdened with this peculiar kind of training, are more likely to, in Mills's terms, "get it straight." They would be more likely to see an event fresh, with the "untrained eye," and describe it accordingly. The well-schooled intellectuals, however, impose a framework taken from another context and, as a result, "get it crooked." It should come as no small surprise that the conceptions present within these intellectual circles tend to be rather simple, black-and-white, stereotypic formulations. Although embellished with a characteristic baroque verbiage, that is to say, with a rich and florid covering, the underlying ideas show impoverishment, not enrichment.

With two significant exceptions, the basic world view of the "centrist" liberals involves a denunciation of all major groups in the society. This holds for the poor and excluded, for the white working classes, for the "ethnics," for the lower middle class, and for the "status-seeking" and consumption-oriented upper middle classes. The world view involves a free, untrammeled, across-the-board denunciation. Rarely does one find, in intellectuals' discussions of these groups, any account of human decency, of generosity, of free and spontaneous openness: in these accounts, there are no redeeming features. Here one sees crude stereotyping of the distant and unknown majority.

It is important to note the exceptions. The first of these involves elites and upper classes. Occasionally, when they are not being denounced for their consumer-oriented materialism, the upper middle classes are also included as deserving of favor. This point has been noted in previous discussion, the attribution of virtue and "responsibility" to those at the top of the society and of ignorance, appetitiveness, and irresponsibility to all others. Once again one sees the typical stereotyping, or, to express the point differently, the inability to take a complex view.

The other group exempted from the sweep of the denunciation is the intellectuals themselves. It will come as no great surprise to know that their self-portrait shows them as pillars of virtue, the saviours of all good things, defenders of the faith, the apostles of all decency—the list knows no end.

The correlate of this belief is the firm rule that they, as a group, are beyond criticism. The gravest sin that one can commit is to be anti-intellectual. Many books and learned articles are written on this subject. These are informed with the same stereotypical analysis of those "others" (that is, of everyone else in the society) in the course of which one attempts to discover the "roots" of this seemingly inexplicable behavior. Anti-intellectualism, it is interesting to note, is explained in "subjective" terms, as being totally without foundation in objective reality. An alternative hypothesis, one seldom entertained, is that anti-intellectual manifestations might be a response to the behavior of some intellectuals. It might, conceivably, be a reaction to the gross and insulting performances of intellectuals themselves.

There is a peculiar irony here. A group of intellectuals make a living by purveying a line, one that involves mass or collective slander. In their collective professional activities they form a rather influential defamation league and that is considered to be right and proper. When others attack them, however, that is felt to be anti-intellectual and entirely illegitimate. Where their interests are touched, they unite to create their own informal anti-defamation league.

All this is rather puzzling when seen from the perspective of their own liberal progressive values. Rather than recognizing the potentials involved in the contemporary scene, rather than seeing or discovering the extent of liberalism and decency in lower middle class ranks and the same in the white working class, the liberal commentators make a very "punitive," from their perspective, a masochistic reading of the situation.

More than disinterested reason appears to be operating in this choice. There is a regular attempt to discount the more positive account or to once again read or interpret it in accordance with the previous punitive understanding. Conceivably reputations and "investments" are at stake: having argued the punitive reading over the course of a lifetime, it is difficult to make the change and argue the contrary. If one accepts the punitive reading of the evidence, another possibility, it provides a justification for quietism or inactivity. The argument is that nothing can be done (all one's hoped-for allies prove to be opposed to progressive change) and that it would be dangerous to mobilize for action (things might easily be made worse). This punitive reading allows one to adopt an appropriate "critical" approach to society and its problems and at the same time it allows one to explain why serious moves to achieve change ought not to be encouraged. This is to see the restraining world views as providing an excuse. If one took away the excuse, then the "concerned" and "critical" intellectual would be obligated to proceed in different directions.

If the adoption of the restraining viewpoints affected only those intellectuals, one might choose to be indifferent. But the implications of the position, in particular the demand for quiescence which follows from the "first principles," involves punishment for others. It means the sacrifice of other people's lives and of their well-being.

NOTES

1. Mills, *The Sociological Imagination* (New York: Grove Press, 1961) p. 126.

2. See Joel D. Aberbach and Jack L. Walker, "The Meanings of Black Power: A Comparison of White and Black Interpretations of a Political Slogan," American Political Science Review 64 (June 1970) 367-388.

3. This result, to be sure, may only be taken as *suggestive* of a causal relationship. It is always possible that the media content is an effect rather than a cause. The media managers, so it is argued in this alternative reading, follow audience preferences closely and adjust the content accordingly. One immediate objection that may be offered is the persistent refusal of publishers to behave in the manner claimed. Although heavy majorities of the American population, for example, favored Franklin Roosevelt in four elections, the newspapers and magazines (Collier's being the only notable exception) steadfastly favored the Republicans.

It is extremely difficult to establish a media effect. One has to know in advance that, let us say, Magazine X is going to take a unique position on a given issue. One has to be prepared to interview a sample of that magazine's audience and be able to compare the result with a control group who have not read that magazine.

It is much easier to test the alternative argument, the audience effect argument. From one's reading of Magazine X one discovers that there has been a change of position on, let us say, the Viet Nam War. From there the research involved is a relatively simple organizational decision-making study. One secures the cooperation of the magazine and interviews the handful of persons involved in making that decision. If the audience's changed position on the war proved to be a salient motivating factor, one might then ask how that was known, what research was undertaken to detect the change, and so on.

4. In addition to chapter 5, see my "Le fondement populaire des solutions militaires dures," Revue francaise de sociologie 10 (janvier-mars 1969) 39-58.

5. This "group-bases" position is discussed, with criticisms, at greater length in Richard Hamilton, *Class and Politics in the United States* (New York: John Wiley and Sons, 1972), chap. 2. The other positions, centrism, pluralism, and the mass society notion, are also discussed here.

6. In 1949, 50 percent of the white population in the United States reported satisfaction with their family income. This compared with 34 percent of the blacks. The levels of satisfaction increased, for whites, to 68 percent by 1963. That level has been maintained ever since. This result provides a rather accurate reflection of real income trends. With the coming of the Viet Nam War and the accompanying inflation, incomes have stabilized. The satisfaction reported by blacks increased to 45 percent in 1966, and that level has been maintained since. See *Gallup Opinion Index,* December 1971, Report No. 76.

A similar development is reported in response to a question about satisfaction with work. Among whites 69 percent reported satisfaction in 1949 with the figure rising to 90 percent in 1963. There has been some fluctuation since then with a decline to 83 percent reported in early 1972. There is a parallel development among blacks beginning at 55 percent satisfaction in 1949 and going to a 1969 peak at 76 percent. Again there was some falloff indicated, to 63 percent, in early 1972. The notions of an upper middle class caught in a "rat race" gain no support or recognition from the relevant populations themselves. Eighty-eight percent of the college educated were satisfied with their work as were 93 percent of those earning $15,000 or more a year.

For whites the level of satisfaction with housing increased from 67 percent in 1949 to 80 percent in 1969. There was an irregular but generally opposed pattern reported among the blacks: the twenty year pattern was 59 percent satisfaction in 1949 and 50 percent in 1969 (from the New York Times, 11 May 1969).

Taking everything together and asking about one's satisfaction with the "quality of life in your community," the result, as of September 1971, was 75 percent reporting satisfaction, 21 percent reporting dissatisfaction, and 4 percent who were not sure.

Despite this general satisfaction with income, work, housing, and the quality of life locally, there is some feeling of malaise. When asked "Is the world getting better or is it getting worse?" a majority, 62 percent, said it was getting worse. It is not clear from these Gallup studies what they have in mind. It does seem to be the case however, that they are referring to some events outside of their immediate localities.

Another extremely useful source is the University of Michigan's Survey Research Center report, *Survey of Working Conditions,* done for the U.S. Department of Labor, Employment Standards Administration, U.S. Government Printing Office, Washington, D.C., 1971.

7. There are, of course, instances one can cite of *persons* reacting in the manner claimed. The trend data reviewed earlier do not deny the existence of such cases. They do deny that they constitute the dominant tendency at present.

For a portrait of the willingness of the white population to improve the condition of the blacks, see Angus Campbell and Howard Schuman, *Racial Attitudes in Fifteen American Cities* (Ann Arbor: Survey Research Center, University of Michigan, 1968). This was a Supplemental Study for the National Advisory Commission on Civil Disorders. See especially the section "Proposals for Action," which begins on page 36.

8. See G. William Domhoff, *Fat Cats and Democrats: The Role of the Big Rich in the Party of the Common Man* (Englewood Cliffs, N.J.: Prentice-Hall, 1972).

9. One widespread assumption is that parties are "constrained" to be responsive, to cater to popular sentiment. For a discussion of the ability of the parties to avoid such constraints, see Hamilton, op. cit., chap. 1, and Donald A. Wittman, "Parties as Utility Maximizers," *American Political Science Review* 67 (June 1973) 490-498.

ABOUT THE AUTHOR

RICHARD HAMILTON is Professor of Sociology at McGill University in Quebec, Canada. He received his M.A. and Ph.D. from Columbia University, and was previously affiliated with Princeton University and the University of Wisconsin before coming to McGill. He has published extensively in the field, with articles in, among others, the *American Sociological Review,* the *British Journal of Sociology,* and *The Nation.* His previous books are *Class and Politics in the United States* (1972) and *Affluence and the French Worker in the Fourth Republic* (1967).

NAME INDEX

Aberbach, Joel D., 285n
Agger, Robert E., 77, 97n
Agnew, Spiro, 227
Allen, Frederick Lewis, 140n
Almond, Gabriel, 212n
Anderson, C. Arnold, 87n
Anderson, Dewey, 93n, 96n
Aronowitz, Stanley, 143n
Aronson, James, 215n

Baus, Herbert M., 238n
Bell, Daniel, 86n, 94n
Bechhofer, Frank, 87n
Berelson, Bernard, 91n, 144n
Berg, Ivar, 96n
Berle, A. A., 64-66, 95n
Bernstein, Eduard, 10, 262
Berwanger, Eugene, 180n
Black, Shirley Temple, *see* Minott,
    Rodney G.
Blank, R., 97n
Bonham, John, 98n
Bonjean, Charles M., 87n
Braun, Siegfried, 139n
Broder, David S., 236n
Brzezinski, Zbigniew, 175n
Buchanan, William, 144n
Bunzel, John, 259

Cain, Leila S., 212n
Campbell, Angus, 87n, 88n, 238n, 287n
Campbell, Joel T., 212n
Cantril, Hadley, 144n
Centers, Richard, 141n
Chester, Lewis, 31n, 178n, 236n, 239n
Cole, Stephen, 146n
Coleman, James S., 144n
Converse, Philip E., 88n, 212n, 238n
Cook, Fred, 176n
Corey, Lewis, 86n, 101, 140n
Cotter, Cornelius P., 238n
Crespi, Irving, 238n
Croner, Fritz, 139n

Davidson, Percy E., 93n, 96n
Denitch, Bogdan, 143n
de Toledano, Ralph, 237

De Vries, Walter, 177n, 236n
Dewey, Thomas E., 223
Domhoff, G. William, 287n
Douglas, Paul H., 134
Dowd, Douglas, 139
Dulles, John Foster, 192

Eberts, Paul, 33n
Elliott, Brian, 87n

Fenwick, Rudy, 178n
Finer, Herman, 192
Fiske, Marjorie, 213n
Foner, Eric, 180n
Fromm, Erich, 86n, 139n

Galtung, Johan, 211n
Gardner, John W., 175n
Geiger, Theodor, 146n
Glazer, Nathan, 146n
Goldrich, Daniel, 97n
Goldstein, Sidney, 86n, 96n
Goldwater, Barry, *see* Subject Index
Gomberg, William, 95n
Greeley, Andrew, 180n
Gurin, Gerald, 87n

Hahn, Harlan, 212n
Halberstam, David, 238n
Hall, Richard H., 86n
Hamilton, Richard F., 30n, 31n, 86n,
    88n, 90n, 92n, 95n, 96n, 98n, 139n,
    140n, 141n, 143n, 144n, 145n, 176n,
    178n, 179n, 180n, 181n, 212n, 214n,
    216n, 239n, 286n, 287n
Hanna, Mark, 232
Harris, Richard, 238n
Hartmann, George W., 93n, 144n
Hearst, William R., 167
Heberle, Rudolf, 146n
Heilbroner, Robert, 95n
Hofstadter, Richard, 180n
Hoggart, Richard, 214n
Humphrey, Hubert, *see* Subject Index
Hyman, Herbert, 180n

Iversen, Robert W., 146n

SUBJECT INDEX

NOTES

NOTES

NOTES

NOTES

NOTES

NOTES